UNSETTLING MEMORIES

For Julius

EMMA TARLO

Unsettling Memories

Narratives of the Emergency in Delhi

University of California Press
Berkeley   Los Angeles

University of California Press
Berkeley and Los Angeles, California

Published by Arrangement with C. Hurst and Co. (Publishers) Ltd.

©Emma Tarlo, 2003

ISBN 0-520-23120-1 (cloth)
ISBN 0-520-23122-8 (paper)

Cataloging-in-Publication Data is on file with the Library of Congress

Printed and bound in Malaysia

10 9 8 7 6 5 4 3 2 1

ACKNOWLEDGEMENTS

This book owes much to the support of different people and institutions. Its greatest debt is to the people whose life and experiences
it describes: the men, women and children of Welcome who were
willing to engage in a complex collective conversation which lasted
on and off for several years. It is hoped that they will find their opinions and experiences faithfully represented and that this text will
help to expose elements of their histories that have previously been
concealed. I am also indebted to officials of the Slum Department of
the Municipal Corporation of Delhi for allowing me access to official
housing files and for assisting me with their interpretation. To the
pigeons whose song enlivened archival work I add my thanks.

The fieldwork on which this book is based would not have been
possible without the help of my research assistant, Rajinder Singh
Negi, who did far more than simply translate. He was a fellow witness
to the stories we unearthed and shared with me the responsibility of
rendering them faithfully. His combination of sensitivity and quiet
curiosity were essential for making people feel at ease and willing to
speak. To Saroj Thappar who made learning Hindi fun, even at 7 in
the morning, I express my gratitude.

To Alveena, who cooked wonderful food and upheld the domestic
front, immeasurable thanks. How I miss your *saag paneer* and prawn
curry!

Of the numerous colleagues with whom I have been in dialogue
I offer special thanks to Christopher Fuller, Patricia Jeffrey, Veena Das,
Véronique Dupont, Denis Vidal and all members of the Delhi Research Group. Our fortnightly meetings at the CSDS in Delhi offered
food for reflection, much of which has found its way into this book.

Some of the findings of this research were presented in seminars held at the Universities of Edinburgh and Cambridge, and at the London School of Economics and Political Science (LSE) and Goldsmiths College, London. They were also presented in the context of the following conferences: 'Violence and Hegemony', South Asia Anthropology Group (SAAG) conference held at LSE in 1995; 'The Anthropology of the Indian State', workshop held at LSE in 1997 and 1998; and 'Delhi Games: use and control of urban space—power games and actors' strategies', conference organised by the Indo-French Delhi Research Group, held at the CSDS in Delhi. I am grateful to all participants who contributed to discussions, in particular to Dhirubhai Seth, Krishna Menon, Roma Chatterji, Saraswati Haider, Jonathan Spencer, Helen Lambert, Patricia Oberoi, Jonathan Parry, Roger and Patricia Jeffrey and Thomas Hansen.

This research has spanned my transformation from a postdoctoral research fellow at the School of Oriental and African Studies (SOAS), to a research fellow at the London School of Economics and Political Science (LSE) and finally a lecturer in anthropology at Goldsmiths College (all colleges of the University of London). I have had the good fortune to have received financial support for research on this book, first in the form of a British Academy postdoctoral research grant, later a two-year research grant from the Economic and Social Research Council of Great Britain and finally the Hoggart Fellowship at Goldsmiths. To all of these institutions and funding bodies, I owe many thanks. I am also grateful to Professors K.L. Sharma and Dipankar Gupta for enabling my affiliation at the Centre for the Study of Social Systems, Jawaharlal Nehru University, Delhi. To members of the CSDS for their conversations and friendship, further thanks.

It remains for me to thank friends and family for their support at different moments; Denis for his ever-stimulating companionship; and Julius for providing a natural deadline for the manuscript.

London, December 2002   EMMA TARLO

CONTENTS

ILLUSTRATIONS

GLOSSARY

bigha	land measurement equivalent to five-eighths of an acre
charpai	string bed
chaudhuri	headman, leader
crore	10 million
dalal	middleman, broker, agent
kabadi	junk
khadi	hand-woven cloth made using hand-spun yarn
khassi	castration
kucha	raw, impermanent, unbaked
kurta	long sleeved knee-length tunic
gali	narrow street, alley
goonda	hoodlum, ruffian
Haj	Muslim pilgrimage to Mecca
Imam	Islamic religious leader
jhuggi	slum shack
jhuggi jhompri	slum shacks
lakh	100,000
Lok Sabha	Lower House of Parliament
nasbandi	sterilisation, vasectomy
pakka	solid, permanent, well baked
pradhan	self-styled local leader
roti	unleavened bread
topi	cap

ABBREVIATIONS

BJP	Bharatiya Janata Party
DDA	Delhi Development Authority
DESU	Delhi Electrical Supply Undertaking
FP	Family Planning
GT Road	Grand Trunk Road
JJ	*Jhuggi Jhompri* (squatter shacks)
JJRS	*Jhuggi Jhompri* Removal Scheme
MCD	Municipal Corporation of Delhi
MLA	Member of the Legislative Assembly
PD-PIB	Photo Division-Public Information Bureau
SC	Scheduled Caste
SSWIG	Selected Speeches and Writings of Indira Gandhi
UP	Uttar Pradesh

1

INTRODUCTION

One Sunday morning in February 1995, I boarded an auto-rickshaw to visit some of the ancient sites of Shahdara in east Delhi. Unfortunately—or fortunately as it turned out—the rickshaw driver lost his way. After we had made several circles through the dense winter smog on the east side of the Yamuna river, I told him to stop the vehicle and drop me off wherever we were. Little did I know at the time that I would return to this place persistently over the next three years.

I had arrived in Welcome—one of Delhi's 47 'resettlement colonies', designed for relocating families evicted from inner city slums. There was nothing spectacular about the place and it was partly for that reason that I contemplated making it a site for fieldwork. At the time I was working on a project about furniture and the uses of the body. I had done a fair amount of research in middle-class areas in south Delhi and now wanted to work in a poorer, less westernised environment. However, my project, like my Sunday itinerary, was soon to change.

What changed everything was a visit to the local branch of the Slum Department of the Municipal Corporation of Delhi (MCD)—a building situated within Welcome. Here my assistant and I had hoped to gather a few background facts about the planning and resettlement of the colony. However, it soon became clear that such general information had never been collated. Instead it lay dispersed in thousands of dusty files. Opening these, I became aware of a wealth of other documents pertaining to the little-studied period known as 'the Emergency'. By the time I closed the files, my research agenda had been redefined.

This book is about unsettling memories: both the process of disrupting and unearthing memories and the unsettling nature of memories evoked. It focuses in particular on events which took place in the

1

Indian capital city of Delhi between June 1975 and March 1977—
a period known in India as 'the Emergency'. Popular and official
narratives of these events are analysed for what they tell us about the
relationship between citizen, state and market in contemporary urban
India. While the immediate aim is to rewrite the Emergency from an
anthropological perspective, the wider objective is to demonstrate
the possibility of producing an ethnography of the state.
The Emergency occupies an unusual place in the Indian past. It
has been much mythologised but little studied. Too recent to be of
interest to historians yet too distant to have attracted the attention
of other social scientists, it has somehow slipped through the net of
academic disciplines. But time is not the only factor that explains the
silence surrounding this brief period. This silence can also be explained in terms of the unsettling nature of what went on during
those 21 months when democratic rights were suspended under Indira
Gandhi and coercive measures brought into play. Press censorship,
arrests, torture, the demolition of slums and tales of forcible sterilisation have all made the Emergency fertile food for fiction,[1] but uncomfortable ground for historical, political or sociological analysis.
While literary writers have been keen to evoke and, at times, embellish the horror of such atrocities, politicians and dominant political
parties have been equally keen to deny their reality and suppress their
memory. The silence that surrounds the Emergency 'as fact' is not
entirely accidental.

This book belongs, then, to a growing body of literature which
seeks to work against the areas of collective silence which often cling
to violent and disturbing events. In particular it seeks to articulate
the experiences and perceptions of ordinary people who found
themselves caught up in the twists and turns of a bleak historical
moment.[2] The key protagonists of the book are men and women

---

[1]Nirmal Verma, 1993, *Dark Dispatches*, Delhi: Indus; Rohinton Mistry, 1995, *A Fine
Balance*, Calcutta: Rupa & Co.; Salman Rushdie, 1983, *Midnight's Children*, and more
specifically, 1994, 'The Free Radio' in *East, West*, both originally published in London
by Jonathan Cape; R.K. Narayan, 1976, *The Painter of Signs*, New York: Viking.

[2]As such, it has affinities with the wealth of recent literature about memories of
the Holocaust and Partition. For two recent examples of books conveying personal
experiences of Partition see Urvashi Butalia, *The Other Side of Silence*, Delhi: Viking,
and Ritu Menon and Kamla Bhasin, *Borders and Boundaries*, Delhi: Kali for Women,
both published in 1998.

who, by dint of poverty and circumstance, were targetted in the mass slum clearance and sterilisation drives, ubiquitous in Delhi during the Emergency. They are people whose lives were profoundly disrupted by these policies but whose personal renderings of the event have not been either written or heard. Other protagonists include the low-level bureaucrats, local leaders and middlemen with whom they negotiated their attempts to retain basic rights and amenities often at the risk of losing others.

A focus on the voices and experiences of the Emergency's most obvious victims does not, however, pretend to offer privileged access to the truth of the event. Like the official record itself, personal memories are fraught with ambiguity and are formulated within the context of wider experiences and agendas—local, national and global. They testify not only to the state's targeting of the poor during the Emergency, but also to the active role played by many of the poor in perpetuating state oppression at that time. The Emergency as fact leaves little space for the romanticisation of the victim.

Though much of this book is concerned with personal narratives, it is equally concerned with other avenues of remembering and forgetting—with government files assumed not to exist, with Emergency propaganda, censored newspapers, post-Emergency resistance literature and political exposés which lead us down the paths of public memory and through the intricacies and inconsistencies of the official record. These various sources offer not only different takes on the event but also different time frames through which to comprehend it. Fieldwork conversations with the sterilised and displaced re-work the past in relation to subsequent events, present circumstances and anticipated futures. The memories they engender are squarely located in the present and are never unmediated. By contrast, government files and official propaganda—both produced during the Emergency itself—lend insight into the present of the past. They offer an official memory still uncensored by subsequent developments and political trends, though such literature was of course subject to a different type of censorship at the time. Located somewhere between these two time-frames, post-Emergency exposés, letters, and judgments which surfaced immediately after the event offer a short-term memory of the Emergency—one which reads strangely now for its lack of historical depth and the imagined futures it evokes. These different time frames remind us of the relativity of all representations

of the past as well as the impossibility of historical perfection. However, they also furnish the basis for the creation of a new multi-textured
narrative of the Emergency, which does not claim to represent the
totality of the event but which, in allowing diversity, seeks to create a
richer portrait of the elements at play.

Although at one level concerned with the specificities of a particular historical moment, this book is also concerned with what
such a moment tells us of the everyday lives of the urban poor in
India's capital city. What seems to characterise their situation is the
extreme precariousness of their relationship to both land and state—
a precariousness which came to light most intensely during the Emergency but is by no means specific to it. The discourse of development
which provided the logic for the mass displacement of some 700,000
people to marginal spaces beyond the borders of the city in 1975–7
did not guarantee either security or entitlement to the displaced. And
although the means by which the poor negotiated 'provisional' land
rights during the Emergency were specific, the fact that they had to
bargain with politicians and bureaucrats for the basic amenities of
everyday life reveals the continuities with both past and present. Such
continuities are all too apparent in the recent re-emergence in Delhi
politics of Jagmohan, the man who had been in charge of slum clearance and resettlement during the Emergency. Now Union Urban
Development Minister, Jagmohan is renewing his stringent efforts to
'clean up' the city by enforcing the closure of thousands of 'non-conforming industries' and removing 'illegal squatters' from the capital.[3]
For the hundreds of thousands of citizens whose lives are inescapably
enmeshed in this major re-development scheme, it must seem that
little has changed since the mid 1970s. In this sense, the Emergency of

[3]In 1996, the Supreme Court ordered the closure and shifting of industrial units
situated in 'non-conforming' residential areas. The precise number of such 'non-
conforming' industrial units in Delhi is unknown but it is estimated at around 100,000.
Following delays in implementation, the Supreme Court served a notice to the
Delhi Chief Minister in November 2000 concerning non-compliance with the court's
earlier instructions. This was followed by a rapid drive to close down industrial units
with a view to eventually relocating some of them. Mass sealing operations are currently
underway, despite organised protest from workers. An estimated 20-lakh (2 million)
people are thought to be employed in these industries. The majority of these will lose
their means to earn a livelihood if the closures continue to function at the current
rate (see *Frontline*, 22 Dec. 2000).

1975 is a trope through which to explore the emergencies of everyday life for poor and marginalised sections of the Delhi population. For those who may be sceptical about the interest in an event which took place over 25 years ago, let me begin by highlighting some key areas of anthropological importance.

The ethnography of events

History has often proved a stumbling block to anthropology and although the relationship between the two is in a process of radical transformation, many anthropologists still endorse (explicitly or implicitly) a false dichotomy between structure and event. Social structure—the seemingly stable state of affairs—was long seen as the domain *par excellence* of anthropologists leaving significant events—especially violent ones—to journalists, political scientists and historians.

Anthropology's refusal to engage with historical events has its origins in a variety of factors. One is anthropology's favoured methodology of participant observation through fieldwork. This method has traditionally consisted of taking up residence amongst a community or people for a period of one or two years and gathering information based on this experience of proximity. Although two years may seem a long time to journalists accustomed to darting in and out of people's lives within a single day, it is of course inadequate for observing historical change and anthropology's reverence of the ethnographic present has often given rise to works which, at best, underplay and, at worst, deny the forces of history. This problem is accentuated by the absence of historical records amongst many of the peoples anthropologists conventionally choose to study. Added to these practical dilemmas is the uneasy nature of what might be uncovered if anthropologists did delve closely into the histories of the people they studied, many of whom have uncomfortable pasts tied with European imperialist interests which anthropologists (who, until recently, were mainly from colonising countries) preferred to ignore.

It was then a combination of methodology and circumstance which served to boost the development of an ahistorical anthropology which generated a string of self-sufficient holistic models—functionalism, structuralism and society-as-text explicable through cultural exegesis. These models left little space for events which tended either to be seen as disruptions, too temporary to interest anthropologists, or as rituals which simply served to boost or reinforce the social structure. Hence in Max Gluckman's famous 'rituals of rebellion' which find their Indian equivalent in studies of the Holi festival, violence and disruption are seen as temporary ritual devices which allow society to let off steam before returning to the status quo.[4]

In advocating the study of an event like the Emergency, I am not suggesting a return to rituals of rebellion although I would endorse Gluckman's obvious point that structure and event are not oppositional terms. Rather, I am interested in the new areas of research suggested by a few contemporary anthropologists who argue for the need for studies which explore the dynamic relationship between moments of disruption and moments of calm.[5] Such studies are necessary because violence and disruption are so integral to the lives of many modern peoples and nations that they are often experienced not as aberrations of the normal state of affairs but as inevitable elements of the everyday.[6] Viewed from this perspective, social structure is not so much a stable force temporarily disrupted by political events, but rather a dynamic form shaped and re-moulded through such events. The fact that the modern nations of India and Pakistan were born through the unspeakable violence that accompanied Partition stands as proof— if proof were needed—of the transformative potential of events.

Veena Das who has led the way in India for a new ethnography of what she calls 'critical events' has argued that a theoretical shift towards events does not so much create new anthropological objects as invite old objects to inhabit unfamiliar spaces and thereby acquire new life.[7] The events she calls critical are those which bring about new modes of action and encourage new social and political formations

---

[4]See Max Gluckman, 1963, *Order and Rebellion in Tribal Africa*, London: Routledge and Danny Miller, 1973, 'Holi-Dhulendi: Licensed Rebellion in a North Indian Village', *South Asia*, 3, pp. 15–22.

[5]See, for example, the arguments raised in John Davis, 1992, 'The Anthropology of Suffering', *Journal of Refugee Studies*, 5, 2, pp. 149–61 and Jonathan Spencer, 1992, 'Problems in the Analysis of Communal Violence', *Contributions to Indian Sociology* (n.s.), 26, 2.

[6]For an exploration of the notion of the violence or violences of everyday life, see Nancy Scheper Hughes, 1992, *Death without Weeping*, Berkeley: University of California Press; Paul Farmer, 1996, 'On Suffering and Structural Violence', *Daedalus* 15, 1; pp. 261–83; Arthur Kleinman, 2000, 'The Violences of Everyday Life' in Veena Das, Arthur Kleinman *et al.*, eds, *Violence and Subjectivity*, Berkeley: University of California Press.

[7]Veena Das, 1995, *Critical Events*, Delhi: OUP, p. 1.

as people are propelled into unpredicted terrains. What her examples of Partition (1947), the Sikh massacre (1984) and the Bhopal gas disaster (1985) share in common is the way these events 'criss-crossed several institutions, moving across family, community, bureaucracy, courts of law, the medical profession, the state and multinational corporations.'[8] Conventional anthropological studies, with their synchronic and location-based focus, can rarely capture the interrelationship between such institutions, yet it is precisely this interrelationship which characterises so much of modern life. 'A description of critical events,' Das argues, 'helps form an ethnography which makes an incision upon all these institutions together, so that their mutual implications in the events are foregrounded during the analysis.'[9]

By making the Emergency the key focus of this book, my aim is to provide just such an ethnography of a 'critical event'. The anthropological value of taking this event as a starting point is, as Das argues, that it provides a view onto a moment of intense social and political dynamism when a whole range of actors—in this case, inner city slum dwellers, displaced peoples, local leaders, professionals, traders, bureaucrats, police and politicians—were brought into interaction and, in many cases, renegotiated their position in the socio-geographic fabric of Delhi. But although it is only at such moments of intense renegotiation that such a range of social interactions becomes apparent, the relationships on which these interactions are based form part of the everyday functioning of life in the capital city. This means that despite the specificity of the Emergency as an event, it provides some sort of privileged access to the semi-obscure social and political structures of everyday life in the capital city.

The anthropology of the state

If critical events have hitherto taken a back stage in anthropological accounts, so too has the analysis of the role of the state in everyday life. The absence of ethnographies of the modern Indian state has been highlighted in particular by Akhil Gupta who uses the concept of 'blurred boundaries' to describe the enmeshed relationships by which local level bureaucrats and rural people interact in a North Indian

---

[8]Ibid., p. 6.
[9]Ibid.

village.[10] He points to the need for further examination of the quotidian practices of bureaucrats which might tell us about the effects of the state in everyday life. He also suggests the importance of analysing how the state is discursively constructed through popular cultural forms including newspapers and TV which inform local perceptions. Anthropological methodology which places a high value on face-to-face encounters and spatial proximity may not, he argues, be well suited to the study of so unwieldy a set of discourses and practices as the state, though a recent collection of ethnographies of the modern Indian state suggests that much can in fact be learned using conventional ethnographic methods.[11]

Unlike Gupta, I suggest that it is precisely its emphasis on face-to-face encounters and spatial proximity that enables ethnographic methodology to offer fresh insights into the lived experience and perceptions of the modern state. Furthermore, far from being ill-equipped for such an exercise, anthropologists are in many ways extremely well placed for investigating the workings of the state as both idea and practice. Not only do they daily and increasingly engage with bureaucratic structures and mythologies within and beyond academic departments, but they also learn to master a variety of relationships with high and low level representatives of the state when organising and conducting fieldwork—whether 'at home' or abroad. Often it is 'face-to-face' encounters with local officials that either open or close doors for anthropologists who are, I would argue, deeply familiar with the concept of 'blurred boundaries'—a term which might be fruitfully used to characterise fieldwork itself.

It would be inaccurate to say that my research about the Emergency led me to engage with local bureaucrats, for it happened the other way round. It was my 'face to face' encounter with local bureaucrats of the Slum Department of the Municipal Corporation of Delhi and my interest in the products with which they deal—official papers—that led me to focus on the Emergency in the first place. This encounter and sustained interaction not only taught me much about the role of the Indian state during the Emergency but provided important insight

[10]Akhil Gupta, 1995, 'Blurred Boundaries: The Discourse of Corruption, the Culture of Politics, and the Imagined State', *American Ethnologist*, 22, 2, pp. 375–402.
[11]Christopher Fuller and Véronique Bénéï, eds, 2000, *The Everyday State and Society in Modern India*, Delhi: Social Science Press.

into the complex relationships of both bureaucrats and ordinary people to the state's administrative structures in everyday life.

My entry into the records room of one of Delhi's regional branches of the Slum Department was not, then, a prelude to my fieldwork but was very much part of the fieldwork itself. These government offices constituted a specific type of ethnographic terrain—a bureaucratic space—in which a particular type of material artefact—official papers— is produced. Like all artefacts, official papers embody social relationships: they have producers and consumers; they circulate between individuals and representatives of institutions; they are rich in symbolism just as they are concrete in form. Anthropologically their interest lies not simply in their content but in the circumstances surrounding their production, circulation and interpretation. And who is better placed to unveil the mysteries of such documents than the people whose profession it is to create them?

Too often anthropologists are prone to treat official records as mere background information and to dismiss bureaucrats and archivists as people who might stand in the way of research. But as the producers and guardians of official documents, government officials can be extremely helpful in decoding the artefacts they have produced as well as demonstrating the techniques of production. It was through conversations with low-level bureaucrats that I was able to establish a basis for interpreting these everyday artefacts of the state. I treat them here, not simply as 'evidence' of what went on before, during and after the Emergency, but as a field of 'paper truths.' The main characteristic of these paper truths lies in the fact that they are malleable and constructed on the one hand yet take on an aura of irrefutability on the other. They highlight the ever-present gap between what is implicitly known and what is officially recorded, a gap open to both negotiation and exploitation as people's experiences during the Emergency make clear.

Bringing anthropological methodology to the Slum Department not only helped expose the everyday technologies and mythologies of state practice but it also shed light on the variegated nature of official memory. Like many other studies, this one highlights the state's attempt to control the production of memory by making its version of events hold and by discouraging the memorisation of particular happenings. The voices of low-level bureaucrats complicate the issue for they maintain a distinction between what they have recorded and

what they experienced. Their status as officials gives their oral testi-
monies some sort of official status, though their accounts are often at
variance with what they themselves recorded in the files. Furthermore, taken together, both the 'paper truths' of the records room and
the memories of bureaucrats provide important material with which
it becomes possible to challenge the state's official master narrative of
the Emergency.

These discrepancies within the official memorisation of the event
also point to the hierarchy and fragmentation found within bureaucratic
structures, where different grades of officials are differently situated
in relation to policies and events. This hierarchy is literally visible in
the allocation of space and resources within government departments
so it becomes possible to read a person's status quite literally from the
size of his desk. Nevertheless, an ethnography of the Emergency which
focuses only on the production and interpretation of 'paper truths'
inside government offices would, of course, be limited. The other
important element about 'paper truths' is their reproducibility outside
Government departments. If documents are the lingua franca of the
state, then citizens wishing to negotiate with the state not only learn
that language but also learn to reproduce it in the form of official
documents 'proving' housing and sterilisation status. The state's demand
for paper proofs generates the popular production of paper truths as
people mimic the very writing technologies that ensnare them. Such
acts of mimesis bear witness to the reach of the state in the everyday
lives of ordinary citizens but they also point to the limitations of that
reach, for ultimately the state risks drowning in the artifice of its own
creation. Government files relating to the Emergency point to the fact
that agents of the state were often unable to interpret the proliferation
of documents that they themselves had set in motion.

The 'paper truths' of the Emergency also bear witness to the multiple violences of the state which they record and embody, however
obliquely. The capacity of the state to act as an implicit or explicit
instrument of violence is something to which anthropologists are
drawing increasing attention. What the personal narratives of victims
of the Emergency bring to this debate is a chilling demonstration of
how state abuses not only produce local worlds but also become
re-worked within them. The process by which the poor were drawn
into participation in the sterilisation campaign as a means of avoiding getting sterilised themselves directly confirms Kleinman's recent

observation concerning the inadequacy of current taxonomies of violence which draw clear distinctions between 'public versus domestic, ordinary as against extreme political violence'.[12] Too often these categories seem to merge. For example, the demolition drives which have been a regular feature of life amongst the urban poor in India's major cities since the early 1960s require demolition workers. These low-level state employees often end up demolishing each others' homes with the aid of a simple iron rod in the interests of 'doing their jobs'.

The plight of the local demolition worker who finds himself displaced and homeless even as he demolishes the homes of others reminds us that large sections of the urban poor, particularly those from scheduled caste backgrounds,[13] earn their livelihoods working for the state which promises them a degree of security, even if the conditions of the promise are subject to change over time. The limits to that security were amply demonstrated during the Emergency when those with two or three children (depending on which branch of the administration) found themselves threatened with loss of employment if they failed to get sterilised. That getting sterilised or paying someone else to do so became, in many cases the only way displaced people could obtain small plots of land in resettlement colonies, reveals the fickle nature of the state's offer of protection. But it also exposes how local people entered into deals with the state by which they negotiated their claims to land on the outskirts of the city.

The rapidity with which the family planning drive of the Emergency transformed into a market for sterilisation in the marginal spaces of Delhi's resettlement colonies is interesting for what it tells us about how people relate to the state at a local level. Situated within the wider context of everyday life in resettlement colonies this trade ceases to surprise for it becomes quite clear that the poor in Delhi relate to the state principally through the market. Basic amenities such as land, jobs, electricity, water and paving are things, not provided, but purchased in exchange for votes, money, or, in the case of the Emergency, sterilisation certificates. That people commonly

---

[12]Kleinman, 2000, 'The Violences of Everyday Life', p. 227.

[13]In the 1950s positive discrimination in public sector jobs and industries was introduced in favour of members of 'scheduled castes' who had previously been classified as 'untouchables'. As a result a large numbers of scheduled caste men and, to a lesser extent, women occupy the lower levels of government posts, working as sweepers, demolition workers, railway coolies and so forth.

pay bureaucrats for gaining access to what ostensibly is their due is a point made by Gupta in the context of development projects in rural India and by Jeffrey, Jeffrey and Lyon in the context of rural women's lack of access to health facilities.[14] It is not that health facilities are unavailable in Uttar Pradesh but that local people feel they cannot gain access to effective treatment without 'heating' the pockets of doctors and nurses.

In effect the market, far from operating outside the state, often features as the vernacular idiom through which ordinary people negotiate with local agents of the state. Furthermore, as Gupta points out, it would be fallacious to assume that it is only at the 'lower levels' that this vernacular idiom is understood. How else might we explain the fact that the unauthorised dwellings of the rich in Delhi too often remain unscathed[15] whilst those of the poor seem to quake permanently under the threat of demolition?

Whether this threat is fulfilled or not depends very largely on the balance of power between representatives of local government on the one hand and the state or municipal authorities on the other. Despite their haphazard and spontaneous appearance most squatter settlements are nurtured by politicians who maintain close relationships of patronage with local *pradhans* (self-styled local leaders) who, in turn, promise politicians the votes of their supporters.[16] It is therefore in the interests of individual politicians to 'protect' settlements or segments of them from demolition in order to maintain these significant vote banks. Here again the fragmented nature of the state emerges as policies of slum clearance are often effectively blocked by representatives of local government. Yet such informal relationships of 'protection' are inherently unstable. A slight shift in the balance of power takes the wind out of the politicians' promise and often has drastic implications for those relying on their protection. This became clear during the Emergency when informal agreements between

---

[14]See Patricia Jeffrey, Roger Jeffrey and Andrew Lyon, 1989, *Labour Pains, Labour Power*, London: Zed.

[15]For discussion of the uninterrupted spread of unauthorised palatial residences in South Delhi, see Anita Soni, 2000, 'Urban Conquest of Outer Delhi: Beneficiaries, Intermediaries and Victims' in Véronique Dupont, Emma Tarlo and Denis Vidal, eds, 2000, *Delhi: Urban Space and Human Destinies*, Delhi: Manohar. The recent crackdown on unauthorised buildings may threaten even these palatial residences.

[16]For discussion of these dynamics see Saraswati Haider, 2000, 'Migrant Women and Urban Experience in a Squatter Settlement' in Dupont, Tarlo and Vidal, eds, *Delhi*.

individual politicians and squatters were overridden by firmly implemented state action under a centralised authoritarian government, backed by force. Current attempts to close down 'non-conforming' industries and displace squatters in response to an injunction from the Supreme Court testify to the enduring sense of insecurity faced by Delhi's urban poor.

Location

The personal and official narratives that inform this text flow predominantly from one particular location—the resettlement colony of Welcome—just one of Delhi's 47 poorly serviced urban settlements created to absorb displaced inner city squatters. The specificity of such spaces lies not only in their social and geographic marginality, but also in the fact that they are made up of fragments of disrupted and dispersed settlements from elsewhere. Arjun Appadurai draws an interesting distinction between 'neighborhoods'(situated communities characterised by their actuality) and what he calls 'locality' (a phenomenological quality or feeling 'expressed in certain kinds of agency, sociality and reproducibility').[17] By creating colonies out of fragments of demolished neighbourhoods, the state authorities lump together people who may share little more in common than their poverty and displacement. As Appadurai points out, such acts of enforced localisation place severe constraints and obstacles on the 'survival of locality'. It must also be remembered that the sense of locality in the inner city areas and squatter settlements demolished during the Emergency was no doubt already tenuous. Most of the people who were displaced to Welcome in the 1970s, had already experienced displacement before, whether in the form of migration or as a response to local or state violence. Many have also experienced further displacement since their arrival in Welcome, for life in Delhi's resettlement colonies is far from 'settled'.

The inhabitants of such fragmented spaces may have difficulty building a sense of shared locality, but in the minds of Delhi's middle-class citizens, they seem to represent a unified group. What they share is the stigma of their association with the slum. Born in the name of slum-clearance, resettlement colonies are rarely ever able to shake off

[17]Arjun Appadurai, 1997, *Modernity at Large*, Delhi: OUP, ch. 9.

this association. Their very existence evokes the 'cleaning up' process out of which they emerged. And if the city is perceived as being cleaner without its poorer inhabitants, then resettlement colonies are inevitably perceived as places of dirt—containers of the city's unwanted elements. In the case of Welcome, this general stigma fuses with the colony's more specific reputation as a 'notorious place' of violence and criminality.

The process by which particular spaces and their inhabitants are characterised as being inherently dangerous has been highlighted by Dhareshwar and Srivatsan in their elaboration of the figure of the 'rowdy' who 'in middle-class imagination...inhabits the dark zone of the city, trafficking in illegal, immoral activities; a zone that is inevitably in need of law and order, and always threatening to spread to the safer, cleaner habitat of the city'.[18] It is difficult to track the specific historiography of Welcome's 'bad reputation' but it is certain that press coverage of the colony's implication in the communal violence of 1992[19] has given Welcome a special place on the map of Delhi's dubious places. This 'fame for infamy' has become a source of local pride to some young men in the colony who boast of how the police can always track a notorious criminal to Welcome. Their words testify to the production of discourses of marginalisation both from within and outside the colony. This popular perception of Welcome as a place 'to be avoided' is to some extent negated by commercial interests. Being one of Delhi's oldest resettlement colonies, it is better situated than most and rising property prices ensure its rapid development even as the reputation for violence and disrepute keeps prices competitive.

The question remains as to the appropriateness of situating a study of wider events, ideas and places—the Emergency, the state, Delhi— within the confines of a single marginal space like Welcome. Increasing

[18]See Vivek Dhareshwar and R. Srivatsun, 1996, '"Rowdy-Sheeters": Subalternity and Politics' in Shahid Amin and Dipesh Chakrabarty, eds, *Subaltern Studies IX*, Delhi: OUP, p. 202.

[19]In December 1992 right wing Hindu activists were responsible for demolishing a medieval mosque at Ayodhya in Uttar Pradesh—an act that unleashed a trail of violence between Hindus and Muslims throughout north India. In Delhi, Welcome became a key site of violence. Areas of the colony, including religious buildings, were set on fire. Once the violence and curfew were over, a halo of fear seemed to linger over the colony, deterring business partners and other visitors from coming to Welcome. The event clearly served to boost the colony's reputation as a dangerous or dubious place.

awareness of the extent to which local sites are produced through translocal power relations and cultural flows has led some anthropologists to advocate multi-locational fieldwork[20] just as it has led others to suggest a shift from location to event.[21] The peculiarity of this study is that it approaches an event through its articulation in the local, arguing that precisely because of its history of displacement, a resettlement colony like Welcome is a suitable location from which to approach wider issues, places and events.

This becomes clear once it is recognised that the inhabitants of Welcome come from over 80 different locations spread throughout the capital, ranging from the southern corners of 'New Delhi' to the historic core of 'Old Delhi'. A map indicating the key sites of demolition may look more like a bombardment plan than a development plan (the similarity is not incidental), but it testifies to the varied spatial trajectories of the displaced. This means that although today the inhabitants of Welcome are based within the confines of a single colony, they carry with them memories and experiences of elsewhere. These were people who lived and worked in varied locations all over Delhi prior to experiencing demolition, and just as many of them built new shelters in Welcome using the bricks and corrugated iron from their demolished homes, so they construct their narratives out of their complex personal trajectories. As a result, this was not a case of the anthropologist having to shift from one location to another in order to encounter the diversity of different experiences of the Emergency. Rather, diverse multi-locational experiences emerged from a single geographic space. The other side of the resettlement equation lies in the concurrent transformations that have occurred to the inner city areas where demolitions took place. Delhi would look quite different were it not for the succession of demolitions out of which the colony of Welcome was born and through which new roads, public buildings and parks were created as part of the 'beautification' of the capital. In this sense the birth of the colony was inextricably bound up with the morphology of the city as a whole, highlighting the fact that the people of Welcome are not so much marginal to Delhi's history as *marginalised* by it.[22]

---

[20]George Marcus, 1995, 'Ethnography in/of the World System: The Emergence of Multi-sited Ethnography', *Annual Review of Anthropology*, 24, pp. 95–117.

[21]See Das, 1995, *Critical Events*.

[22]For more specific discussion of the history and development of Welcome within

Once we re-establish the links between those resettled in Welcome
and the places where they once lived and worked, it becomes less
surprising that their narratives should lend insight into places and
events of wider national importance. In fact, elsewhere I have argued
that, far from standing outside national policies and events, the urban
poor often find themselves deeply implicated within them for they
lack the political, economic and educational resources with which
to build a shield in moments of crisis.[23] This was blatantly obvious
during the Emergency when an estimated 700,000 people (15 per
cent of the local population) were dispersed outside the city and over
161,000 were purportedly sterilised. Whether singled out as the key
targets of state policies, or simply exposed to critical events like wars
and so called 'communal riots', the people of Welcome have often
found themselves caught at the centre and drawn into the action. From
this viewpoint, they no longer seem so marginal. Their narratives
confirm Appadurai's point that in a contemporary world of complex
dislocations and relocations, there is nothing 'mere' about 'the local'.

Voice and image

Much has been made in recent years of a paradigmatic shift in
anthropology from the visual to the verbal, from seeing to listening,
from observing the lives of others to giving them voice. Though much
of this book is devoted to just such an exercise, it is important to stress
that the opposition often implied between the visual and the verbal
is both artificial and unhelpful. We live in a world in which we constantly
interpret a complex variety of words, images and material forms which
sometimes communicate in different ways and sometimes in unison.
In the first chapter, I take the reader on an imaginary tour of Delhi in
order to track how narratives of the Emergency and its forgetting are
visibly inscribed in the city's layout, its street names, its museums and
monuments. Similarly, when listening to people recount their personal
experiences of the Emergency, I was aware not only of what was said
and how it was said but also of the wider circumstances including the
visual field: who said what in front of whom, in what types of places,

---

the context of national policies and events see Emma Tarlo, 2000, 'Welcome to History:
A Resettlement Colony in the Making' in Dupont, Tarlo and Vidal, eds, *Delhi*.
    [23]Ibid.

with what gestures and so forth. Like other anthropologists I have tried to be sensitive to the discrepancies between what people say and what they do, between how they want to present themselves and how we observe others reacting to them. These visual observations, far from belittling the research process, are essential to it. They provide a context to voices which, disembodied, can too easily be used uncritically by writers/ethnographers as a simplistic device to support the story they want to tell.

None the less the recent incorporation of different 'voices' in anthropological and historical texts has been important in all sorts of ways. Voices not only convey the subjectivity of experience, but they also disrupt the homogeneity and closure of texts as well as enabling a rejection of the spurious old anthropological assumption that all members of a given culture necessarily represent it in a direct and unproblematic way. Voices, then, allow for controversy and debate; they leave space for different personalities and they carry the potential to challenge the anthropologist's prior assumptions. Their insertion into texts seems particularly important when the subjects of research are mostly illiterate and when the events under investigation have been largely suppressed.

However, as has often been pointed out, researchers, both as ethnographers and as writers are in a position of power which enables them to be selective, to take heed of some voices and ignore others, to re-arrange different narratives within the text. For this reason some modern ethnographic writing is accused of being deceptive on the grounds that it gives the impression of allowing others to speak when ultimately these others are always subjected to the author's will. This seems inevitable, but the question remains as to whether such authorial control is necessarily a negative thing. Surely the point of researchers devoting years to a particular project is that they develop the competence to be able to follow leads intelligently, to select appropriately from different types of material, to recognise the difference between the person whose opinions are informative and the one who tries to lead them up the garden path? One striking peculiarity of the predicament of ethnographers is that they often find themselves able to mix with a much wider variety of people than any one member of the community they are studying is ever able to do. Outsider status lends at least some degree of immunity to internal factions or social divisions, whether these are based on gender, religion, class, caste or other criteria.[24] Hence, in my research about the Emergency I found myself able to discuss with all sorts of people who would barely, if ever, interact among themselves and it is this variety of encounters which I hope lends a certain legitimacy to the nature of the collective narrative which, as author, I have orchestrated.

The use of voices in this text and the conversational form in which they are often included reflect, then, the nature of my fieldwork experience in Delhi. This was an experience based much more on talking than on participation in the classic anthropological sense. I was not living in the resettlement colony of Welcome; neither would it have been appropriate for me to do so. My outsider status—an obvious disadvantage in terms of language—was advantageous to the extent that people were often as curious to speak to me as I was to them. This outsider status was explicit throughout my fieldwork and remains so in the book. Where the questions I asked seem relevant to the types of answers people gave, I have included them in the text; where they seem insignificant, I have chosen to omit them and at times I simply report conversations which were triggered off by my initial inquiries but in which I barely participated. This was a fieldwork which bore the character of one long collective, open-ended conversation based on people's accounts of their own experiences and it is precisely this quality that I seek to retain in the text.

Ultimately the narrative I have produced is not without its imperfections: some voices may dominate more than they should; others will always remain inaccessible; official records reveal much, but there are also things that they conceal. This is a text made up of many fragments which, put together, will never make a perfect whole. None the less, I was struck throughout the research by the high degree of coherence between official papers, bureaucratic interpretations, photographic documents and personal narratives which, when critically examined and pieced together, are mutually supporting in the story they collectively tell even if they tell that story in very different ways and add different elements to it.[25] In this sense, this account of what

[24]Following Kiran Narayan, I would argue that the very process of doing ethnography creates both intimacy and distance between researcher and researched, making all ethnographers both part-insiders and part-outsiders, whatever their ethnic background (Kiran Narayan, 1998, 'How Native is a Native Anthropologist?' in Meenakshi Thapan, ed. *Anthropological Journeys*, Delhi: Sangam).

[25]In his attempt to rewrite the history of a violent event which took place in

went on during the Emergency takes distance both from fiction and from earlier stereotyped renderings of the event in spite of the fact that it relies on the notoriously complex and imperfect instrument of human memory and its verbal and material embodiments.

The photographic sequences between chapters are intended not so much to illustrate the text as to run parallel to it. They make visual observations on the themes of memory, marginality, state policies, leadership and everyday life. Like other forms of documentation, they should be interpreted as a powerful form of paper truth.

The book begins by examining the various means by which the memory of the Emergency has been handed down, distorted or suppressed. The first chapter is intended to introduce those unfamiliar with Delhi and the Emergency to the existing master narratives of the event. As a moment of national shame, a blot on India's democratic record, the Emergency has been built more as a moment for forgetting than as one for remembering. This agenda for forgetting the Emergency is marked by the lack of public monuments which might invoke its memory as well as by memorials which encourage a very different reading of the past. Inviting the reader on an alternative guided tour of the city—I trace the material deposits through which the Emergency might be remembered but also the contours through which it has become forgotten. The chapter is also intended to provide a taste of the early stages of the research process characterised by moving about from place to place, meeting with different people and working through existing literature. The aim is not to analyse the rhetoric of the Emergency but to give a sense of the ingredients with which the ethnographer starts and from which she eventually departs.

Those already familiar with the rhetoric of the Emergency may wish to move straight to chapters 3 and 4 which lay the foundations for the emergence of a new narrative of the event. Based on an analysis of official documents and letters pertaining to slum clearance and sterilisation, these chapters trace the role of the state bureaucracy in

---

Chauri Chaura in 1922, Shahid Amin suggests the impossibility of surmounting the high levels of discrepancy, distortion and fragmentation which exist between official records and different personal narrations of an event. My own research, though by no means suggesting the possibility of historic perfection, does imply a far greater degree of coherence between the various fragments of history with which a researcher can work, see Shahid Amin, 1995, *Event, Metaphor, Memory: Chauri Chaura, 1922–1992*, Delhi: OUP.

carrying out Emergency measures. Unlike existing renditions of the event, bureaucratic memories portray it, not as a moment of wild unfettered violence, but as a period of meticulously orchestrated state oppression. They also problematise conventional dichotomies drawn between the official and unofficial, between victim and agent, highlighting the many grey areas, not only in state policy but also in popular responses to it. These issues are examined more closely in the remaining chapters which take us out of the Slum Department and into the homes of the people of Welcome—craftsmen, vendors, rickshaw pullers, sweepers and other low level government servants and their husbands and wives. Their personal accounts reveal the links and disjunctions between political intentions and lived realities. Taken together they provide a powerful collective critique of the Emergency even if this critique remains fragmented and retains many contradictions. Though focused principally around a specific historical moment, their narratives tell us much about the dynamics of life amongst the urban poor in Delhi.

2

FORGETTING AND REMEMBERING
THE EMERGENCY

'Nothing that happens in the future can undo this past.' (*John Dayal and Ajoy Bose*)

The history of Independent India can, like all history, be read as a history of remembering and forgetting. Certain characters, moments and events are splashed large across the canvas of public memory; others are watered down, diminished, reduced, faded out of the picture altogether. One such faded moment is the Emergency of 1975–7. So much has it slipped out of public discourse that today it is remembered, if at all, for the extent to which it has been forgotten. Yet, such forgetting is not without significance. It has its own history. As Ashis Nandy recently commented: 'Enormous political effort has gone into wiping out the Emergency as a live memory.'[1]

The Emergency does not lie alone in India's pool of forgotten moments. Neither is it unique. Such moments share at least one common factor: they do not fit comfortably into the national picture of how things are meant to be. Hence, as Shahid Amin has demonstrated, the violence that occurred at Chauri Chaura in 1922 has been sidelined in the 'nationalist master narrative' of the freedom struggle which seeks to uphold an image of non-violence.[2] Similarly, the horror that accompanied Partition in 1947–8 has been underplayed or passed off as a brief 'moment of madness' because it does not fit the 'history of progress' as we want to see it.[3] The Emergency

[1] Ashis Nandy, 'Emergency Remembered', *Times of India,* 22 June 1995.
[2] Amin, 1995, *Event, Metaphor, Memory.*
[3] Gyanendra Pandey, 1995, 'Nation and Masculinity: Some Reflections on Gandhi and the Partition of India', paper presented at a conference on Gandhi held at SOAS,

is another violent moment. Like Chauri Chaura and Partition, it is difficult to digest. Not only does it threaten the precarious image of India as 'essentially non-violent'—an image increasingly difficult to sustain—but it also implicates the state as the key agent of violence. More threatening still, the Emergency challenges the discourse of democracy which claims an unbroken hold over India's past from the present day right back to the attainment of Independence in 1947.

But the Emergency cannot be forgotten without leaving some casualties in the discourse of democracy, for to forget it is also to forget what was once described as 'democracy's finest hour': the vote which dramatically overthrew the Emergency government in March 1977. At the time this event was projected as a historic victory, a genuine 'people's struggle' on a par with the attainment of Independence. One British journalist even went so far as to state '22 March 1977 may be recorded by future historians as one of the most significant dates in the second half of the twentieth century'.[4] His words read oddly now, as if in the process of entering history, they somehow got deleted.

Recent trends in historiography teach us to take an interest in such deleted moments. We are no longer concerned only with what is written but also with how it is written and what has been excluded. This creates an awareness of the processes by which certain events become significant through the activation of memory whilst others become insignificant through the institution of forgetting. Forgetting, like remembering, can be public as well as private. Whilst public memory is triggered off by collective symbols that often take on physical form, public amnesia operates through producing absences or substitutes; absences which serve to discourage the construction and survival of memory, and substitutes which serve to redirect memory along alternative routes. Public forgetting is a subtle process, not least because we tend to forget what it is we have forgotten. And that is when forgetting is most successful—when we are no longer aware of what is absent.

The visitor who arrives in Delhi is offered a tour of the monuments

---

October 1995. It is only in very recent years that attempts are being made to recover Partition narratives and to recognise and analyse the levels of violence they contain. See also Butalia, *The Other Side of Silence* and Menon and Bhasin, *Borders and Boundaries*.

[4]Michael Henderson, 1977, *Experiment with Untruth: India Under Emergency*, Delhi: Macmillan, preface.

of public memory. For the modern period these include Parliament House, Rashtrapati Bhavan, India Gate and the memorials and cremation sites of great national leaders, notably Mahatma Gandhi, Jawaharlal Nehru, Indira Gandhi and Rajiv Gandhi. It is a tour which traces history as it is meant to be remembered, replete with physical markers inscribed in the landscape of the city. What is proposed here is a guided tour of how a certain moment, the Emergency, has been forgotten, and how its forgetting is equally imprinted in the capital's landscape. It is a tour which takes us to places which might have become sites for remembering the Emergency but which, in the course of history, have become sites for forgetting it. We begin our tour by following a bus of Indian tourists to Teen Murti Bhavan, the residence of the Nehru family, just a short distance from Parliament in the heart of New Delhi.

Teen Murti Bhavan

Teen Murti Bhavan is a handsome cream coloured mansion built by Edwin Lutyens in the 1920s as part of the new imperial capital. It is situated in a luscious tree-filled garden, one of the few places in contemporary Delhi where peacocks literally strut. Jawaharlal Nehru lived here during his 16 years as India's first Prime Minister and much time was also spent here by his daughter Indira and her sons, Rajiv and Sanjay. Until 1948, however, it had been the official residence of a British Commander in Chief. History has since smoothed over these imperial edges by converting the building into a memorial museum 'dedicated to the nation'. Walking around this gracious home-cum-museum one can see Nehru's study and living rooms, frozen in time since his death. One can also begin again at his birth and follow his steps through a photo montage of the freedom struggle and the founding of the Indian Republic. It seems an ironic place for tracing memories of the Emergency, a period which most intellectuals consider a blot on the noble Gandhi-Nehru legacy. But history has kindly intervened on two occasions to save posthumous Nehru from exposure to his daughter Indira's politics: once in 1971 when close associates prevented her from fulfilling her plan to take up residence in the mansion; and again in 1974 when the library, which used to be inside the mansion, was transferred into a new modern building around the corner. All of this means that when Indira Gandhi declared the

Emergency, she was living not in Teen Murti Bhavan, but in the nearby residence of 1 Safdarjang Road, and when literature about the Emergency began to surface, it was shelved, not in Jawaharlal Nehru's home but in the modern new library next to it.

The library, moulded in sandy concrete, may lack the historic grace of the mansion, but it serves our purpose well as a repository of the past. Whilst the tourists continue to follow the arrows of public memory in Teen Murti House, we shall make a brief detour in search of things once remembered but since forgotten, for it is only through reviving memories that we can comprehend what their forgetting is about. Rummaging through the shelves marked 'Constitution', it is possible to trace the duration of the Emergency both as an experience and as a written memory. The books, though jumbled together, slip easily into two categories: those which welcome the Emergency, generally published between 1975–6, and those which deride it, generally published between 1977–8. The overlap is minimal since censorship had prevented people from openly criticising the Emergency at the time, whilst simultaneously pushing criticism underground from which it re-surfaced after the event. What we have, then, are two alternative narratives, each with its own vision; one which projects the Emergency as a step into a brighter future; the other which remembers it as a bleak and shameful past. Each narrative creates its own time-scale, re-arranging past and present to suit its future, yet neither dominates for more than 21 months. These are phantom futures and ghostly pasts. By 1979 they are already subsiding. By 1980 their demise is marked by the absence of new additions that year to the Emergency shelf.[5]

Stepping into the future: the official narrative of the Emergency

'I am sure you are all conscious of the deep and widespread conspiracy, which has been brewing ever since I began to introduce certain progressive measures of benefit to the common man and woman of India,' Indira Gandhi announced in her first Emergency broadcast

[5]Occasional books on the Emergency trickled into the library in the 1980s such as *Voices of Emergency*, Bombay: Popular Prakashan, a collection of resistance poems edited by J.O. Perry which did not come out until 1983 owing to the difficulties that had been involved in collecting poems from across the country.

on 26 June 1975. 'Certain persons have gone to the length of inciting our armed forces to mutiny and our police to rebel...How can any Government worth its name stand by and allow the country's stability to be imperilled? The actions of the few are endangering the rights of the vast majority.'[6]

'We were not happy to declare Emergency,' she announced some six weeks later in her Republic Day speech, 'but we had to under the compulsion of circumstances...Stringent measures were taken just as bitter pills have to be administered to a patient in the interest of his health...No one can prevent India marching ahead.'[7] These were themes she was to repeat throughout the Emergency; that temporary hardships were necessary in order for India to speed up the march of progress. They were themes splashed across the newspaper headlines and posted onto billboards and stickers throughout the city:

THE NATION IS ON THE MOVE!
EMERGENCY USHERS IN ERA OF DISCIPLINE!
MARCHING TO A BETTER TOMORROW!
EMERGENCY FOR A STRONGER MORE PROSPEROUS FUTURE!

Integral to this vision of the future was the notion that democracy had been derailed and that the country was spiralling towards unprecedented disaster. Jayaprakash Narayan was identified as the chief conspirator intent on provoking full scale rebellion and encouraging 'anti-Congress parties' to obstruct not only economic development, but all normal functioning of the administration and economy. They were inciting people not to work, encouraging the non-payment of taxes, preventing farmers from selling their produce to the government, encouraging mass strikes and rousing children and students to violence. They had created 'the kind of climate' in which it was impossible for any nation to survive, let alone prosper.[8] The Emergency was therefore a constitutional necessity. It gave the Prime Minister the much needed right to deal harshly with disruptive elements and to set the nation back on the path to progress at an

---

[6]Broadcast on radio, 26 June 1975, included in Indira Gandhi, 1984, *Selected Speeches and Writings (SSWIG)*, vol. III, 1972–1977, Delhi: Ministry of Information and Broadcasting; pp. 177–8.
[7]Speech from Red Fort, 15 August 1975, *SSWIG*, pp. 200–1.
[8]Interview, 3 July 1975, *SSWIG*, p. 180.

accelerated rate. 'Whatever we are doing is pro-India, it is pro-Indian people, it is pro-the direction of the future of India,' she told the Lok Sabha (Lower House of Parliament).[9]

By portraying the recent past as a descent into catastrophe, Indira Gandhi not only justified 'stringent measures' but also proclaimed them as a duty: 'It is incumbent on a democratic regime to remove obstacles and impediments...for social, political and economic progress.'[10] The arrest and detention of opposition leaders, social activists, journalists, students and academics 'were necessary' for the preservation of democracy. So too was the banning of certain organisations and groups 'wedded to terror and murder'. Similarly press censorship had become 'a necessity'. 'I am not happy that we had to impose regulations on newspapers,' she told M. Shamim in an interview, 'but some journals had shed all objectivity and independence and allied themselves totally with the opposition front and did anything to spread doom and defeatism.'[11] For some time they had 'deliberately distorted news', 'made provocative comments', 'hurled allegations' all of which had to be stopped in order 'to restore a climate of trust'.[12] As for foreign journalists, they had long enjoyed maligning India and spreading vicious rumours so their trumped up criticisms were not to be heeded.

Slogans in the streets of Delhi reiterated these messages:

> GRAVE MISCHIEF HAS BEEN DONE BY IRRESPONSIBLE WRITING!
> SILENCE IS GOLDEN!

Conditions restored to 'normalcy', Indira Gandhi was then able to 'GET ON WITH THE JOB OF NATION BUILDING!' by introducing a new 20–point economic programme aimed at hoisting the country forward. 'The Emergency provides us with a new opportunity to go ahead with our economic tasks,' a government pamphlet announced. Plans were oriented towards improving the social and economic conditions of the poor. They included lowering the price of essential commodities, providing land-sites for the landless and weaker sections, banning barbarous customs like bonded labour, reviewing agricultural minimum wages, expanding irrigation, accelerating power schemes, developing

---

[9]Speech in Lok Sabha, 22 July 1975, *SSWIG*, p. 187.
[10]Interview with Indira Gandhi in *Souvenir on Emergency and Social Justice*, 1975, Delhi: Council of National Affairs.
[11]Interview, 3 July 1975, *SSWIG*, p. 181.
[12]Broadcast on radio, 27 June 1975, *SSWIG*, p. 179.

the handloom sector, implementing agricultural ceilings and liquidating rural indebtedness. They also included income tax relief for the middle classes, control of prices for books and stationery, and harsh measures intended to tackle tax evasion, smuggling and various types of 'economic crime'. The overriding message was that through hard work and mass co-ordination, India could enter a new and successful era of socialism.

THE ONLY MAGIC TO REMOVE POVERTY IS HARD WORK!
YOU TOO HAVE A ROLE IN THE EMERGENCY!
WORK HARD! PRODUCE MORE! MAINTAIN DISCIPLINE!

While slogans, stickers and newspaper headlines codified the basic message into succinct and memorable phrases, government pamphlets with titles like *Timely Steps* and *Preserving our Democratic Structure* spread the word. Meanwhile books and seminar proceedings lent the weight of academic approval with titles like: *Freedom is not Free* (1975), *Era of Discipline* (1976), *Thank you, Mrs Gandhi* (1977) and *Emergency: Its Needs and Gains* (1976). Such books, along with newspaper and magazine reports of the time, should be read, not as witnesses of the past but as mouthpieces of the dominant narrative of the then present. Take for example the commemorative booklet *Souvenir on Emergency and Social Justice*, 'presented to the great leader of masses, Indira Gandhi' on her 58th birthday (19 November 1975). Here the Prime Minister's words are echoed in the praise of successive chief ministers and important dignitaries who proclaim the Emergency 'a necessary measure', a 'good opportunity for the poor', 'a wise and timely action'. Meanwhile Indira herself is admired for her dynamic leadership, her pursuit of truth and her dedication to the nation for which she will never be forgotten. 'The coming generation will feel extremely proud of the name of Indira Gandhi. They will worship her as [the] personification of Sita, Laxmi and Durga [Hindu goddesses]. Long live Indira Ji,' predicts an enthusiastic Virendra Khanna, General Secretary, Council of National Affairs.

By 1976 the 20-point national economic programme had been joined by an equally promising five-point programme, to be implemented by the Youth Congress under the 'dynamic leadership' of the Prime Minister's youngest son, Sanjay Gandhi. So apposite was this smaller programme that Indira Gandhi even suggested that the 20-point programme could do with borrowing some extra points from it! Some, in their enthusiasm, began to refer to 'the 25-point programme'.

Sanjay's points were short and pithy: Each One Teach One—to achieve complete literacy; Family Planning—for a prosperous future; Plant Trees—for ecological balance; Abolish Dowry—to end a social evil; Eradicate Casteism—to destroy social prejudice.

The speed with which Sanjay Gandhi was rising to prominence was heralded as 'a symbol of the new emerging youth power', made possible through the favourable conditions brought on by the Emergency. It was in the enthusiasm and actions of this newly roused Indian youth that the country's future lay. 'Significantly and happily', wrote the journalist of a reputable fortnightly magazine, 'Sanjay Gandhi today has leapt out of the wings...and raced to the centre of the Indian political theatre. He has won this prize race within a span of 12 months, or even less...He is ensconced today in a position of political leadership which comes naturally to him. He is in the key-slot of authority: both political and organisational.'[13] This magnificent leap to power at the age of only twenty-nine, and without any previous political experience, showed his extraordinary energy, his 'hard-as-nails approach' and his 'accurate perception' of India's urgent problems. Like his mother he seemed to magnetise the crowds through his projection of a better future: 'As a catalyst he is a vital and necessary political bromide to organise Indian youth. Appropriately large numbers of Indian young men and women have increasingly gravitated towards Sanjay Gandhi. They have all gravitated for a reason. And they will remain with him for a reason.'[14]

In Delhi Sanjay's praises were sung for two main 'reasons'. His close involvement with the Delhi Development Authority (DDA), and his personal dedication to beautification of the city, had resulted in the planting of thousands of trees and resettlement of thousands of squatters who had previously lived in miserable and wretched slum conditions. Such slums could no longer be tolerated with callous indifference. Demolition and resettlement were the prerequisites for development, and Sanjay Gandhi was visibly at their forefront. But most importantly of all, Sanjay Gandhi was praised for his deep commitment to family planning. At the 'Hum Do Hamare Do' (We are two, so let's have two) Family Planning seminar in August 1976, he was acknowledged as one of the driving forces behind the new priority

---

[13]'Sanjay Gandhi: A Driving Force', *India Today*, 1–15 Sept., 1976, p. 20.
[14]Ibid.

given to this urgent economic problem. The conference pamphlet contains Sanjay's photograph on the frontispiece, along with those of the President and the Prime Minister. The cover of the pamphlet, typical of government publications of the time, portrays a panorama of the vast, uncontrollable Indian 'masses'. Inside we are confronted by the horrifying urgency of the population explosion, as the chief ministers of various states compete with alarmist statistics. 'Every 19th second a child is born in West Bengal, every minute, 3 new born babies, every hour, 180 new born babies and by the time you leave the conference today—today we shall be spending two hours—we shall have 360 new born babies in West Bengal...Can you see how dangerous the problem is?' There was unanimity that vasectomy was the most efficient means of tackling the terrifying birth rate which would lead India to ever more grinding poverty if not forestalled. Vasectomy camps were already spreading throughout the country, and incentives in the form of cash, ghee and electrical equipment were offered as appropriate. Sterilisation was heralded as the means by which every Indian, rich or poor, could contribute to a better and more prosperous future.

The dominant narrative of the Emergency was bold and unmistakable. It flowed not only from the mouths of Indira Gandhi and her son, but also from the mouths of politicians, bureaucrats, officials and journalists. In Delhi, it was quite literally plastered in the streets in hoardings, stickers and bold slogans painted on the back of rickshaws and buses. By controlling population growth, increasing production, boosting agriculture, encouraging industry, abolishing socially backward customs, clearing slums and rooting out corruption, India could achieve new levels of greatness. Modernity was the goal and the Emergency was the means to attain it. It provided India with the discipline she so desperately needed. But, despite the clarity of this message, certain people deliberately chose to 'misunderstand' it. They went about spreading rumours of 'forcible sterilisations' and of people 'crushed to death under bulldozers'. They delighted in exaggerating the occasional mishap and spreading fear amongst the people who were basically in favour of the Emergency.

By the end of 1976, the dominant narrative had become increasingly defensive. It was losing its hold. Despite censorship and imprisonments, voices of dissent were beginning to surface which could no longer be glossed over as the discourse of the traitor. Previously reduced to the hushed tones of underground literature, the muted criticisms of the few Indian newspapers with editors brave enough to risk their careers[15] and the blatant but distant rumblings of the foreign press,[16] these voices of dissent were getting both louder and closer. By early 1977, they seemed to be emanating not just from subversive activists, many of whom were in prison, but from the ordinary citizens, from the very crowds who had previously cheered so loudly, not least because they had often been paid to do so. Attempts were made to adjust the dominant narrative to suit the apparent change of atmosphere. A halt was called on family planning activities and prominent individuals began to alter their tone. Bansi Lal, the Defence Minister, made a public apology to the people of Haryana, promising, 'no more sterilisation'. Increasingly ministers began to speak of 'overenthusiastic officials' getting carried away. Indira Gandhi decided to calm fears of a permanent dictatorship by relaxing censorship and announcing a general election in January 1977, but the tide had already turned. At her first election rally on 1 March 1977, her speech was shaky. It began with references to 'reactionaries and vested interests' bent on attacking her, but continued with an admission that certain 'excesses' had been done, not only by officials, but also by politicians.[17] Her words were drowned out by a disgruntled crowd. During the election campaign that followed, counter arguments gathered strength in the merging of the opposition forces under the Janata Party. These forces were speaking a new discourse of vengeance.

The election results were announced on 22 March 1977. They

---

[15]During the Emergency the two national newspapers which most successfully withstood censorship restrictions were the *Indian Express* and the *Statesman* whose editors, V.K. Narasimhan and C.R. Irani respectively, retained their commitment to the idea of a free press.

[16]Foreign newspapers played an important role in publishing critical material about the Emergency, much of which fed back to India through underground channels. Foreign correspondents were at first expected to submit drafts of their articles for inspection by official censors. Later they were permitted to censor their own dispatches according to official guidelines. Peter Hazelhurst (*The Times*), Mark Tully (*BBC*), Lewis Simpson (*Washington Post*) and Lorens Jenkins (*Newsweek*) were amongst those foreign correspondents who were expelled from India for their controversial reporting.

[17]Since the main source of Indira Gandhi's speeches is a 'selected' rather than a 'collected' works (*SSWIG*), it contains very few of the speeches she made during the Emergency. This means that we are obliged to rely on the reports of journalists and writers for their content.

recorded a massive Janata victory. Indira Gandhi revoked the Emergency the following day. Her march into the future had been abruptly halted. It was time for a new narrative to assert its dominance.

Anatomising the past: the post-Emergency counter narrative

'On 25 June 1975, Indian democracy was put to death'—so reads the cover of B.M. Sinha's *Operation Emergency,* a slim paperback completed only 10 weeks after the March elections. The book purports to be 'an uncensored sweeping narrative of the terror, oppression and resistance during those dark days'. The words are sprawled dramatically in black and yellow on a white background. In the right-hand corner a blood-red splash contains the words 'Topical Hard Hitting Political Best-seller'. On the back cover is a potted history of the Emergency experience, printed dramatically in heavy black ink:

- POLITICAL LEADERS AND WORKERS, INTELLECTUALS AND JOURNALISTS NABBED IN MIDNIGHT SWOOP, AND JAILED
- PRESS GAGGED, AND EMASCULATED
- PRISONERS SUBJECTED TO TORTURE AND UNHEARD OF BRUTALITY
- HOUSES AND BAZAARS BULLDOZED INTO RUBBLE
- MEN AND WOMEN DRIVEN LIKE CATTLE INTO FP [FAMILY PLANNING] CAMPS
- THE 'CAUCUS' STRIKING TERROR, UNHINDERED BY THE LAW
- SYCOPHANTS AND HANGERS-ON CALLING THE TUNE

We have entered a new body of literature, enthused with outrage and the desire to expose. As if to compensate for the burden of censorship during the Emergency, this new literature seems to have virtually flooded the market in the years 1977–8. Whether in the form of prison memoir, official judgement, resistance literature or political exposé, this new literature is concerned primarily with remembering the Emergency in such a way that it can not and will not be forgotten. 'Because we tend to forget,' writes Rajmohan Gandhi in his foreword to Michael Henderson's *Experiment with Untruth,* 'we must be reminded of what it was like to miss the air of liberty.'

This elevation of memory to the status of a national imperative had the effect of cancelling out Indira Gandhi's presentation of the Emergency as a transitory phase designed to usher in a new future— a tough means to a more glorious end. The new post-Emergency narrative spins the focus back in time. We are no longer concerned with the projected ends but with the actual means. In the new atmosphere of political post-mortem, the 'bitter pills' which Indira Gandhi had administered as 'a cure' are now identified as a form of poison. The new prerogative is to track the progress of that poison as it seeped into the veins and arteries of the nation, thereby infecting the entire system. Unlike the official Emergency narrative, the new master narrative cannot be traced back to a primary source. Rather, it is multi-vocal and has been cobbled together from a mixture of personal experiences, underground literature, prison memoirs, public hearings and newly uncovered government documents. Above all, it is part of a vast collective exercise in memory with a view to judgement. This is not to argue that the elements of such a narrative had not existed earlier. Voices of dissent had of course been present throughout the Emergency, but political conditions had rendered them fragmented and dispersed. Arrests, censorship and the climate of fear had not only prevented the circulation of alternative views, but had also cultivated a series of blanks which had worked against the formation of a single coherent narrative. It was only after the Emergency, when the fear of repercussions had been lifted and new information uncovered, that such a narrative could be established and elevated to a position of dominance.

After the nightmarish experience of nineteen months of terrifying darkness, the nation awoke to the clear bright sunshine of a new day...The dawning of this new day brought to light the gory sequence of that night...And those who were the perpetrators of the horror, those whose hands shaped the pattern of events, will not be let off lightly—Justice will take its toll![18]

One strand of this new master narrative lay in recovering fragments of dissent originally expressed during the Emergency under what were then conditions of danger and adversity. *The Smugglers of Truth*, for example is a selection of articles and drawings taken from *Satyavani*, an underground paper that was published in London and New York during the Emergency. It contains the writings of foreign journalists and resistors whose controversial words and opinions had been 'smuggled' in a two-directional process both in and out of India. 'It is a selection of what people in India could not read at the time.' Although the articles it contains were originally written during the Emergency,

[18]N.D. Rawla and R.K. Mudgal, 1977, *All the Prime Minister's Men*, Delhi: Pankaj, preface.

the volume itself belongs to the post-Emergency era and is part of the collective exercise of asserting a dominant interpretation of the recent past. So too is *Voices of Emergency*, an anthology of resistance poems. Its retrospective quality is highlighted by the fact that some of its poems turn out not to have been written during the Emergency at all![19] A recurring theme throughout the volume is people's inability to speak out against the Emergency which imposed an eerie silence just as it imposed an all-engulfing darkness. Jimmy Avasia's short poem 'Emerging' expresses in a few words what others say in many:

> *One day we woke,*
> *Free to do as they wanted.*
> *Ideals collapsed in smoke.*
> *Nobody spoke.*
>
> *On the way to an answer*
> *they selected a truth*
> *but all suggestion of question*
> *died en route.*

A volume of the intellectual journal *Seminar* is quite literally the publication of critical voices that were silenced until the final phase of the Emergency.[20] But here the silence signifies resistance rather than compliance. The editor of the review, Romesh Thapar, had originally prepared the volume in 1976 but, refusing to submit to censorship restrictions, withdrew the manuscript from publication. His decision to publish it six months later, when Emergency restrictions had been lightened, makes it part of the retrospective exercise of remembering the past.

There are three principal overlapping genres of this post-Emergency discourse: the political exposé aimed at making visible what was previously hidden; the prison memoir providing the intimate account of personal experience,[21] and the public judgement aimed at

---

[19]The journalist, Dhiren Bhagat, later criticised the validity of some of these so called 'resistance poems'. Having found one of his own adolescent ramblings in the collection, he was well-placed for making such a criticism, especially since his own poem had been written long before the Emergency. (See Dhiren Bhagat, 1990, *The Contemporary Conservative: Selected Writings*, Delhi: Viking.)

[20]*Seminar*, 210, February 1977.

[21]This book is concerned less with the prison experiences of the literate than with the unwritten narratives of the urban poor. Those interested in prison memoirs

interrogation of the guilty. Barely two weeks after the Janata victory, the Home Minister, Chaudhuri Charan Singh had asserted that justice must be done 'by bringing to book all those guilty of excesses, malpractices and misdeeds during the Emergency from the highest down to the lowest functionary of the Government'. On the basis of this statement special commissions were established to bring the past under the microscope of the law. The most famous judgement was that of the Shah Commission, which opened its enquiry on 30 September 1977. It received as many as 48,000 allegations of abuses which it whittled down to 2,000 cases for investigation. The scale and scope of the commission was compared with that of the famous Nuremberg trials. But long before it had published its slow and ponderous conclusions, the framework of the new master narrative had already been established in books with dramatic titles like *An Eye to India: The Unmasking of Tyranny* (1977), *Black Wednesday* (1977), *Nineteen Fateful Months* (1978), *What Price Perjury?* (1978), *Democracy Redeemed* (1977) and *Experiment with Untruth* (1977). Such books may sit together with Emergency publications on the library shelves, but the story they tell is a very different one.

Like the official narrative, the new narrative takes us back to the period immediately before the Emergency. But this time Indira Gandhi is portrayed as a corrupt and tyrannical leader trying to assert her already fading power, whilst Jayaprakash Narayan (popularly known as JP) is described as the noble and ageing people's hero, encouraging the masses to assert their discontent through non-violent protest in the Gandhian style. Justice had seemed destined to prevail when on 12 June 1975 the Allahabad High Court had found Indira Gandhi guilty of corrupt election practices and debarred her from office for a period of six years. The crowds had been expectant as J.P. Narayan and opposition leaders had demanded the Prime Minister's resignation, but their hopes had been shattered by an unforeseen event. Obsessed by power, and egged on by her ruthless son, Indira Gandhi had chosen not resignation, but dictatorship.

---

of the Emergency should consult the following: Jayaprakash Narayan, 1977, *Prison Diary*, New Delhi: Popular Prakashan; Lal K. Advani, 1978, *A Prisoner's Scrap-Book*, New Delhi: Arnold-Heinemann; Kuldip Nayar, 1978, *In Jail*, New Delhi; Vikas; Primila Lewis, 1978, *Reason Wounded,* New Delhi: Vikas; and Mary Tyler, 1978, *My Years in an Indian Prison*, London: Penguin.

The declaration of Emergency features both as a moment of revelation—the time when Indira Gandhi's real intentions become apparent—and as a descent into utter darkness. 'We were caught unawares in this unexpected treachery undermining all our constitutional provisions, parliamentary practices and public institutions,' recalls P.G. Mavalankar, a member of the Lok Sabha. Others, like the journalist V.K. Narasimhan refer to the Emergency as 'the long dark night' when 'free people lost their basic liberties and were subjected to a regime of terror and suppression they had not known even under the British'. What is unanimous in all of these accounts is the view that Indira Gandhi declared the Emergency in order to stamp out opposition voices which she could no longer control by democratic means. The arrest and detention of thousands of men and women conveniently classified as 'conspirators' provides indication of her sinister intentions. So too does the sudden termination of the electricity supply to major newspapers for a period of three nights—thereby enabling her to prevent adverse publicity in the short term and install press censorship for the long term. The Emergency therefore features as a device through which Indira Gandhi obtains access to the basic tools of dictatorship: the ability to ban all meetings, processions and agitations that did not work in her favour; the ability to arrest and detain people without trial and the ability to gag the press and to use it as an agent of personal propaganda. It therefore represents a complete subversion of democracy.

The 20-point economic programme, which features prominently in the official Emergency narrative, becomes a minor detail in the post-Emergency exposé. The programme is dismissed as old plans dressed up in new populist discourse. Socialist talk about 'helping the weaker sections' and 'going to the masses' is interpreted as mere rhetoric whilst the fact that food prices dipped in 1976 is explained by the heavy rains which had resulted in a successful harvest. But none of this, we are told, could deceive the masses into thinking that the Emergency worked in their favour. 'People were, no doubt, terrorised but certainly their thoughts could not be checked,' Sinha suggests. 'They were aware [even before the Emergency] that the Government was slowly turning them into slaves by promising them the bread of plenty. The 20-point programme was another attempt to fool them into believing that long-awaited millennium had come. This resulted in hate for her and her coterie. How could they accept somebody as their leader who had thrown to the winds all ideals of truth and justice, and on false ground claimed to be the most virtuous person in the world?'

As it unfolds, the new narrative becomes like a play, endlessly repeated with minor variants but with the basic roles well defined. Indira Gandhi is the new 'Hitler' otherwise known as the 'Durga of Delhi'.[22] Dominated by an oedipal passion for her own son, she is seen to support his rise to power despite his well-known history of failure and corruption. The fact that Sanjay dictates orders without holding any official position is an indication not only of his ruthlessness, but also of the insatiable greed of the politicians and officials who surround him. They feature in the play as an ever-flattering chorus of sycophants, singing the praises of the powerful with unholy gusto. Not much better are the journalists and editors who readily bow down to press censorship, crawling when only asked to kneel.[23] Last, but by no means least, petty officials and bureaucrats populate the stage like small but lethal spiders, building the bureaucratic web with which to ensnare the populace.

The role of intellectuals in this tragi-comedy is more ambiguous. Though some are perceived as being guilty of complicity, many feature as the emotional sufferers of the Emergency; the men and women burning with indignation but unable to speak out either because they are already in jail or else because they fear arrest. 'For India at that point was a country where mail was opened, phones tapped, movements watched, and dissenting views punished with imprisonment without trial.' Thus wrote Michael Henderson, a foreign journalist who had tried to publish a critique of what was happening during the Emergency itself, but had been unable to find a foreign publisher willing to accept the manuscript for fear of the damage it might do to their commercial links with India. When, after the Emergency, such critiques became hot commodities, Henderson's newly expanded manuscript joined the growing body of post-Emergency exposés.

The new narrative also features victims and resisters, the bulk of whom are poor and illiterate. Indeed speculation even arose as to

---

[22]Durga, the powerful and vengeful goddess renowned for having slain the buffalo-demon, Mahishasura.

[23]A phrase used by Lal Krishna Advani and much-quoted in the post-Emergency literature.

whether Sanjay Gandhi's resettlement and family planning measures were not part of a systematic plot to obliterate the poor. 'Was Sanjay trying to wipe out the harijans and the tribals and the poor through vasectomy?' asks Raj Thapar in an article in *Seminar*, concluding that he was. Writing in more sociological bent, Anirudha Gupta declares, 'It was the poor, the illiterate and the depressed who suffered the most. The rich—either because they had the money or the influence—mostly escaped.' [24] Just what the poor suffered is made explicit in the numerous accounts of how, in the effort to fill sterilisation targets, chief ministers and others anxious to please Sanjay Gandhi instilled terror by imposing forcible sterilisation. 'People were rounded up at random, from the streets, the tea shop, and the bazaars, and taken to the family planning camps to be sterilised. No distinction whatsoever was made between old men and young boys, between married and unmarried men—the forced sterilisation just went on and on!'[25] Many books feature an assortment of nightmarish incidents of death by sterilisation. In the northern states of Uttar Pradesh and Haryana, located in the so called 'vasectomy belt', there were tales of entire populations of village men hiding in the fields to escape police raids in the night. There were also instances of police firings and innocent protesters killed. Most post-Emergency writers identify the fear and fury over sterilisation as being the primary cause of resistance to the Emergency. 'Please do not think I am exaggerating,' an old Congressman is reported to have told a journalist during the 1977 election campaign, 'but these damned vasectomies have become something like the greased cartridge of 1857.'[26]

In the Delhi version of the post-Emergency narrative, the poor suffer a form of double victimisation. Not only are they sterilised, but they also lose their homes in the massive slum clearance project directed by Sanjay Gandhi in the name of resettlement. David Selbourne's eye-witness account, published during the Emergency, and republished after it, sets the scene: 'In clouds of dust, and with children weeping beside their smashed and bulldozed hovels, as I saw myself, trucks

---

[24]Anirudha Gupta, 1977, *Revolution through Ballot*, Delhi: Ankur, p. 85.

[25]N.D. Rawla and R.K. Mudgal, 1977, *All the Prime Minister's Men*.

[26]Gupta, 1977, *Revolution through Ballot*, p. 83. This is a reference to the famous Indian Rebellion of 1857 which is said to have been sparked off by the rumour that cow's fat was used to grease the cartridges used by Indian sepoys.

now drive the displaced away and dump them without food, sanitation, water or building materials for "resettlement" in the name of a new politics of "discipline" and "development". Writing in more controlled language, the Shah Commission concludes: 'The manner in which demolitions were carried out in Delhi during the Emergency is an unrelieved story of illegality, callousness and of sickening sycophancy by the senior officers to play to the whims of Sanjay Gandhi.' Within a mere 21 months an estimated 700,000 people were displaced from slums and commercial properties, including large areas of the Old City. And it is here, in one of the ancient Muslim strongholds known as Turkman Gate, that Delhi's counter-Emergency narrative reaches its climax as the dual forces of sterilisation and demolition unite. 'Turkman Gate is where it came to grief,' chronicles Henderson. 'People speak the words now in the way that they spoke of Jallianwala Bagh after General Dyer's massacre in 1919.'[27]

What exactly happened at Turkman Gate on 19 April 1976 remains open to speculation as each playwright revises the script. But the overall theme is clear: local resistance to family planning and demolitions precipitated a brutal massacre of innocent citizens. Some litter the stage with as many as 1,200 corpses; others are more restrained. The version we shall follow here is that of John Dayal and Ajoy Bose[28] who, after conducting 'two months of tough and continuous investigation' put the death toll at 12. Their tale winds its way between two nearby localities of the Old City: Turkman Gate on Asaf Ali Road and Dujana House near the Jama Masjid. It begins in mid-April with the inauguration of a family planning clinic in the Muslim-dominated area of Dujana House. The clinic is run by a glamorous socialite turned 'social worker' whose name is Ruksana Sultana to some, and *rundi* (whore) to others. She is Muslim herself and goes about trying to persuade Muslim women of the area to get their husbands sterilised. As the week progresses, the people of the area watch in horror as beggars are rounded up in the streets and bundled into a basement

---

[27]Henderson, 1977, *Experiment*, p. 59. In 1919 General Dyer ordered troops to fire on a crowd of protesters gathered at Jallianwala Bagh in Amritsar. This resulted in the death of 379 unarmed civilians and the wounding of over 1,000 others. This event became a major rallying-point around which many Indians united in the freedom struggle.
[28]J. Dayal and A. Bose, 1977, *For Reasons of State, Delhi Under Emergency*, Delhi: Ess Ess Publications, pp. 35–65.

clinic, from which some never emerge. The story advances to Turkman Gate, only a mile away, where demolition squads show no sign of leaving the area and residents begin to realise that their homes may be next on the list for devastation. Some try to enlist the help of Ruksana Sultana, knowing her influence with Sanjay Gandhi, but she is only willing to support their case if they set up a family planning clinic at Turkman Gate and supply her with 300 sterilisation cases within a week. As fears spread a delegation of local residents try to approach Jagmohan, then Vice-chairman of the DDA (Delhi Development Authority), asking amongst other things, if the Turkman Gate people might be resettled together in a single colony known as 'Welcome' or the nearby colony of New Seelampur in east Delhi. Jagmohan is angered by the idea of displaced Muslims building up their strength by huddling together in particular locations. He is said to have replied, 'Do you think we are mad to destroy one Pakistan to create another Pakistan?'

The tension is mounting. At Dujana House the knives are out; at Turkman Gate, the bulldozers are preparing to roll. Women of Dujana House begin to protest. A *burqa*-clad (veiled) woman lies on the road, blocking a van full of sterilisation victims who have been collected randomly off the streets. The police try to intervene and end up arresting one man. The crowd raises a protest and a general strike is called throughout the area including Turkman Gate. When Ruksana Sultana next arrives at Dujana House, she is besieged by furious local women but manages to escape. 'It was around this time,' report Dayal and Bose, that the message from Turkman Gate was flashed to Dujana House. 'They are massacring us here at Turkman Gate. Come and help us if you can.'

The message took the family planning camp right out of the mind of the people of the Jama Masjid. Men, women and children ran through the lanes and by-lanes towards Turkman Gate. The people of Turkman Gate were their relatives and friends. If they were being attacked, that was where they would fight the police...The two parallel dramas of Turkman Gate and Dujana House had at last converged.

So the scene is set for the ensuing onslaught. At its centre are women and children squatting on the road in the hot April sun, trying to protect their homes from demolition. Facing them are demolition squads; men wielding pickaxes and backed by bulldozers. Close by the Central Reserve Police Force (CRPF) is standing guard, arms in hand and ready for use. Violence finally erupts when some women and children get up to pray. Seeing the sudden movement, the chief of the Nehru brigade incites his men to prevent the crowd from throwing stones. This they do by throwing stones themselves only to be met with fierce retaliation. What follows is a stiff police crackdown, first with sticks and then with a teargas shell which lands in the midst of the women and children. 'An eerie scream went up amongst them. It was not a cry of fear,. It was a battle cry.' Someone, nobody quite knows who, incites the police to fire and a bloody conflict follows. Some flee into the Faiz-e-Elahi Mosque only to find themselves gassed out and physically and verbally abused. 'In just half an hour the Masjid had become an abattoir. Blood lay in pools on the ground and the air was noxious with fumes of teargas and groans and moans of the injured congregation. Doors, windows and furniture had been smashed and the cash box of the Masjid, containing a few thousand rupees had been looted by the marauding policemen. It had been a wholesale affair.'

Outside in the street the desperate crowd is throwing stones and is aided by new arrivals who attack the police from behind, taking control of the police *chowki* (post). The Commissioner of Police orders reinforcements, which, armed with bayonets, aim to kill. 'The Western horizon was red. Four o'clock in the afternoon and blood flowed down Turkman Gate. Their short-lived jubilation had turned sour as bullets cut them down one by on. Nobody, not even the people of Turkman Gate, could take so much punishment.' At 5.30 in the afternoon a curfew is declared, leading to a systematic wave of rape and looting as foul-smelling constables break into the homes of defenceless women whose husbands have been arrested or have fled. It is a tale which ends in darkness—literally and metaphorically. The electricity has been cut off, leaving only the shadow of bulldozers grinding through the night. 'The rubble of Turkman Gate was scooped up into trucks and thrown behind the Ring Road where buzzards and jackals were seen rummaging through the rubble. Only the stink of stale meat which hung for days together over the thrown rubble remained to tell the story of the life and death struggle of the people of Turkman Gate.'

Who threw the first stone and for what reason? Was it the Nehru brigade or the people of Turkman Gate? Were the latter resisting sterilisation or demolition or a mixture of both? The unanswerable nature of such questions does nothing to diminish the symbolic value of the story. For, of all Emergency tales, the story of Turkman Gate contains the most dramatic elements for a tragedy. It begins as the state versus innocent women who fight for the basic right to retain their homes and reproduce. The fact that they are veiled highlights their sanctity and emphasises the state's violation of it, whilst the fact that they are accompanied by children reinforces the image of innocent lambs to the slaughter. It becomes the state versus the community as residents of the old city rush to support one another, willing to unite and die together in the face of such oppression. It is also the state versus the minority, with the suspicion that this is a deliberate attempt to remove Muslims from one of the few areas where they are dominant. The reference to 'a second Pakistan' creates an echo of the bloody massacre that accompanied Partition. In this cruel drama the people are poor and unarmed; but the state does not hesitate to use the technology of violence, crushing the people with guns, gas and machinery. Most accounts contain at least one incidence of a person who is crushed to death by the bulldozers. In many accounts it is a breast-feeding mother and her new born baby who are the victims. As far as symbolism is concerned nothing is lacking: the bureaucrats are callous and speak like villains; the police murder innocent citizens and rape women; homes, bodies and religious property are systematically and brutally violated, leading Sinha to conclude: 'Never was such a great human tragedy caused in any part of the world.'[29]

The post-Emergency retrospective ends with a people's victory as the victims of the Emergency rise up to overthrow the dictator. It is the victory of right over wrong. Many dedicate their books to the millions of victims and resistors who made this victory possible. *Nineteen Fateful Months* for example is dedicated 'to those valiant sons of the Indian soil who refused to submit to the forces of tyranny, high handedness and authoritarianism and preferred misery, humanitarianism or even death'. Similarly *The Emergency: Future Safeguards* is dedicated to 'the victims of the Emergency whose sufferings roused their countrymen to sweep out of power governments which had caused those sufferings.' With the victory India's new future is realigned with her noble past. Jayaprakash Narayan is the new Gandhi,

[29]Sinha, 1977, *Operation Emergency*, p. 153.

and just as Independence Day had heralded a new era of optimism for India, so the March elections promised a fresh reawakening after the lengthy darkness. However, the discourse of judgement breeds its own controversies. The institution of the judge splits the people not only into the roles of witness and accused, but also of defendant and approver. Many of the ministers brought before the Shah Commission claimed that they had simply been following orders and had been unable to resist the terrible pressures placed upon them. Even prominent men like Kishan Chand, Lieutenant Governor of Delhi and B.R. Tamta, Commissioner of the Municipal Corporation of Delhi claimed a combination of ignorance and helplessness. Some even wept with humble apologies; others sought to alleviate their own guilt through implicating their colleagues. 'During the Emergency many people like me had to mortgage their conscience,' remembers Congressman Shankar Dayal Singh, 'but the truth is I have often been smitten by a feeling of repentance over all that happened during the period.' He presents his book, *Emergency, Fact and Fiction*, as an attempt to redeem his conscience by revealing the inside story of what really happened. His foreword is humble but inside the book he devotes much time to denigrating his colleagues whilst remaining relatively silent about his own position. He is also highly cautious in his critique of Indira Gandhi, recognising (and perhaps hoping) that she may still rise again.

More radical is the discourse of defence which surfaces in the works of those who refuse to don the mantle of guilt and shame. Jagmohan, for example, the 'villain' behind the DDA's demolitions, not only defended his actions before the Shah Commission, but also published a book aimed at proving his innocence. In *Island of Truth*,[30] he portrays himself as a lone honest man surrounded by hypocrites and buffeted by concocted accusations. He dismisses much of the dominant narrative as 'inaccurate', 'an injustice to history and public information', a product of 'hypocrisy and superficiality'. He claims that the Turkman Gate episode in which he, as Vice-chairman of the DDA, was directly implicated has been blown out of all proportion and embroidered with erroneous facts. The riot was caused, not by demolitions, but by the threat of family planning at Dujana House. He supports his

[30]Jagmohan, 1978, *Island of Truth*, Delhi: Vikas.

argument by pointing out that out of the six people killed, only one lived in the Turkman Gate area and he happened to be someone whose home was not scheduled for demolition. Jagmohan insists that the entire resettlement drive conducted during the Emergency was in line with DDA policy which was created back in the 1950s. His language is emotive: 'Mine is an island of truth—truth in its essence, truth in its basic framework. I intend to take you to this island...I hope to show you a few spots from which the reality may emerge, and you may be able to see true reflections even in a cracked mirror. You may realise that what was done in Delhi during the Emergency was development and not "demolition". It was a dawn, not a doom.'[31] Similarly in response to David Selbourne's dramatic accusation that 25,000 displaced people could only get new plots through compulsory sterilisation, he argues: 'Not in a single case, compulsory sterilisation was made a pre-condition for allotment of land or plot to those who were affected by the clearance-cum-resettlement operations.'[32]

But the most effective challenge to the post-Emergency narrative came from Indira Gandhi herself who refused to submit to the role of dictator that had been ascribed to her. Her arrest on 3 October 1977, and subsequent release the following day, acted as a buttress to support the idea that she was not guilty after all. Meanwhile, by claiming that the Shah Commission was politically motivated, she justified her refusal to comply with it. Eventually, when pressurised, she did attend the court but refused to come to the witness box and be sworn in for testimony. This resulted in Justice Shah ordering a case to be filed against her, thereby delaying the procedures of the commission. Meanwhile, Indira Gandhi continued to wield power within the Congress Party and was beginning to reassert her importance by promising to devote herself to the service of the nation. Some blamed the Janata Party for failing to make use of the atmosphere of revenge that had prevailed immediately after the Emergency. Dayal and Bose who wrote a second Emergency book, this time about the Shah Commission, conclude: 'The developing political scene made time a valuable commodity, the public memory a political force of considerable magnitude.

[31]Ibid., p. 1.
[32]Ibid., p. 82.

The public which had suffered was crying for justice. It had shed blood and it wanted blood...The appointment of the Commission in those blood-thirsty times was an anti-climax.'[33]

Even before the Commission opened its enquiry in September 1977, the post-Emergency narrative was already subsiding against a backdrop of rising prices and political chaos.

The euphoria of March steadily gave way to bitterness and cynicism by August. The victims of the Emergency like the people of Turkman Gate or the resettlement colonies outside Delhi still continued in their misery and sorrow. To make things worse, prices of almost all essential goods had started rising alarmingly. There had begun to circulate already among some the dangerous logic that perhaps Mrs Gandhi was right in saying that the Emergency was a bitter pill needed by the country.[34]

Our excursion through the book shelves of the Nehru Memorial Library ends with a Janata Party publication entitled *Will we let her do it again?* Published in late 1979, the pamphlet bears witness to the decline of the post-Emergency narrative. It is a desperate attempt to convince the electorate not to allow Indira Gandhi back to power. It ends with a plea: 'Shrimati Indira Gandhi imposed Emergency on an unwary people; if the people vote for her in the coming elections, she would, true to style, argue that the people have endorsed a return to fascist, dynastic rule. Ponder over it.'

After 1980, the shelves marked 'Constitution' fill up mainly with books on other themes; communalism, regionalism, minorities. The Emergency has ceased to be either journalistic coup or scholarly preoccupation.

1 Safdarjang Road

It is time to leave the library and to converge with the coachload of tourists back on the heritage trail. Our brief detour through one of the more neglected shelves of the Nehru Memorial Library has reminded us of what it is we might be looking for as we track the forgetting of the Emergency in Delhi. Just a few hundred yards away

---

[33]J. Dayal and A. Bose, 1978, *The Shah Commission Begins*, Delhi: Orient Longman, p. 3.

[34]Ibid., p. 6.

from Jawaharlal's home is the residence where the adult Indira Gandhi lived and died. We are at 1 Safdarjang Road, a comparatively modest bungalow in another leafy bird-filled garden. In the early 1970s Indira Gandhi had considered it too modest; hence her plans to set up residence in her father's loftier abode. But her plans had been thwarted by the Nehru Trust and she remained at 1 Safdarjang Road which now serves as a museum and memorial both to herself and to her eldest son, Rajiv.

To those familiar with the Emergency literature, the address alone is poignant with memories. A scene from the post-Emergency epic immediately springs to mind:

'1, Safdarjang Road. Late 1975. "They come quite early, by 7.45 a.m. Municipal Commissioner B.R. Tamta, Delhi Development Authority Vice-chairman Jagmohan, V.S. Ailawadi of the NDMC, Minister H.K.L. Bhagat, Lt Governor's Special Secretary Navin Chawla. Police DIG P.S. Bhinder is also occasionally here.

They wait in the ante-rooms, sometimes with Dhawan (Prime Minister's Secretary) and talk about Delhi affairs. They eye each other with rabid suspicion. He (Sanjay) calls them in one by one. He listens to their situation reports, and tells figures. Sometimes he taunts them that the other fellow is far more active. The person promises to be better by tomorrow.

Sometimes he calls all of them together. This is when the big schemes are chalked out. This is when the officers bid for more portion of the work to be done. It is like a grand auction."' (An eye witness)[35]

We are standing at the entrance to the place where Indian democracy went to the highest bidder. This was the infamous den of secret meetings, conspiracies and unconstitutional goings on; the home of the monstrous two-headed tyranny of Delhi. But when we join the crowds waiting at the entrance we find, not surprisingly, that we are queuing for an entirely different play.

We are greeted by a photograph of a smiling Indira Gandhi who, like us, stands at the doorway of the house. Below a plaque reads, 'Indira Gandhi lived in this house with her family as Minister for Information and Broadcasting from 1964 to 1966, and as Prime Minister from 1966 to 1977 and 1980 to 1984. Rajiv Gandhi, sworn in as Prime Minister 31 October 1984, lived here till March 1985.' Where Indira lived between 1977 and 1980 we are not told. Who

---

[35]Cited in Dayal and Bose, 1977, *For Reasons*, p. 33.

took up residence in the house during that period is also omitted. Such details have no place in this new drama. For this is the Life and Martyrdom of Indira Gandhi. The exhibition begins with a photograph of her addressing a vast crowd of people in Orissa. With it is an extract from her patriotic final speech:

I am here today, I may be gone tomorrow. But the responsibility to look after national interest is on the shoulders of every Indian citizen. Nobody knows how many attempts have been made to shoot me, lathis [sticks] have been used to beat me. In Bhubaneshwar itself, a brickbat hit me. They have attacked me in every possible manner. I do not care if I live or die. I have lived a long life and am proud that I spent the whole of my life in service of my people. I am only proud of this and nothing else. I shall continue to serve until my last breath and when I die, I can say that every drop of my blood will invigorate India and strengthen it. I hope that youth, women and others, will all think together. They should shoulder the responsibility and it cannot be done by accepting others as leaders. (30 October 1984)

Next, we are confronted by screaming newspaper headlines in various languages:

MRS GANDHI SHOT DEAD
End comes soon after outrage at house.
Assassination by 2 guards: One killed

NATION MOURNS INDIRA
Dastardly Killing by Security Men.
Funeral and 12 day Mourning

INDIRA GANDHI ASSASINATA DAI SIKH. IL FIGLIO
RAJIV NUOVO PRIMO MINISTRO

This is a room dedicated to her brutal death in the garden of 1 Safdarjang Road where she was shot by two of her own security guards. The shelves contain posthumous awards from foreign dignitaries. A photograph of her distraught son, Rajiv Gandhi, at the funeral pyre links the grief of the individual to that of the nation. We, too, should mourn the death of the mother. A display of stones and crystals emphasises the durability of her soul.

Room 2 whisks us through her political career in startling black and white. A three-tier display bombards us from every direction.

Lining the top of the walls up to ceiling level are panorama shots most of which show Indira with the masses; receiving garlands, shaking hands, visiting villages and handing out flowers. Beneath are portraits demonstrating her various moods and attributes. In younger portraits she is shy and demure; later she is strong and authoritative, sometimes pensive, always dignified. At eye level is a montage of newspaper headings and selected articles. Since this is only the second room of the exhibition, it is quickly choked with people and the museum staff have little patience with those who loiter to read the headlines. 'Move on! Form a line! Quickly! Go through!' an authoritative male voice bellows out in Hindi. 'There's nothing to see in here. Move on!' Soon the jostling crowd of adults is replaced by a train of uniformed children who trot past, hand to shoulder, with the occasional teacher to direct the stream.

I have been granted special permission to go at my own pace which enables me to read the headlines: UNANIMOUS ELECTION OF INDIRA GANDHI. YOUNGEST WOMAN TO BE CONGRESS CHIEF (*Indian Express*, 8 February 1959); INDIRA GANDHI ELECTED AS PARTY LEADER INDIA'S FIRST EVER WOMAN PRIME MINISTER (*National Herald*, 20 January 1966); PRESIDENT ASKS MRS GANDHI TO FORM GOVERNMENT (*The Tribune*, 13 March 1967); NATION GIVES PRIME MINISTER MASSIVE MANDATE FOR CHANGE (*Patriot*, 12 March 1971); MRS GANDHI LOSES. SANJAY, BANSI LAL AND GOKHALE DEFEATED (*Statesman*, 21 March 1977); MRS GANDHI WINS BY 77,333 VOTES [at Chikmagalur] (*Hindu*, 9 November 1978); 'MASSIVE MANDATE FOR INDIRA. SANJAY, SHUKLA, CHAVAN WIN. PAI, DHARIA, GOREY LOSE' (*Amrita Bazaar Patrika*, 8 January 1980).

We arrive at a plaque which informs us of various important decisions that were made at 1 Safdarjang Road. From now on the display is thematically arranged under headings: Self-sufficiency in Food Grains; Devaluation of the Rupee; Bank Nationalisation; Abolition of Privy Purses Privileges, Congress Split, Indo-Soviet Treaty, Liberation of Bangladesh; Emergency; Election Defeat; Election: Come back; Punjab.

We stop at the heading 'Emergency' and read: NO BAR ON INDIRA CONTINUING AS PRIME MINISTER (*Times of India,* 25 June 1975); PRESIDENT PROCLAIMS NATIONAL EMERGENCY; SECURITY OF INDIA THREATENED BY INTERNAL DISTURBANCES; PREVENTATIVE ARRESTS: PRESS CENSORSHIP IMPOSED (*Hindu*, 27 June 1975); INDIRA GANDHI DEFEATED (21 March 1977). A photograph shows her sitting cross-legged on the ground, haggard and humiliated after her election defeat in 1977. Another of the same year shows her being taken under arrest. Next she emerges victorious and traditional, this time in a coloured photograph. She is dressed in the orange of renunciation with the end of her sari pulled modestly over her hair. On her forehead is a red *tilak* (mark). We have passed on to the next section where new headings confront us: MASSIVE VICTORY...

In case we should be overwhelmed by the political face of Indira Gandhi, we are reminded of her simplicity by a low level display of objects which 'formed an intimate part of Indira Gandhi's daily life'. These are ordinary things: family snapshots, a scrabble set, knitting needles, a Beatrice Potter plate, an artificial cockroach and some butterflies, binoculars and books on wildlife. They seem to inform us that despite her greatness, she was an ordinary human being like you or me. As we leave the room we are confronted by a large black and white photograph of the urns containing her ashes, and then we arrive at the central exhibit which stands apart. Later we shall see it again from other directions. It is the sari she was wearing at her death. Reminiscent of other exhibits in the capital, such as Mahatma Gandhi's blood-stained dhoti, the pale yellow sari contains the bullet holes of the assassin. It is accompanied by a colourful embroidered bag and a pair of rather worn black sandals which highlight the sense of missing body. The perforations in the sari are discreetly encircled in what looks like pencil. There is no blood. The man beside me is pointing out the bullet holes to his son. Two women are discussing the sari, commenting on how the dirt has turned the yellow to grey. A braising quotation from Rajiv Gandhi leads us to the next room: 'Indira Gandhi died as she lived; unafraid with courage abiding'. (*Young Patriot*, 7 November 1984)

Having begun with her death, we now swing back to her life. First we are confronted with Indira Gandhi in context. We see her noble ancestors and their family homes, one of which we have already visited. We see her in genealogical perspective, with her parents and grandparents on the one hand and her children and grandchildren on the other. We are reminded that, not only she but her father before her and her son after her were Prime Ministers of India. Having set the frame we now go back to Indira Gandhi's childhood. We see her as a wide-eyed baby, a serious school girl; a budding nationalist; a coy adolescent and self-conscious student. Later we also see her as a courting youth; a married woman and mother. Her wedding sari, woven from yarn spun by her father and the vessels used for the nuptials form one of the major attractions to women tourists, leading the museum staff to chivvy people on again. This time I am whisked along with the crowd but the word 'population crisis' has caught my eye and I stop in front of the relevant cabinet. This causes a pile up as a group of young men crowd around hoping to see something of particular interest. I am looking at a brass plaque presented to Indira Gandhi by the Population Council 'in recognition of her fostering support to solve the world population crisis through a demonstrated commitment to share ideas, knowledge, and experience towards the ultimate objective of reducing population growth and creating a better life for all the world's people.' (New York, 2 August 1982) With it is 'The United Nations Population Award—an affirmation by the international community of the importance of population in development, is presented to Her Excellency Mrs. Indira Gandhi, Prime Minister of India for her outstanding contribution to the awareness of population questions and their solutions.' (New York, 30 September 1983)

Past more certificates, this time indicating honorary degrees, and past gaudy gifts from foreign dignitaries, we enter the room 'Indira Gandhi and the World' in which we see photographs of her on world tours or entertaining foreign politicians and diplomats. Soon we are with the diplomats and politicians at her funeral, reading the lines of Fidel Castro, the President of Cuba: 'We saw her disappear amidst flames, while her people, her descendants, and statesmen from all over the world surrounded the funeral pyre in respectful silence. And we recalled the august calmness with which, years earlier, she had indicated that one day she also would, with resignation, give up her life in a holocaust for the unity of her nation.'

The last image shows her as a frail but determined figure walking into the distance. It is reminiscent of a famous pose of Mahatma Gandhi who, like Indira, sacrificed his life for the nation.

We step outside and then re-enter the house and file past her study which contains unexceptional office furniture and a few easy chairs. 'Indira Gandhi's study was her sanctum. It was filled with well loved books and pictures and she often worked here at her desk late into the night.' A quotation from Indira reads, 'A tree must have roots. Though the roots go deep into the ground, the tree itself grows up into the sky towards the sun. So must we turn our faces and our steps towards the future though our roots remain in the past.'

We step outside again and this time re-enter the house in the section where Rajiv Gandhi used to live with his wife and children. The exhibition is primarily photographic, accompanied by extracts from Rajiv's own writings, speeches and interviews. Again, we begin with death. First we see Rajiv carrying the ashes of his father, Feroz Gandhi. Next we see him with the ashes of his grandfather Jawaharlal. Next he is performing the last rites at his brother Sanjay's funeral, and finally he is at the funeral pyre of his mother. Above each photograph is a smaller image of Rajiv with the person portrayed in happier times. By seeing these deaths in quick succession we are invited to participate in his grief and to understand how he was compelled to enter politics. The context established, we swing back to his birth in 1944 and his childhood. He is a sensitive and pensive boy, sometimes seen with his mother; sometimes seen playing with his younger brother in the gardens of Teen Murti House. Later we see him as a schoolboy, a healthy adolescent in sports gear, a student at Cambridge and a young pilot with Indian Airlines. His marriage to Sonia is noticeably more prominent than his mother's marriage to Feroz Gandhi. What we get is a sense of Rajiv's carefree existence as a happy family man; an existence which ended abruptly with the death of his brother in a plane accident in 1980.

'I wanted to be left to myself. That was very much the case when I was flying. Then my brother Sanjay was killed in the prime of his life. My mother called to me in her loneliness. I went to her side. She urged me to respond to the insistent demand from the constituency and the party to take my brother's place as Member of Parliament for Amethi.'

A sequence is established. First we see the adult Sanjay beside his mother. The photo has been taken *contra jour* making Sanjay little more than a silhouette in the darkness. Next we see Rajiv comforting his mother after Sanjay's death. Then we see Rajiv's letter of resignation to Indian Airlines and finally we see him addressing the crowds. White *khadi* (hand-spun hand-woven cloth),[36] which he previously wore mainly

---

[36]*Khadi* was popularised by Mahatma Gandhi who elevated it to the status of national dress in the 1920s. The cloth still plays an important role in politics, though today it is associated as much with hypocrisy as with morality. For a history of *khadi* and its relevance, see Emma Tarlo, 1996, *Clothing Matters*, London: Hurst, chs 3 and 4.

on ceremonial occasions, now becomes his everyday garb. His adoption of it marks his acceptance of the burden of political office and his entry into the service of the nation.

His collection of intimate objects is noticeably more postmodern than his mother's. It contains a personal computer along with his travel bag and *khadi* outfit. We see him addressing the people in various locations and read extracts from his speeches until finally we arrive at the clothes he wore at his death. Unlike Indira Gandhi's discreetly ruptured sari, Rajiv Gandhi's *kurta pyjama* (tunic and trouser) seems to scream the violence of his death. It has been exploded into fragments, hideously stained. Only his trainers remain intact—stalwart and unscathed—their durability horribly reminiscent of those advertisements for products strong enough to endure anything.

The exhibition which began with Rajiv performing the last rites for his father, grandfather, brother and mother ends with Rajiv's son, Rahul, performing the last rites of his father. Rahul's face is seen through the flames, magnified but faint; almost ghostly. A tragic continuity is established. An anticipation of the future perhaps? One last fleeting glimpse of Rajiv's smile, then we are back outside, following the arrows to the drawing room and dining room of 1 Safdarjang Road. Both are tasteful and unostentatious, with fairly simple furniture and a few choice works of Indian art on the walls. As we leave the house yet again, we catch another glimpse of the sari in which Indira Gandhi was assassinated. Outside we arrive at the path on which she was actually shot. 'Every morning Indira Gandhi walked this path to her daily *darshan*[37] at which she met people from all corners of India and the world.' It is now covered over in gleaming crystal glass, donated by the Czechoslovakian government. Flower heads are placed at both ends and at the spot where she was shot. The sun makes patterns on the crystal as we walk to the far end where two uniformed guards stand alert. And here we read an excerpt from her undated handwritten notes.

If I die a violent death as some fear and others are plotting, I know the violence will be in the thought and the action of the assassin, not in my

---

[37]*Darshan*: sacred sight. In the Hindu religion gods and important mortals make themselves visible to people who imbibe their holy sight. Indira Gandhi used to make herself visible by greeting members of the public in her garden everyday and answering their queries.

dying—for no hate is dark enough to overshadow the extent of my love for my people and my country; no force is strong enough to divert me from my purpose and my endeavour to take this country forward. And the final statement: 'Here Indira Gandhi fell martyr to the bullets of 2 assassins on 31 October 1984.'

This is the spot where those with cameras take photographs before passing on to the book shop where Indira Gandhi key rings and post cards are available along with works about her and other Indian leaders. But I have taken a detour and cut back through the exhibition in order to meet the director who is sitting behind a desk in a pristine office near the entrance to the bungalow. He is young, welcoming and somehow more helpful than I expect.

'This is the smallest Prime Minister's house in the world,' he informs me. 'She liked things to be simple. When people tried to persuade her to move to Teen Murti Bhavan or some other grander place, she said she preferred this small bungalow.' I remark on the crowds and ask if it is always as crowded on a weekday morning. He replies that the museum gets between 5,000 and 10,000 visitors a day; sometimes as many as 20,000.

'Thousands come out of love for Indira Gandhi. The fact that she died here also counts for a lot. They think of her as a *devi* [goddess] and want to see the place where she was killed. They just want to bow down and pay their respects, especially the old women. I used to sometimes interview the people queuing up outside and I found that they really consider her a goddess. Its the blind faith of the people—well I don't know if its blind or not—but their faith is really incredible.'

Pushing through the gates I leave the compound, noting the swelling queue accumulating in the street outside, as organised groups arrive by the coach-load from all over north India and possibly beyond. The figures may be exaggerated but I have never before seen such a huge queue outside a museum in India.

It is not difficult to trace the historical events through which this new master narrative took over and ultimately effaced both of the narratives that preceded it. Indira Gandhi's return to power in January 1980 is the first significant marker, followed shortly by Sanjay's death. With his plane accident in July 1980 one of the most controversial stars of both Emergency dramas ceased to exist. Meanwhile Indira Gandhi's assassination in 1984 transformed any lingering shadow of dictatorship into a halo of self-sacrifice whilst at the same time establishing Rajiv's legitimate right to rule. His assassination at a time when his image was badly tarnished led to a purification process which enabled him to join Mahatma Gandhi and Indira as the martyrs of the nation. The 'dynastic dictatorship' of the post-Emergency narrative has slipped smoothly into 'dynastic democracy': benign, authoritative and protective. India's new fortunetellers now speculate as to which of Rajiv's children will don the mantle of power which some see almost as a birthright.[38]

Convenient deaths and brutal assassinations may have helped to push the Emergency narratives out of focus, but politics has also played a part. If it had been in the interest of the Janata Party to build the memory of the Emergency in the months that succeeded it, it was also in the interests of the Congress Party to establish its forgetting. The exhibition at 1 Safdarjang Road not only provides us with alternative memories but also encourages us to forget the Emergency, which features as little more than an empty hollow. It appears first in the form of a declaration and next in the form of an election defeat. Nothing is told of what went on between this beginning and this end. Instead we simply jump from beginning to end to new beginning with Indira Gandhi's return to power. Viewed within the broader perspective of her lengthy political career, the Emergency is a mere hiccup, one of those brief but insignificant disruptions that every politician has to face. There seems no need to mention that the Janata leader, Morarji Desai, also lived at 1 Safdarjang Road, from which he too governed the country, albeit for a short while. Neither, of course, is there any mention of the Shah Commission, nor of the fact that the Congress Party is suspected of having bought up most copies of the Commission's final report in order to prevent its circulation.

And what of the glorious future that Indira Gandhi had promised during the Emergency? What of the revolutionary 20-point programme? The 5-point programme? Sanjay Gandhi's fantastic leap to fame? All of these have been effaced for they cannot afford to be remembered without running the risk of invoking the post-Emergency

---

[38]When Rajiv Gandhi's widow, Sonia, entered the general election campaign in 1998, she was thought by many to be paving the way for her children and in particular, her daughter, Priyanka. Sonia Gandhi's recent acceptance of leadership of the Congress Party has further exacerbated speculations about the resurgence of the Gandhi/Nehru dynasty.

narrative which encourages us to remember them in a certain way. This no doubt explains why at 1 Safdarjang Road Sanjay Gandhi's political career is entirely absent. His role is restricted to that of Rajiv's little brother and of Indira's son. The only adult photograph which portrays him in a political context has been taken in such a way that his face is reduced to a faint blur beside that of his mother. Death soon transforms him from beloved son to figure of tragedy and reason for Rajiv to enter politics. After his death Sanjay reappears briefly as an icon on a poster accompanying Rajiv on a political rally. Nothing is said of Sanjay's own participation in politics except that he once held the Amethi seat which Rajiv is now obliged to fill. With a curious irony the misdemeanours of the past have helped legitimate the presentation of the past in the present. The fact that Sanjay's power was largely unconstitutional during the Emergency becomes a valid reason for excluding him from an exhibition which aims to establish a legitimate master narrative. Similarly, press censorship and government propaganda of the past operate retrospectively. The occasional newspaper cutting from 1976 works in Indira Gandhi's favour since public criticism had been unpublishable at that time.

Safdarjang Road gives us the new master narrative in concentrated form, but it should not be supposed that this is its only physical refuge. Wherever Indira Gandhi's memory is publicly evoked within the city, it is done so within the framework of this narrative. The international airport and the indoor stadium, both of which bear her name are gigantesque monuments in her honour, symbolising her own hugeness. With the recent renaming of Connaught Place the narrative has been officially inscribed at the very heart of the city. Connaught Place has become Rajiv Chowk and Connaught Circus, Indira Chowk, thereby placing the mother's embrace of her son at the very centre of the capital city and nation. Needless to say, it is the son whose power was legitimate who features in the renaming of the streets. Monuments to Sanjay are conspicuous by their absence; the Sanjay Gandhi Memorial Hospital being an exception.

In search of memories

Like the tourists, we shall pass through 'Rajiv Chowk' and 'Indira Chowk,' but, like Delhites, we shall continue for the time being at least to refer to them by their original names. We are passing out of New Delhi and heading for the Jama Masjid at the very heart of the old city, otherwise known as Shahjahanabad. As we proceed, the roads become narrower and more crowded; Marutis, Ambassadors and auto rickshaws begin to mingle with cycle rickshaws and ponies and traps. The Jama Masjid towers majestically above us, its black and white minarets lending a fresh look to its ancient form. But we are not here to visit the Masjid. It is time once more to wander off the tourist path, this time in search of one of the central localities of the post-Emergency narrative, Dujana House. My map, though useful in New Delhi seems instantly inadequate in Old Delhi and I find the way by asking. The directions are clear. Opposite a small police booth, in the midst of the food and vessel sellers I must take a left turn. As I arrive at the police booth, I see a sign, Dujana House and walk under an unimpressive gateway, checking as I go past to see if there is any reference to the Emergency experience. Inside is a courtyard with shabby concrete apartments on one side and a beautifully maintained garden on the other. Cycle rickshaws are lined up in the entrance but the space remains open, populated only by the occasional passer by and a few men polishing enormous *biriyani* vessels used for wedding banquets. The people, mainly men, follow my movements with their eyes, indicating that this is not a space for foreigners; not a place for unaccompanied unveiled women either. I too am casting my eyes about, looking for visible reminders of the Emergency; a statue to the sterilised perhaps? A simple memorial plaque?

By now a middle-aged man in a *kurta pyjama* is looking at me as if he wants an explanation, so I begin to explain and soon find myself standing in a group. My knowledge of Hindi—though by no means perfect—is adequate for converting me from mere object of curiosity to curious subject with an enquiry. I ask the men if I can see the spot where the family planning clinic used to stand during the Emergency. They lead me to the end of the courtyard and into a neglected alley where they point to a derelict building, locked behind a metal grill. 'It was there, in the basement,' a man points. 'That was where they used to cut them up. Do you want to see inside?'

A young bearded man is sent off to find the key, but when we enter the building we find there is no electricity, making it difficult to see. A black cavern with white tiles on the walls of the staircase. Nothing spectacular. A third man is pointing to an empty space nearby: 'This is where they set up the camp. The main officer used to sit round about here.'

What do you mean by 'camp'?

'It was a wooden shed. It was here they gave out the certificates and money. They were also offering a pot of ghee and a clock for *nasbandi* [sterilisation] at the time. They would grab the people by force, take them into the tent, make them sign papers, then take them into the basement. At first there was no toilet, but then they built this.' (He points to a shabby concrete building opposite the clinic.)

Who used to take them by force?

'The police. Who else? If the police get you, you can't do much.'

Were many people from Dujana House sterilised?

'No. Not us. They brought the men from outside. They say some went in and never came back.'

So what happened to the camp after the Emergency?

'When the Janata came to power they came here and pulled the whole lot down.'

Conversation flows along familiar lines as the men begin to reiterate episodes from the post-Emergency narrative. Their eyes are enthusiastic as if recalling an old wife's tale they have not heard for a long while. Their memory is more collective than personal, but it is not public. No official attempt has been made to publicly inscribe the memory of the Emergency at Dujana House. It is a place empty of connotations to those who do not know.

Our final destination is Turkman Gate, the centre stage of the post-Emergency narrative; the ultimate symbol of oppression and resistance. If the Emergency is to be remembered anywhere it is surely here. We arrive in a stream of traffic going down Asaf Ali Road on a Thursday afternoon. Opposite is the tourist camp, one of the cheapest places for visitors to stay in Delhi. It brings back personal memories of when, as a student, I had spent a full two weeks in the camp, driving past Turkman Gate everyday, oblivious then of what had occurred there some ten years earlier. Was it that I had ignored the signs or was it that there were no signs to ignore?

Today there is something written on the gate. It reads: 'Regional

Defence'. Behind it is an enclosure for the police. Yet again the police headquarters acts as an indicator that we have come to the right place. Another Muslim area in the Old city. Guarded. Under surveillance. Later enquiries inform me that the police were located there even before the Emergency and that this was the police *chowki* that had been captured by the people during the struggle.

As we take the road that leads behind Turkman Gate, we again enter a region of cycle rickshaws, *burqa*-clad women and *topi*-wearing (cap-wearing) men. The architecture is unspectacular, consisting of four storey concrete blocks painted in a pale violet blue. These apartments correspond neither to the noble ancient homes described in the post-Emergency rhetoric nor the filthy stinking slum of the Emergency rhetoric. This is hardly surprising since these are the buildings that were erected after the controversial demolition, leaving the two narratives to dispute over the area's past appearance.

I talk to an old bearded man, dressed in a blue checked *lungi* (waistcloth), white *kurta* (long-sleeved, knee-length tunic) and *topi* (cap). He makes a wide gesture with his arm to indicate the extent of the area demolished during the Emergency. He sends a small boy to search for the person who will tell me 'the entire story'. A stalwart man appears and introduces himself as the local *chaudhuri* (leader) and Head of the Turkman Gate Committee. He tells me that he spent several months in prison following the demolition and protests at Turkman Gate on 19 April 1976. Our conversation on a street corner inevitably attracts a crowd, leading the original man to offer his scrap metal shop as a quiet place for discussion. Four of us go in: the *chaudhuri*, the iron merchant, a *burqa*-clad woman who turns out to be a local social worker and I. A conversation ensues:

CHAUDHURI
'Turkman Gate became a famous name during the Emergency. People came from all over Delhi to see what had happened. Even foreigners used to come and visit our houses. But look at the mess we are in now.'

SOCIAL WORKER
'The government makes promises but they don't do anything.'

CHAUDHURI
'This is a Muslim area so nobody bothers.'

The conversation swings back and forth between the Emergency drama and present-day neglect. New details embellish the post-Emergency narrative which has become even more spectacular over time.

CHAUDHURI
'400 people were killed, at least.'

SOCIAL WORKER
'The bulldozers crushed the people to death, grinding them into the ground. There was one man, he had just got married the night before, and the next day he was gone.'

What about Sanjay Gandhi? Did he ever visit this place?

CHAUDHURI
'Yes. He came. He took one look at our homes, which were bigger and more beautiful than anything you see here today, and he said, "These are all *jhuggis* [slum shacks]. They must be demolished". He wanted to build Sanjay Minar in the place of our houses but we did not let him. He never came back.'

What do you mean, Sanjay Minar?

CHAUDHURI
'One of those restaurants that spins round and round. A revolving hotel—that's what they call it.'

I ask if I can see the remains of the Faiz-e-Elahi Mosque which they tell me has been largely destroyed. We cross over the busy road, pass by the street vendors selling cloth for *hajj* (pilgrimage to Mecca) and enter a large empty space of dusty barren ground. 'All the buildings here were demolished.' We stare about at the vacant space, a space fertile for forgetting. The *chaudhuri* is walking with his head down, pointing out stone traces of old foundations—traces of demolition to those who know; mere stones in the sand to those who don't. In one corner stand some mature trees 'which got saved' and a section of the mosque. 'They would have destroyed the whole lot,' the social worker adds, 'but one of the bulldozers got stuck in the ground and the person driving it was killed so they got scared and called it off.'

Next we re-cross the road and they take me around the residential area, pointing out the dodgy electric wiring which twists and turns from one building to another.

Are there any signs to indicate what happened during the Emergency to passers-by like me who might not know?

CHAUDHURI

'No. Nothing like that.'

SOCIAL WORKER

'We couldn't do that. If we did they would make us take it down. They would say it was a provocation.'

They?

SOCIAL WORKER

'The government'.

They take me to the nearest equivalent; a brick arch standing in a derelict park which has turned to dust. We all squint at its faded plaque, unable to detect what is written there—something about Morarji Desai dedicating the garden to the people. A goat strolls by.

'But we do have a film,' the *chaudhuri* adds, 'a film which tells the truth about Turkman Gate and Dujana House.' He invites me to return for a screening on the evening of 19 April, the day of the famous battle at Turkman Gate some 20 years earlier.

Fragments of the past for the future

19 April 1996. Turkman Gate. Chairs fill the main lane, transforming it into an open theatre. Above the stage, a black and white banner bears an inscription in Urdu, 'Day of the Martyrs.' At 10.30 p.m., the head of the Turkman Gate Committee makes his way to the microphone and begins an impassioned speech which stretches on until midnight. It soon becomes clear that this is not an occasion for showing films but a political rally aimed at levering votes for the Janata Dal in the forthcoming local election. As the *chaudhuri* raises his voice, he swings his arms furiously like a prophet of old. His cries, hideously amplified by badly rigged loudspeakers, reverberate into the night, bouncing off the tenement buildings that line the street. His words are met by cheers and applause from a responsive audience composed almost entirely of Muslim men and boys.

'When our houses were being demolished, Jagmohan and Sanjay Gandhi came here. They threatened to cut me up into tiny pieces...No one can come here and wipe out our houses, sweep us off the streets just because this is a Muslim area...For almost four hours we faced the bullets...'

We have stumbled across an act of remembering, live and vibrating. This is memory with a purpose. Like the demolition of the Babri Masjid by right wing Hindu extremists in 1992, the demolition of Turkman Gate in 1976 is invoked as proof of the betrayal of Muslims by the Congress Party and of the need for all Muslims to unite under the Janata Dal:

'All three stripes of the Congress flag have been stripped away leaving only the stick which they will use to beat us with. The Janata must win. The Congress try to buy us with favours but I am offering you my blood. I am prepared to die for you...'

The *chaudhuri*'s impassioned speech is followed by vehement words from the local MLA (Member of the Legislative Assembly) and two other Muslim notables. Like the *chaudhuri*, they invoke memories of 1976 and 1992 as evidence of an anti-Muslim plot and the need for solidarity. The speeches go on for several hours. All are in Urdu.[39] They speak a discourse of vulnerability channelled for collective action:

'All of you have come together tonight. If we scatter, we may have to face bulldozers and bullets again. Stand together on the same platform. Today is the day of the martyrs. The real tribute to the martyrs will be when we honour them with our deeds.'

20 April 1996, just one day later. I come across an election leaflet written in Hindi. Jagmohan, ex-Vice-chairman of the DDA, villain of the post-Emergency narrative, is standing in the local elections as a candidate for the right wing pro-Hindu BJP (Bharatiya Janata Party). The leaflet lists his many achievements, heralding him as 'the man who laid the foundations for making Delhi a modern city and for setting a world standard in development'. A newspaper article published the same week in an important national daily bears the heading 'BJP plays Turkman Gate card to woo voters.' Underneath, it claims, 'Jagmohan, *the* demolition man of the Emergency days, has turned Messiah for the uprooted residents of Turkman Gate.' The

---

[39] I am grateful to Rajinder, my research assistant, for accompanying me to hear these speeches and for translating extracts from them.

article goes on to claim that those people from Turkman Gate whose homes were demolished and who were taken to resettlement colonies in outer Delhi during the Emergency are now grateful to the ex-Vice-chairman of the DDA for having made them landowners. Jagmohan 'the Saviour' is now appealing to such people to remember his good deeds by supporting the BJP in the forthcoming election.[40] Two fragments of memory of the same event. Both elaborated to suit present day political agendas, both used as resources for engineering futures, neither of which took shape. The Janata Dal failed to muster adequate support from the Muslims of Old Delhi in the 1996 elections just as Jagmohan failed to get elected for the BJP that time round, although he has since been elevated to the position of Union Urban Development Minister . The Turkman Gate Massacre, once so central to the post-Emergency narrative, has today shrunk to the status of a localised grievance which may raise passions amongst those individuals who were directly affected in 1976, but failed to capture the imagination of the electorate two decades later.

Our guided tour of the forgetting of the Emergency is over. What we have encountered in the city of Delhi is a series of absences in time and space—phantom futures that never happened; ghostly pasts whose relevance to the present has either been effaced or distorted and reworked to different ends; physical blanks or substitutions where houses were once demolished; where the conception of unborn children was prevented; and where political decisions were taken by a man who has since been edited out of history altogether.

Travelling around the city of Delhi we will pass many more spaces where demolitions once perforated the urban fabric, clearing the way for new homes, shopping centres, roads and parks, many of which already seem old. Demolition or development? I hear the echo of past narratives, fragments of which are discretely guarded and embellished in different corners of the city. But is there an alternative perspective from which we might begin to view the Emergency? One which speaks a language less tainted by the master narratives of times gone by? One in which the central characters are not the stars of Safdarjang Road, Turkman Gate and Dujana House, but the hundreds of thousands of ordinary Delhi citizens and bureaucrats whose lives were or were not disrupted by the Emergency?

---

[40] *Pioneer*, 17 April 1996.

3

PAPER TRUTHS

It is time to enter another space. Not New Delhi this time, nor Old Delhi but a space which seems to defy such classifications. You could call it the 'margins', if margins can be denser than the centre, the location of which is itself difficult to place. One of Delhi's peculiarities is, in fact, its absence of a clearly defined central point. For this is not a city that developed organically, like a cell multiplying outwards, but one which grew in fitful spurts of destruction and relocation. Crumbling monuments of the past litter the urban landscape at considerable distances, as if to remind us that Delhi's centre often changed in the past, and may still change again.

When the British decided to move the imperial capital from Calcutta to Delhi in 1911, they did little to improve the city's disjointed development. Having already established a settlement known as Civil Lines north of the existing city of Shahjahanabad (nowadays known as Old Delhi), they then set about establishing a new colonial settlement south of the city. Hence, 'New Delhi', with its gracious avenues and well-planned shopping centres grew up in contrast to 'Old Delhi' with its narrow lanes and congested markets. Although New Delhi has since expanded upwards and outwards, the contrast between the two Delhis remains. So too does the controversy over where the centre lies. If the people you meet tell you it is in Connaught Place (they are reluctant to call it 'Rajiv Chowk'), then that is because the people you meet probably come from New Delhi where the Westernised middle classes are concentrated. But Delhi has many stories which can be told from many perspectives. This one favours the vantage point of those who once inhabited the 'inner city slums' of both New and Old Delhi but who were expelled eastwards and outwards to the 'kalapani' (black waters)[1] of a 'resettlement colony'. It is the off-centre perspective of people thrown well beyond the margins of a city which has since expanded to re-incorporate them within its dense and ever spreading urban fringe. Many such people still look to Chandni Chowk in Shahjahanabad as the centre of Delhi.

The colony to which we are heading is locally known by the somewhat unlikely name of Welcome. We have already encountered it, not only in the introduction to this work, but also in the post-Emergency narrative. This was one of the places where the Muslims threatened with demolition at Turkman Gate had asked if they could be resettled—the colony purportedly 'saved' from becoming 'a second Pakistan' by Jagmohan, then Vice-chairman of the DDA, who had been opposed to the idea of members of a single community clustering together. We know it, then, as the place where the people of Turkman Gate were not resettled but where others were—a place which almost played a significant role in the post-Emergency narrative, but which, as it turned out, occupies no more than a sentence in what is already a forgotten history.

Contrary to what might be imagined, 'Welcome' got its name, not from over-enthusiastic town planners trying to disguise the horrors of resettlement, but from the first wave of people who settled there in the early 1960s. They chose it, neither out of pleasure at their new surroundings, nor out of irony at the lack of facilities there, but rather out of sheer practicality. 'The Welcome Hair Oil factory was the only building for miles around when we were first dumped here,' an old man explains, 'so when we used to give directions about how to reach the colony we would tell people: "Go along the main road until you get to Welcome and then turn left. So the name Welcome got stuck!"' The old man's version of the tale is as good as any. The Welcome Hair Oil Factory, which opened in 1954, was closed down in 1970, leaving its large brick structure as a warehouse for chemicals. Those who joined the colony in the second major wave of resettlement during the Emergency never knew the Welcome factory, but the name, Welcome, remained.

---

[1]'Kala pani' is a reference to the Andaman Islands where Indian prisoners used to be banished, a punishment dreaded because it violated the Hindu taboo of crossing the ocean. It is a phrase frequently used by people who found themselves displaced from Delhi slums. Its European equivalent would be 'Siberia'.

Given that Welcome was developed in the 1960s and 70s one might imagine that it belongs to what is known as New Delhi. But this is not the case. 'New Delhi' is a space defined not merely by temporal criteria but also by social connotation and geographic location. Welcome fails to qualify on both counts. It belongs instead to another space, commonly defined as *Jamuna par* (Trans-Yamuna), meaning the area across the River Yamuna. The phrase is revealing; it assumes one is standing west of the river where both 'Old' and 'New' Delhi are located. Like rivers in cities all over the world, the Yamuna draws a boundary which is both social and geographic. When slum dwellers were first displaced 'across the river', they were left in the back of beyond, in forgotten spaces once reserved for hunting. So even if it is not clear where the centre of Delhi is, we know for certain where it is not. It is not east of the river in the area known as Trans-Yamuna.

Population pressures in Delhi are such that even the Trans-Yamuna's profile is changing over time. It is no longer just the home of evicted slum dwellers in over-crowded resettlement colonies. Today it also attracts middle-class Delhiites who, in the interests of obtaining more space at cheaper rates, are constructing luxury colonies 'across the river'. These pristine colonies with their uniform architecture and standardised white concrete stand in stark contrast to the dense brick patchwork and turquoise-blue paint so characteristic of poorer housing settlements. But the latter predominate. East Delhi remains the city's poorest constituency, where illiteracy rates are highest and urban amenities most scarce.

So how does one get to this colony named Welcome? One has to cross the river of course. These days there are various bridges, but there used to be only one which, even today, remains the most congested. To reach this bridge you take the road which runs along the back of one of Delhi's most famous monuments—the seventeenth century Red Fort, built by the Mughal Emperor Shah Jahan. Its sturdy pink walls mask the fact that its inner structure was blown up by the British for use as an army base. And so another centre rises and falls. Today it still functions as a base for the army and is also the location for Independence Day speeches, retaining some of its earlier importance. Just beyond the fort, avoiding the vendors who offer coconut segments which gleam an incongruous white in the suffocating traffic, you work your way round to the right and enter a congested medley of vehicles trying to edge onto the 'Old Bridge' (*Purana Pul*)—a vast

Left Celebrating the Emergency—full page spread in the *Hindustan Times*, 26 June 1976. *Right* Cover of B.M. Sinha's book, *Operation Emergency*, published just 10 weeks after Indira Gandhi's defeat in March 1977.

MEMORIES OF THE EMERGENCY

A YEAR BECOMES AN ERA

UDYOG MELA '76

opp. Tagore Garden, Najafgarh Road

Celebrates the successful year of National Discipline and Socio-Economic Peaceful Revolution ushered by our Prime Minister Smt. INDIRA GANDHI with her historic declaration of 26th JUNE 1975

A grateful Nation Salutes her for initiating the 20' Point Programme of Socio-Economic Resurgence

We pledge to Implement the 4 Point Programme of action of our dynamic youth leader Shri SANJAY GANDHI

Organised by : AJIT SINGH CHADHA
President: District Congress Committee, South Delhi

DELHI PUBLICITY

Above Press interview of Indira Gandhi arranged by the National Broadcasting Corporation, 20 August 1975. (PD-PIB, New Delhi)

Below Resistance cartoon by R.K. Laxman, December 1976. Reproduced from *Satyavani*, an underground newspaper published in New York and London during the Emergency.

Above A model Delhi. Indira Gandhi overseeing proposed development plans before the Emergency, 1972. (PD-PIB, New Delhi)

Below Delhi for foreign dignitaries: Jagmohan, Vice-chairman of the Delhi Development Authority (DDA), flanked by Margaret and Denis Thatcher, visiting a DDA housing project, 24 September 1976. (PD-PIB, New Delhi)

Above The other side of the DDA's resettlement scheme. Displaced people cobble together shelters using old bricks in one of Delhi's resettlement colonies, 27 December 1976. (PD-PIB, New Delhi) *Right* Advertisement in the *Hindustan Times*, 1 May1976.

Above Men register their names for vasectomy at Dujana House Family Planning Clinic in Old Delhi, 6 September1976. (PD-PIB, New Delhi)

Below Sterilised men are given ghee and clocks as rewards for undergoing vasectomy, Dujana House, 6 September 1976. (PD-PIB, New Delhi)

Above Forgotten space, 1996: where the family planning camp at Dujana House once stood. (PD-PIB, New Delhi)

Below Janata Party Prime Minister, Morarji Desai, lays the foundation-stone of the new housing complex to be built at Turkman Gate, 19 January 1977. (PD-PIB, New Delhi)

Above The new housing complex at Turkman Gate 20 years on, 1996.

Below Women of Turkman Gate cast their votes in the election which brought down the Emergency government, March 1977. (PD-PIB, New Delhi)

Top Jayaprakash Narayan and the new
Prime Minister Morarji Desai with
members of the Janata Party, 24 March
1977. *Above* A face forgotten: Sanjay
Gandhi during the Emergency. (Both:
PD-PIB, New Delhi) *Right* Cartoon
by Abu, censored during the
Emergency. The censors added the
'd' after 'Save'.

iron structure, a tribute to colonial engineering, which carries trains at its upper level and road traffic at the lower. It used to be one of the major points of exit from the city, leading onto the Grand Trunk Road which stretches across the flat plains of Uttar Pradesh. It is not difficult to imagine something of the sense of expulsion that must have been felt by the truckloads of displaced people who were taken across the bridge in the 1960s and 70s and left some miles over the other side in the name of resettlement.

Today, as then, the riverbank remains a liminal space, dotted with a mixture of temples, cremation grounds, sacred *ghats* and shacks. As one nudges across the bridge in a lethal combination of scooters, trucks, bicycles, cars, auto rickshaws, cycle rickshaws and fat Harley Davidsons with passenger room for eight—one can look down through the iron railings and observe the fringes of the riverbed—occupied mainly by slum dwellers and washermen steaming clothes. Known as a notorious spot for drug-taking, it represents one of the more sordid faces of Delhi—a hidden face overturned by the unusual perspective offered by the bridge. Some of the residents of Welcome had once cobbled homes together in this very spot, using a patchwork of mud, wood, brick and straw. Those homes have long since been demolished and replaced by other slum clusters waiting for the next flood, fire or government scheme to wipe them away. Like other stretches of vacant land which line riverbeds and railway tracks in the city, this is one of the spots where the slum population seems irreducible, despite the regular attempts at 'slum clearance'. Once over the bridge, you work your way onto the Grand Trunk Road until you reach the old Welcome factory building a few miles before the border with Uttar Pradesh. The building no longer stands alone as it did in the 1960s. Today it is submerged within a vast urban jigsaw that stretches far beyond, but it still remains a landmark to those who know. From here, as the old man says, you just turn left and you are in Welcome.

Entering the colony from this southern entrance you see, to your left, people splitting coconuts and arranging the fresh white segments of flesh on steel plates—the same people perhaps who earlier in the day supplied the vendors who weave their way through the traffic behind the Red Fort. And strolling through the colony you see many familiar Delhi sights: men mending the rickshaws they have hired for the day; women queuing for kerosene; fruit vendors arranging their fruits; paper pickers sorting out bundles of waste paper and plastic for recycling; women washing steel utensils and clothes over the open gutters of their narrow, densely packed brick homes; people lounging on string beds and children playing, defecating or just roaming in the streets. As you proceed to the north side of the colony, the population shifts from predominantly Hindu to predominantly Muslim. On the whole the buildings are taller, often containing three or four storeys, though many houses are shared by several families. Here goats and hens become more numerous and the number of craft activities sharply rises. You can see rough hewn furniture being made from low quality wood, metal pots being hammered with decorative designs, and above all denim jeans, of every size, shape and description being cut out, stitched up, dyed and dried in small workshops located mainly in the front room or ground floor of houses. Denim jeans for sale all over India—Welcome's major product.

Denim jeans and the Emergency! There is no obvious connection unless, perhaps, that the students of anti-Emergency rallies wore denim jeans with their *khadi kurtas*. After all, it was the 1970s when cheesecloth and denim were beginning to grab the collective imagination of urban youth all over the world and middle-class Delhi kids were no exception. But Welcome did not start manufacturing jeans until the 1980s. The colony's relationship to the Emergency lies elsewhere. Like the other resettlement colonies developed or expanded during the mid-1970s, Welcome contains people whose homes were demolished by the DDA at the instigation of Sanjay Gandhi. The interest in tracing memories of the Emergency in such colonies lies in the fact that for those resettled, the Emergency was not so much a fleeting event as a time when their conditions of existence in the city were radically, if not permanently, altered. Welcome, like other resettlement colonies, offers the possibility of viewing the Emergency from a different perspective. We are no longer in the city centre observing the blanks and empty spaces left behind, but on the periphery where new futures were built, reluctantly or otherwise, upon the rocky foundations of the Emergency.

We begin our quest in the clapped out offices of what is known as the 'Slum and JJ [*Jhuggi Jhompri*][2] Department' of the MCD, East Zone

[2] *Jhuggi* or *jhuggi jhompri*: colloquial terms for squatter shacks. In housing policy parlance, this usually implies a building slung together from impermanent materials. By contrast the term 'slum' is often used to refer to a more permanent structure that has fallen into disrepair. However the terms are used inconsistently by different authors and, following common usage, I use the term 'slum' to cover both types of dwelling.

B. The name is curiously evocative of the place it describes, conjuring up an image of both slum conditions and bureaucratic verbiage. This is indeed a place where heavily-worded papers pile up and proliferate in sordid heaps under a mixture of accumulated dust and bird droppings. The main headquarters of the Slum and JJ Department is located in a more salubrious complex which, as one might expect, is situated in New Delhi. It is there that major planning decisions are sketched out and important orders issued. The building we have entered is, however, only a local branch and bears the stamp of neglect appropriate to its unglamorous location in Welcome. This is not a place for planning resettlement colonies on crisp white paper, but a place where the remnants of past policies lie about in crumbling files and where current procedures are half-heartedly carried out by those officers who have the energy and willpower to bother.

This two storey concrete block was built in the early 1980s but suffers from severe and premature ageing. The Slum Department occupies three rooms on the first floor: one reserved for the assistant director whose appearance is limited to a few hours a week; another occupied by the main staff—a 'head clerk', an 'upper divisional clerk' and three 'lower divisional clerks', and a third which serves as a record room. Lower-grade staff such as the two peons, the cleaner and the sweeper generally hang out in the corridor unless required on duty.

The Slum and JJ Department is an intensely hierarchical male-dominated space; its structure replicating that of bureaucracies all over north India and probably many other parts of the world. The only women employed are the sweeper and the cleaner whose social inferiority is marked not only by their occupations but also by the fact that they generally squat or sit on the floor in the corridor. Hierarchy is physically embodied here, with relative status demarcated both through the allocation or non-allocation of space, and through the presence or lack of consumer durables. The importance of the largely absent assistant director is inscribed in the cooler and curtains which grace his office, which is generally kept locked for most of the week. These stand in sharp contrast to the basic fans and boarded-up windows of the main office and the dysfunctional fans and non-boarded empty window frames of the records room (the domain of the peons when they are not in the corridor). Desk size also establishes relative status whilst the peons' superiority to both the cleaner and sweeper is marked by the former sitting on chairs. After all, they too are men of paper.

There is nothing exceptional in this sort of hierarchical arrangement. It is, on the contrary, typical of office structures all over the world. The British Embassy in Delhi, I am told, classifies its staff into three grades, distributing not only office furniture but also household furniture according to status. But the sense of importance that is evoked by the presence of a desk and chair is particularly significant in a place like Welcome, where many would never have sat behind a desk and where the use of chairs is reserved principally for special occasions. The Slum and JJ Department is by local standards an intimidating space for men, and even more so for women. It is a space where vital papers (most of which cannot be understood by local inhabitants for reasons either of medium, language or wording) are passed around by important men behind desks—men who have the power to alter the path of your destiny.

Traces of such altered destinies lie in the records room which contains personal files recording the allocation of plots and tenements in seven resettlement colonies. Although the building is comparatively recent, the records date back to the first wave of resettlement in the 1960s and go on to cover the period of the Emergency up to the present day. Why begin by looking through these dusty files and not by talking with the residents of the colony about their personal experiences? I begin here simply because this is where I did begin. It is these files, on which I accidentally stumbled, that first provoked my interest in the Emergency, for here the period is portrayed not as a moment of explosive drama, but as a humdrum fact of bureaucratic existence—a time when paperwork was prolific and when housing rights were redefined.

What the records of Welcome give us is an official memory of the Emergency within the context of housing policies which precede it and succeed it, the Emergency in historic and administrative perspective. Viewed from this angle, the distinguishing feature of the period is not so much the fact of slum clearance (although demolitions were hugely accelerated at that time),[3] as the fact that many people secured

---

[3]Contrary to what is often imagined, the slum clearance programme was not a product of the Emergency years. It was first initiated back in 1958 with the establishment of the *Jhuggi Jhompri* Removal Scheme (JJRS) designed to demolish squatter settlements, resettle the inhabitants and deter new migrants from squatting on government land. The scheme has undergone considerable modifications over the years and responsibility for its implementation has been shunted back and forth

their rights to housing through participation in family planning. Case by case and file by file the records pertaining to Welcome bear witness to the granting of housing rights on the basis of sterilisation—a fact previously imputed by the journalist, David Selbourne, but hotly disputed by Jagmohan. However, the precise nature of the relationship between resettlement and sterilisation seems difficult to define. Far from simplifying the image of the Emergency, the yellowing papers of these files create confusion, posing at least as many questions as they seem to answer and blurring clear cut distinctions between victims, persecutors, conspirators and resistors.

To stumble across such records is surprising—not so much because of their subject matter which post-Emergency authors to some extent anticipate,[4] but rather because such records are not meant to exist. It is part of the mythology of the Emergency that controversial things like details of the Delhi administration's participation in family planning were not recorded in anything other than general terms. Once again the silence of the past works to reproduce the forgetting of the Emergency in the present—this time by denying the existence of 'the evidence'. When a middle-aged Indian journalist recently informed me that the idea of the DDA having been involved with sterilisation was just a baseless rumour spread by sensation-hungry foreigners (a category to which I was clearly assigned), it led me to reflect on the hold of this distorting silence both in the past and the present. This was a man who had been writing for a respectable national newspaper in Delhi during the Emergency, albeit under conditions of censorship. Still the notion that censorship conceals seems somewhat feeble when applied to a journalist who surely knows what it is he is hiding. Equally, one is led to question why contemporary books which purport to give a history of the resettlement scheme in Delhi[5] fail to mention the explicit link between housing and sterilisation during the Emergency which was, after all, the time when the greatest number of people were resettled.

---

several times between the Delhi Development Authority (appointed by central government) and the Delhi-focused Municipal Corporation.

[4] See Dayal and Bose, 1977, *For Reasons*; Selbourne, 1977, *An Eye to India* and Sinha, 1977, *Operation Emergency*.

[5] See Giresh Misra and Rakesh Gupta, 1981, *Resettlement Policies in Delhi*, Delhi: Institute of Public Administration and Ali Sabir, 1990, *Slums within Slums: A Study of Resettlement Colonies in Delhi*, Delhi: Har Anand.

The existence of the records therefore leads us to probe the nature of the silence that is said to have characterised the Emergency experience, haunting the daily lives of the intelligentsia who felt immersed in an all-engulfing darkness. Were family planning abuses as hidden during the Emergency as many like to imply? Or was it partly in the interests of those who condemned the Emergency retrospectively to take refuge in the notion that they had not known how to distinguish rumour from reality or exaggeration from fact at the time? Most post-Emergency authors attribute Indira Gandhi's election defeat to the people's fear of sterilisation, but on what was that fear based? Where were the educated classes whilst the sterilisation wave was sweeping through Delhi and across the northern states? Could it be that the sterilisation of 'the masses' (a favourite term in those days) was of little concern to the average middle-class Indian except when it came to mustering their support against Indira Gandhi in the election campaign? The ease with which many today dismiss past tales as 'grossly exaggerated' or 'based largely on rumour' seems to suggest that the silence characteristic of the Emergency was, and still is, far from innocent. Hasn't silence always acted as an excuse for non-intervention? And hasn't it equally provided a refuge for those who were not as inactive as they might retrospectively have wished—the bureaucrats and many others who sought to escape the burden of sterilisation by imposing it on their social and economic inferiors perhaps? And isn't such ambiguity of behaviour in times of crisis often compensated for after the event through the elaboration of horror stories which serve to remove what happened from one's own doorstep, bundling it into violent episodes or simplistic anecdotes which can later be recounted with amusement or dismissed as exaggerations? Whatever the reality, the presence of sterilisation records in the Slum and JJ Department provides some threads with which it is possible to begin weaving an alternative narrative of the Emergency. Lifting off the veil of secrecy, which in this case has proved more fictional than real, we are left with the records—previously unexplored and unacknowledged.

A first glimpse at the files

The records for Welcome are, like most records, incomplete. They consist of 3,733 personal files which represent 80 per cent of the allotments in the colony. It was the contents of these files that my assistant and I studied over a period of six weeks—aided by the periodic intervention of the clerks and peons who answered our queries, translating legal and administrative jargon into common language and explaining not only the rules of the system but also the techniques by which they are circumvented. In this sense, despite being officials, they gave insights into the unofficial history of the colony, explaining what the files concealed as well as what they revealed.

A Slum Department personal file comes into being when a plot of land or built-up tenement is allocated to a family whose home has been demolished usually as a result of slum clearance policy, occasionally as a result of flood or fire. Since files correspond to allotments rather than demolitions, it is impossible to judge from them how many of the displaced failed to obtain a plot or tenement. What we have here are files which begin with the successful attainment of a plot but which often contain information relating to several different families as the plot changes hands either officially or unofficially over the years. By tracing the paperwork relating to the plot, we can simultaneously learn something of how housing policies changed over time and how both the inhabitants and officials dealt with these changes. Some files contain only minimum information about the original allocation of land; others give rich and varied insights into the various techniques through which plots have been obtained, lost or retained in the colony.

Our first encounter with these files came about when a helpful lower divisional clerk decided to take us through one, explaining the system as he went along. 'All plots have been allocated on a leasehold basis to people who could prove that their *jhuggis* were demolished by the MCD or DDA under the *Jhuggi Jhompri* Removal Scheme. Only if you are the original allottee or a blood relation of the allottee can you pay the licence fee for the plot. You *must* have the proofs.' He points to two slim pieces of paper, one entitled a 'demolition slip' which records the details of the person's dwelling prior to demolition, and the other entitled an 'allotment order' which gives the details of resettlement. 'In order to distinguish genuine allottees from impostors, the MCD also decided to issue photos of each allottee which we keep in the files.' He points to two passport sized black and white photographs of a man standing rigidly and staring blankly into the camera. In front of his chest the man holds a mini blackboard on which is chalked his name, his father's name, the initial of his block and number of his plot. The photo is peculiarly evocative of the penal system, as is the language of some of the documents. A census of squatters[6] form, dated 1960, for example, demands the number of 'inmates' in the man's previous *jhuggi*. 'When people come to pay the licence fee, we use these photos to check that they are the genuine allottee', the clerk continues, tapping the photographs authoritatively. 'But in actual fact, many of the people in the colony are not the original allottees so we cannot accept lease payments from them. But if, as in this case here, the new occupant is in possession of all the relevant documents of the original allottee, then we generally tell him that as long as he pays the licence fee *in the name of* the allottee, then we won't make a fuss.' He smiles, sees my surprise, then clarifies: 'The slum wing's main concern is to collect the licence fee.'

'But in some cases we do send out eviction orders—that is when it comes to the official notice of the department that the person residing in a plot is not the original allottee.' He shuffles through a small pile of files on his desk until he finds one appropriate for demonstrating his point. 'You see here' he points to a document called 'Show Cause' which seems to have been issued from the department's old headquarters in Seemapuri. He reads out paragraph 4 which turns out to be one long convoluted sentence in contorted legalistic English:

Whereas it is reported that you _____, have occupied the said quarter/plot without the prior approval of the Competent Authority and such occupation is illegal, you are required to show cause within seven days from receipt of this notice why should you not be removed from the said plot/quarter, failing which further necessary action will be taken against you ex-parte without reference.

'This means that the man has seven days to state why he should be allowed to remain on the plot. If he does not come forward, then

[6]The census of squatters was carried out in 1960 to distinguish between two categories of squatters: the 'eligible' consisting of those who had been squatting in Delhi since before July 1960 and the 'ineligible' consisting of those who had settled in Delhi after that date. The intention was to shift 'eligible' squatters to resettlement colonies where they would be expected to pay lease payments and nominal rents either for built up tenements or, if they were unable to afford the rent, for plots of government land. Meanwhile the ineligible squatters were to be chased out of the city altogether with the idea that this would discourage new migrants from thinking they could squat in the capital. Difficulties in distinguishing the eligible from the ineligible led to the later abandonment of this distinction.

action goes ahead.[7] But in this case here, the man has come forward and has produced these documents.' He flicks through a pile of papers which include photographs along with photocopies of a ration card, an application for regularisation of the plot and power of attorney documents, covered in signatures and rubber stamps, recording details of the sale and purchase of the plot. 'You will see these documents in a lot of files,' the clerk continues. 'This man here has paid 12,000 rupees for the plot in 1981, but the sale is totally unauthorised. One of the terms and conditions of the resettlement is that the plots cannot be transferred to anyone except a close blood relative—that is called a "mutation case" for which you need a death certificate. But here the purchaser is not a relative. This means we cannot grant his request to transfer the leasehold into his name. So what we have done is ask for damages. Damages are calculated at one rupee per square yard per month. Most of the residential plots are 25 square yards, so that makes 25 rupees a month. It's not much, but the licence fee is less—only eight rupees a month. But since in this case, the man is what we call an "unauthorised occupant", we cannot accept the licence fee from him.'

We ask what proportion of the plots have been sold in this fashion. He estimates that at least half of the original allottees have left the colony. He goes on to tell us how the first plots given by the MCD back in 1960 were 80 square yards each, but that the authorities found that far from solving the '*jhuggi* problem', they had actually increased it, since almost all the people resettled had sold their plots and returned to *jhuggis*; sometimes even getting resettled a second time. So in order to put a stop to this practice, the MCD had reduced the size of the allotments, first to 50 square yards, and then to 25 square yards, thereby reducing their value and making them less appealing to developers. All of that had happened in the first few years of the *Jhuggi Jhompri* Removal Scheme which had been initiated back in 1958 when the slum population of Delhi first began to be perceived as a serious 'problem' requiring drastic action. Welcome's neighbouring colony, New Seelampur (technically known as Seelampur Phases I and II) contained some of the earlier large plots, but Welcome (technically Seelampur Phases III and IV) was founded in 1963 just after the change of policy. This meant, as the lower divisional clerk explained,

[7]The usual action would be to prosecute the accused under the Public Premises Act of 1971.

that there were only three types of allotment in Welcome: the 25 square yard residential plot; the 12.5 square yard shop plot and the 40 square yard built up tenement. In the case of plots, which formed over 90 per cent of the colony's official area, the resettled people had been allotted a rectangular strip of land on which they were expected to build their own home. In the case of the tenements, they were housed in one-room flats with a kitchen, bathroom and terrace, for which they were expected to pay not only the lease but also some rent. They were the wealthier people of the colony and represented less than 5 per cent of the population. Welcome also contained a large number of unauthorised *jhuggis* clustered together at the back of the colony in an area known as the Janata Colony. This unofficial sub-colony had grown up immediately after the Emergency. Its unofficial nature means that there are no files pertaining to it.[8]

This first conversation with the clerk gave us an excellent introduction to the complex workings of the Slum Department where there was clearly no simplistic dichotomy between the 'legal' and the 'illegal'. Even the line separating the 'official' from the 'unofficial' seemed difficult to draw, since this was an official giving us an unofficial version. The status of the documents seemed equally ambiguous. The power of attorney papers, for example, seemed to function simultaneously as proof that an illegal purchase had taken place and as evidence of the purchaser's right to become officially recognised as an 'unauthorised occupant.' Similarly, possession of the original allottee's documents seemed to give unofficial entitlement to a purchaser to pay the licence fee in somebody else's name. Clearly this was a system with considerable room for manoeuvre, both on the part of residents and on the part of officials.

The clerk's introduction also provided important indications concerning how the records should be perceived. Evidently, what we would face in the records room was not so much truths, nor even 'official truths' (since these were refuted by officials), as 'paper truths' whose status as truths was intrinsically linked to their symbolic value as official papers. These were the tokens which, it seems, mediated between the official's requirements and the occupant's needs. Judging

---

[8]For a more detailed account of the distribution of space in Welcome and its relation to urban policy, see Emma Tarlo, 2000, 'Welcome to History: A Resettlement Colony in the Making' in Dupont, Tarlo and Vidal eds, *Delhi*.

by the clerk's explanations, both officials and occupants recognised the constructed nature of these 'paper truths' and at times, colluded in their making. Yet the files also suggested that such truths must have a very different meaning depending on one's position in the system. To officials, the documents were obviously familiar, bulging repetitively out of every file—the daily fodder of the system. But such familiarity and comprehensibility seemed unlikely for the residents of the colony despite the fact that their personal security clearly depended on possession of the papers. Judging from the two files examined so far, this was a system which had no place for the paperless, and yet the papers that residents were expected to produce came across as being peculiarly alien. The thumb-print 'signatures' of applicants seemed to indicate the layers of distance that separated them from the bureaucracy: distance marked not only through the heavily coded official language, but also through the choice of language (English), the medium of writing and the very fact that the truths had taken on a paper form. For 'paper truths', despite their flimsiness and elasticity, despite their potential to be forged or destroyed, none the less have authority, belonging as they do of the world of the modern state where the written word reigns supreme.

Unfortunately, since the record room was at some distance from the main office, our contact with the helpful clerk was more limited once we sat down to explore the records in detail. Instead, we had the company of one of the peons who watched us laconically—occasionally asking us why we bothered or demanding to know where we lived and what we were paid. The ambiguity of our status seemed to bother him far more than our curiosity. I had a card which revealed I was a 'doctor' from the University of London—all of which suggested that I should not be getting my hands dirty rummaging through filthy files which the peons themselves were reluctant to touch. Furthermore, my assistant, Rajinder, seemed to work more diligently than was reasonable, tolerating the grim conditions of the records room without complaint despite the fact that his English was fluent, indicating a high level of education. Our other company was in the form of wildlife: mainly birds which made their nests on the dysfunctioning fans and flew about the room throughout the day, using the shelves of files as perches for sleep and other activities. Ironically, the MCD head office had failed to respond to its own regional department's frequent applications for money for repairs.

As a consequence each time the pre-monsoon winds rose, they brought in a new blanket of dust which sugared the files, and each time the clouds burst, the room became flooded. None the less, the presence of so many pigeons ensured that, despite the unfavourable conditions, this was an archive with non-stop live singing!

Since each file began with an allotment, some dated back to the early 1960s when the colony was founded, whilst others dated back to the Emergency years when an additional 1,483 plots were created, making a grand total of 4,034 residential plots, 415 tenements and 198 shop plots. Some files were almost empty, containing only an allotment slip which gave the name, block and plot of the resettled person. But most files contained some form of demolition slip, an allotment order, a possession slip, a list of MCD or DDA terms and conditions (depending on which body was running the Slum Department at the time), two photographs, an affidavit signed or thumb printed by the original allottee and a few receipts for licence payments and sometimes the back payments of damages relating to a person's previous residence.[9] The precise wording of the documents varied from year to year, largely in accordance with changes in policy and administration. The headings at the top of the pages bore witness to the fact that the Slum Department has long been caught in an on-going tug of war between the MCD and the DDA with the result that most files contain a mixture of papers from both administrative bodies. Also included in some files were death certificates, applications for mutation, documents of purchase, eviction orders, papers relating to court cases and, from time to time, a survey form, dated 1989, which was aimed at establishing how many of the original allottees had left the colony.

A fair amount of general information can be gleaned from this material despite the gap between paper truths and realities. From the names of allottees, one can usually guess their religion, thereby establishing that the majority of people resettled in Welcome prior to the Emergency were Hindu whilst a large proportion resettled during the Emergency were Muslim. One can also learn, from the demolition slips, that whilst most pre-Emergency allottees came from *jhuggi* clusters all over the city, many of those resettled in 1975–6 came from ancient

---

[9]A system by which squatters were expected to pay retrospective damages for each year they had been living illegally on government land was introduced in 1960 at the time of the census of squatters.

areas of Old Delhi, suggesting that probably they were not recent migrants but long-standing residents of the city. The documents of purchase, mutation cases and the 1989 forms bear witness to transfers of properties over time although they cannot tell us of those purchasers who continue to pose as original allottees. Conversation with the lower divisional clerk has taught us to be wary of such information. What, for example should we assume from the missing files or from those files which contained a paucity of documentation?—a family which has left the colony; the arrival of a squatter; an allottee who never paid the licence fee; a purchase unrecorded; lethargy on the part of housing officials; the discreet acceptance of a bribe; a file that went astray? The options are so numerous that it would be dangerous to assume too much.

Perhaps of greater value than this general data, which lends itself all too well to the production of potentially dubious statistics, are the glimpses of alternative voices which from time to time creep into the files. These usually appear in the form of letters, sometimes handwritten in Hindi, but more often typed in English, presumably by professional letter writers. These letters usually consist of requests for changes of plot, either within the colony or from one colony to another. They demonstrate not only the space for negotiation, but also the language within which negotiations take place. Take, for example, the following letter addressed to the executive officer of the Slum Department:

Respectfully, I beg to bring to your kind notice that my *jhuggi* at Arjun Nagar was recently demolished and in lieu of that I have been allotted a plot in Madangir...In connection, I may state that I am a 'Balmiki' scheduled caste[10] and my relatives mostly live in Shahdara. Due to my backwardness I am

[10]Balmiki is the self-chosen respectable name adopted by a number of people whose conventional caste occupation was and, in many cases still is, sweeping. The name was selected in order to identify the community with Maharishi Valmiki, author of one version the classic Hindu epic, the *Ramayana*. Welcome contains a large proportion of Balmikis, most of whom earn their living working as government-employed sweepers. In Hindu hierarchies of occupation, sweeping is considered one of the most polluting tasks and the people who performed it were conventionally regarded as impure. The Balmikis, along with other low-status groups who were previously classified as 'untouchable' are today included within the government classification of 'scheduled caste'. Positive discrimination in terms of access to education and government jobs was introduced in the 1950s to try to improve the status of scheduled caste groups but the social stigma associated with occupations like sweeping continues to exist. When the Balmiki author of the above letter says he is

unable to live alongside with other well-placed people in Madangir. I therefore request that I may kindly be allowed a suitable plot in Silampur Area in lieu of my existing allotment. I shall be highly thankful to you, Yours etc.

The fact that this letter is accompanied by an allotment slip which allocates a plot in Welcome indicates that the Balmiki's request was successful. So too was that of a 'private sector worker' who submitted the following letter in 1969:

With due respect and humble permission I beg to state I have been granted a plot in Rajori Gardens...Sir, I inspected the site...and it is among the sweepers and evil-minded persons. I applied for getting a plot in Rajori Gardens as a good colony, but the plots are lying among quarrelsome persons. I don't want to get an allotment in this absurd locality. It is requested that I may be given a plot in Seelampur...Thank you, Yours etc.

Although these letters appear to reveal all too blatantly the orthodox social values of their senders, I would suggest that they may tell us as much about the expectations of their recipients as about the attitudes of the applicants. Both are framed within an idiom of social hierarchy which professional letter writers clearly consider appropriate for approaching the hallowed offices of a government department. The Balmiki's request hangs on his self-confessed sense of inferiority whilst the private employee's hangs on his sense of superiority. From the fact that both were successful in attaining transfers to Welcome we can surmise that this is an idiom which officials of the Slum Department understand. So too is the language of deference within which almost all letters are couched. This language combines archaic formulae from nineteenth century British bureaucracy with apparently indigenous formulae of worship and adoration. Sometimes the executive officer is appealed to within the framework of legal rhetoric—as in the formulation 'I earnestly request your honour concerning the aforesaid case' or 'I would most respectfully like to submit that I saw your honour in person in the afternoon...' At other times, the rhetoric is more religious—'May the goddess of prosperity and success keep her constant smile on you for this timely service...' or alternatively 'I pray to God for your longevity and prosperity'. At other times, an appeal is made to the officer's feudalistic sense of responsibility—as in a letter

---

'unable to live alongside with other well-placed people', it may well be that he is suffering intimidation from his better-placed neighbours.

where a man recounts two ancient parables about the king's duty to his subjects before stating his request for a plot. In some cases, legal, religious and feudalistic formulae are all rolled together with expressions of the applicant's utter worthlessness: 'I am a poor and poverty stricken man having liability of 6 daughters and 2 sons...Therefore again, I request your honour that kindly having mercy upon my pathetic position please consider my case in my favour...so that I may pass my remaining life under your kind shelter.'

The correspondence in such files provides insight into the functioning of a system in which the participants speak in clearly defined codes. The official documents are worded in the pompous and archaic language of Slum Department bureaucracy—a language of demolitions, allotments, affidavits and mutations. To this, the residents respond with equally archaic but deferential letters, written usually by professional letter writers who mediate between the literate and the illiterate. In response to the humble appeals of the applicants, the officials communicate with each other in largely monosyllabic formulas, like 'Put up', 'granted' , 'submitted for approval', or 'refused'. All of this means that despite the 'human element' introduced by the letters, the ensuing dialogue attains a high level of predictability. By 1976, however, signs of a new language have penetrated the bureaucratic discourse of the Slum Department.

The language of family planning
The new language finds its most direct expression in a small and unpretentious looking document called the DDA Family Planning Centre Allotment Order which is found in over 28 per cent of the files. It is reproduced below.

DELHI DEVELOPMENT AUTHORITY
FAMILY PLANNING CENTRE

Allotment order

1. Name and Age
2. Father's name
3. Plot
4. No. of family members
5. Date of voluntary sterilisation
6. Nature of assistance claimed
7. Order

Signature of applicant   *Officer in Charge*
Date

Here, the allotment order is just an empty form, devoid of details, but since each form must have been empty before being filled, it is interesting to pause to contemplate it first in its blank state. No doubt, the title alone gives official acknowledgement of the fact that the DDA was issuing plots on the basis of family planning. But what does it mean by 'family planning'? For this we have to go to point 5 which demands bluntly 'Date of voluntary sterilisation'. So 'family planning' is defined as 'sterilisation' and 'sterilisation' is defined as 'voluntary' even before the person has begun to fill in the form. What we find in this small piece of paper is a fragment of the dominant Emergency narrative—a token of official family planning euphemisms in action at a local level.

On first encounter the presence of these allotment orders would appear to confirm Selbourne's claim that those whose homes were demolished in the slum clearance scheme could only get alternative plots through being forcibly sterilised at the hands of the DDA. But there are various facts which seem to suggest that the simple formula, demolition → sterilisation → plot, cannot fully explain the complexity of the situation. First, there is the fact that the FP allotment orders are not found in all the files pertaining to residential blocks created during the Emergency and are not restricted only to the files which date from 1975–6. On the contrary, well over half of the sterilisation cases recorded refer to plots which date back to the 1960s. This not only suggests that some of those who experienced demolition during the Emergency managed to obtain plots without getting sterilised, but it also implies that some of those who did get sterilised through the DDA had not just experienced the demolition of their homes, since it is unlikely that the DDA would have been destroying plots it had officially created only a decade earlier. Second, the details on the allotment orders seem to suggest that not all of those who participated in the DDA family planning scheme were in fact sterilised themselves. When one looks at the answers given in response to point 5 of the form, one finds not only a date and sterilisation number, but also one of two phrases: either 'self-sterilisation', or 'motivated case'.

The term 'self-sterilisation' seems clear enough, suggesting that in return for sterilisation a person was able to obtain a plot. But the term 'motivated case' is by no means self-explanatory, and led my assistant and I to turn to the peon for an explanation. 'Those were the people who gave a case,' he explained, rather too briefly. He was using the language of family planning, a language with which we were not yet familiar. What did it mean to 'give a case'? Further prompting led to the explanatory statement, 'You could get a plot by motivating others for sterilisation.' This cleared the picture to some extent, but it still left a number of questions unanswered. Why did the plot go to the motivator? Did the person who was sterilised get a plot too? The peon gave a tired smile at these ignorant questions. He was beginning to get impatient. 'Of course the motivated person did not get a plot. I've already told you, the plot went to the motivator for motivating the other to get sterilised.' I was still confused. Why would anyone be willing to be 'motivated' when they could get a plot themselves if they went in for 'self-sterilisation'? The peon raised his right hand and rubbed his fingers against his thumb in a gesture which spoke clearly enough: 'Money'.

'People were told they could get a plot either by getting sterilised or giving a case. This meant that they had to make some sort of private deal with the person concerned. If I want to motivate you [he points to Rajinder], then I'll offer you this much money to get sterilised. You might say you want more, so we strike a deal. I have to accompany you to the hospital as proof that I am the motivator. You get sterilised, and I get the plot. That's the incentive.'

I notice that we are all laughing. Laughing at what? Was it that we were enjoying a good story—another little escapade into the unofficial? Or was it rather that we felt uncomfortable talking about something as physical and personal as sterilisation? Was it a mixture of both? Certainly, for my part, I felt that we had entered complicated territory on which it was dangerous to tread. Should I be asking so many questions about what was turning out to be a government-initiated market for infertile bodies? Might not the peon start getting nervous about my curiosity? He had already asked us, naturally enough, why we were interested in the files. Did I even know why I was interested? When I had initially asked to consult the records, I had not had any idea that they would contain information on sterilisation. I had simply been looking for general background information about the colony. But now that I did know, I was curious. At the same time, I felt that my curiosity should not be too explicit—a hangover from the Emergency perhaps? There seemed to be something clandestine about uncovering details which had been so effectively effaced. Another product of silence? I seemed to be laughing partly to make a joke of my ignorance, and partly to keep the conversation light, as if to say, you can tell stupid ignorant me. I was also responding to the peon's laughter which seemed to say, I am speaking from outside my role as an official of the DDA—I am telling you things you should not really know but this is how it worked. There also seemed to be a strong element of irony in our laughter—'appreciation' perhaps of the grotesque absurdity of a government policy which explicitly encouraged illicit deals in human infertility.

It was this encounter which had first led me to consult the forgotten volumes of the post-Emergency narrative. I was looking for explanations. Although the idea of displaced slum dwellers buying each other's sterilisation fitted ill with the narrative's general projection of the poor as either passive victims or active resisters, there were, none the less, many useful insights to be gained. In particular Dayal and Bose gave an excellent description of the structure of the family planning policy in Delhi: its centralised grip over all government institutions, including hospitals, schools, police stations, transport authorities, the MCD, the DDA and even over civic bodies.[11] They demonstrated how those at the top of institutions were set sterilisation targets which they were encouraged to fulfil by accumulating sterilisation cases from their staff. While the MCD demanded that all employees with three or more children should be sterilised, the DDA set the limit at two. Such targets were sanctioned by a package of 'incentives' and 'disincentives' which generously rewarded those employees who accumulated large numbers of cases and which penalised those who refused to participate by threatening to withhold their salaries. Once the DDA had exhausted its own staff, it turned to its clients as a potentially lucrative source of sterilisation cases.

[11]cf. Dayal and Bose. For a concise account of the variation in family planning policy from state to state, see Gwatkin, 1979, 'Political Will and Family Planning: Implications of India's Emergency Experience', *Population and Development Review*, 5, 1, pp. 29–59. See also ch. 3 of V.A. Pai Panandikar, R.N. Bishnoi, and O.P. Sharma, 1978, *Family Planning Under the Emergency: Policy Implications of Incentives and Disincentives*, New Delhi: Radiant Publications. That Delhi functioned as the centre of Emergency measures is confirmed by Davidson Gwatkin's observation that the sterilisation achievements of different states varied in relation to their proximity to Delhi, with the highest rates found in neighbouring states and lowest rates in states physically distanced from the capital. This was partly owing to the fact that fertility rates were already in decline in the southern states where family planning activities had been concentrated prior to the Emergency.

Dayal and Bose reproduce an official government order issued on 15 May 1976. Under the heading 'Provisions for the General Public' it reads: 'Allotment of houses, flats, tenements, shops and plots in all income groups...will be made only to "eligible persons" or eligible couples...An ineligible person can become eligible on production of the sterilisation certificate in respect of him/her or his wife or her husband from the prescribed authority.'[12] They interpret this as meaning that it was impossible to get DDA housing facilities without getting sterilised. However, our recent encounter with the records of the Slum Department raises the possibility of another interpretation. When the statement reads that a sterilisation certificate is required 'in respect of' the husband or the wife, it does not categorically state that it is the husband or wife who must get sterilised. Rather it seems to suggest that one of them must submit a sterilisation certificate in their name. But whose certificate? In this vague and ambiguous wording there seems to be space for the motivator, that evasive figure we have briefly encountered in the Slum Department files at Welcome. This is not to argue that the existence of the motivator has hitherto gone unacknowledged. On the contrary, the motivator is a familiar figure in writings on family planning in India before, during and after the Emergency. But the identity and scope of the motivator has, until now, remained unexplored. Usually it is government employees like nurses, doctors, teachers, and family planning officers who are described as 'motivators'. These professionals have been set sterilisation targets and are paid small bonuses for their motivation work. They are not expected to buy sterilisation cases but to persuade people of the benefits of contraception. Sometimes they are seen to employ touts who are paid petty sums for rounding up people for sterilisation. But there is not, to my knowledge, any recognition of the fact that anybody, whatever their identity and whatever their status or lack of it, could become a motivator during the Emergency. Neither is it recognised that by motivating a single person a man or woman could get the same benefits as someone who came forward for self-sterilisation or that, in effect, motivators went about purchasing sterilisation cases so that paying someone to get sterilised became a means of buying a plot.

This brief detour into the post-Emergency narrative has familiarised

---

[12]Dayal and Bose, 1977, *For Reasons*, appendix, p. 223.

us with the language of sterilisation with its vocabulary of 'incentives', 'disincentives', 'motivators', 'eligible' and 'ineligible' people. It has also provided insight into the structure of the family planning policy. Returning to the files of Welcome, it is now possible to try to unravel how the DDA perpetuated and interpreted this policy at the local level. The first thing to establish is which files contain DDA FP allotment orders and to what use were these orders put. We begin with a fat pile of files pertaining to a residential block created in 1969. It is one of a number of blocks with the prefix 'JB'. 'Why JB?' we ask the peon. 'Because the people in these blocks used to live in Jamuna Bazaar. That was a famous slum on the banks of the Jamuna.' His response bore witness to the short-sightedness of housing policies in which 'slums' were demolished only for their residents to be resettled in new areas which are given the same name and hence connotation as the original slum. The fact that the official body that administers 'resettlement colonies' is called the 'Slum and JJ Department' is equally indicative. As far as the administration is concerned, resettlement colonies are just another kind of 'slum' even if they were developed in the interests of 'slum clearance'. When DDA officials and policy makers proclaim that over one-third of the population of Delhi is living in slums, they include these colonies in their calculations. Keeping slum statistics high is important. It acts both as a magnet to international development funds as well as providing an excuse for why the 'slum problem' can never be resolved.

JB15[13] is the only residential block in Welcome for which every file is available and where the level of information in each file is unusually high. The slum wing had been transferred from the MCD to the DDA by 1969, and the latter had introduced a form which demanded a number of details of the resettled. As a result information is given concerning, not only the names and ages of applicants, but also their family members, their occupations, their incomes and their previous residence. From these forms we learn that some of the resettled were engaged in low level government employment such as sweeping or gardening, whilst the vast majority worked in the informal sector as tonga drivers, rickshaw pullers, fruit vendors, cobblers, labourers and so forth. Demolition slips suggest that all of them had their homes demolished in March 1968 whereupon they were left in a 'camping

---

[13]In the interests of preserving anonymity, I have inserted a false number here.

site' in Seemapuri, a colony a few miles further towards the Uttar Pradesh border. From there, they succeeded in being transferred to Welcome after an intermediary period of one year. In order to qualify for the transfer they had to prove that they had been squatting in Delhi since before 1960. This made them 'eligible squatters.' Some also provided clearance certificates to show that they had paid damages on their previous *jhuggis*, although this does not appear to have been a pre-requisite to transfer since some had not yet been assessed for damages. What is clear is that the people of JB15 represent only a selection of those whose *jhuggis* were destroyed in Jamuna Bazaar in 1968. These are just the 'eligible' squatters at a time when 'eligibility' was defined, not in terms of sterilisation, but in terms of the length of one's stay in Delhi.

There are 254 files for the block. Of these, 28 contain DDA FP allotment orders, all of which are marked with dates between August and October 1976. We begin with a file which contains the demolition slip of a fruit seller. Judging from his name, he is a Hindu. Like others in the block, his *jhuggi* in Jamuna Bazaar was demolished in 1968 but he was not allocated a plot in Welcome until 1969. The file contains the usual documents: a demolition slip, a few receipts for license payments, a census of squatters form, a clearance certificate to say that he has paid damages on his previous residence, a photograph, an application for allotment, a list of terms and conditions and an affidavit swearing, amongst other things, that he does not posses any other property in Delhi. However, it also contains a FP allotment order which is in the name, not of the fruit seller, but of a Hindu woman who appears to be unrelated. From the order, we learn that she is aged 35 and has four children. She has applied for 'self-sterilisation' and the number and date of her operation is recorded in response to point 5 on the form. The 'nature of assistance claimed' under point 6 is filled in with the formula 'regularisation of residential plot'. Under point 7 'order', the DDA officer has written the words 'allowed provisionally'. Like all other DDA FP allotment orders found in the files of Welcome, the order is signed and dated by K.K. Nayyar, then executive officer of the DDA for this region. It is also signed by the applicant. A survey form, dated 1989, clarifies the situation. It states that the woman had purchased the plot some time before 1976 and that she had transferred the leasehold to her name through getting sterilised. Using the vocabulary of the family planning policy, we can say that she has become 'eligible.' The 1989 form reminds us however that such eligibility may not be permanent. It recalls that the regularisation was 'provisional only'. All of the DDA FP allotment orders found in this block turn out to be 'regularisation' cases. Some record 'self-sterilisation'; others record 'motivated case.' All except one refer to residential plots. In each case, the name on the FP allotment order is different from that of the original allottee, suggesting that the properties had changed hands prior to or during the Emergency and that the new purchasers made themselves 'eligible' through participation in the 'family planning' programme. The only exception is that of an original allottee who got sterilised in order to 'regularise' a temple she had constructed on a plot adjoining her own. There is a brief note on the FP allotment order stating that the woman in question had already constructed the unauthorised temple on the plot. The 'nature of assistance claimed' reads 'allocation of religious plot'. The order reads 'approved provisionally', and is further stamped with the words 'attested'. What is apparent from these cases is that sterilisation had become a medium through which 'irregularities' could be ironed out. A DDA FP allotment order had the capacity to transform illegal purchasers into 'eligible' license holders. All of the 25 pre-Emergency blocks have files containing similar orders. In one block as many as 60 per cent of the files contain the orders; in another block, as few as 2 per cent. However, my aim is not to enumerate the 'facts' of each block, but rather to demonstrate the different types of cases that emerge and the different situations in which they seem to occur. The most significant finding at this stage is that DDA FP allotment orders are contained most frequently in those files where the paperwork suggests that the original allottees were no longer residing in their plot at the time of the Emergency.

Let us turn, now, to the files of the three blocks which were created in 1975 during the Emergency months. Taken together, these blocks contain 1,084 plots, for which 889 files are available. The people resettled during this period seem to have come from a variety of different locations all over Delhi. A large number are from a place called Gandhi Camp, near the British School in New Delhi. Others are from central locations of Old Delhi, such as Chandni Mahal, Kalan Mahal, Jama Masjid and the infamous Dujana House. Yet others have curious incomprehensible addresses such as 'Bombay type latrine'.

In the 889 files available, we find only 110 DDA FP allotment orders, suggesting that in 1975, sterilisation was not yet a requirement for resettlement. Again those FP orders that do surface are dated 1976 and do not, in most cases, correspond to the formula: demolition → sterilisation → allotment.

Here again we find a number of regularisation cases of which just under half are classified as 'motivated'. One FP allotment order reveals that the applicant is a 23-year-old Muslim man without children. He had purchased a plot in January 1976 and regularised it in September 1976 by 'giving a case', thereby avoiding being sterilised himself at such a young age. Apart from 'regularisation cases', we also find 'transfer cases'. These are often accompanied by a small note, as in the case of a sweeper who states that he wants to transfer to Welcome because he has relatives there and because he works in Wellington Hospital. He achieves his request through getting sterilised. In another transfer case, there is a letter from the applicant in the file. This file is interesting since it bears witness to the moment of transition when sterilisation papers became incorporated into DDA policies. The applicant's letter reads as follows:

Most respectfully I beg to state that I am the resident of ___, J.J. Colony Seelampur IV. My hut was demolished by the DDA from Humayun Road on 31.10.1975, but the demolition slip was not issued on that day. The officers told us that the demolition slip will be issued later, when all the camp will be demolished. Only a few huts were demolished on that day. Some were given demolition slip and some were not. The demolition was stopped on that day due to Diwali Festival.

Due to correspondence with the Vice Chairman, DDA, Ltd Governor of the Implementation Committee and Shri Arjun Das, MMC, we got provisionally allotment in Seelampur by the Executive Officer in December 1975. When the full camp was demolished, all the people from Humayun Road were allotted plots in Trilokpuri. On my demolition slip was also written Trilokpuri wrongly instead of Seelampur. I brought this mistake to the notice of the officers but they said that this will be done later in their office.

Sir, it is requested that my case may please be seen sympathetically and that my plot in Seelampur be regularised instead of Trilokpuri as I have already constructed it by spending some money in these hard days. I shall be highly thankful to you, Yours etc.

The executive officer of the DDA responded to the letter by scrawling a note to his subordinates: 'Please furnish a report, 7.6.1976.' To this the concerned officer replied on the same day: 'All families were resettled in Trilokpuri. We are not allowing changes in such cases, 7.6.1976.' This appears to be a definitive answer, but at the very bottom of the same page, another officer has added: 'Vasectomy case. Change to Seelampur allowed.' This additional note is dated 21.8.1976. By August 1976, sterilisation had clearly become a medium through which people could negotiate their housing rights with officials of the DDA.

Another form of negotiation is apparent in those cases where husbands are recorded as having motivated their wives, or wives their husbands. There is also a case of a young man motivating his brother and two cases of children motivating their parents. When we asked the peon about the logic of this, he gave a practical explanation. 'Suppose you have one plot already, then you cannot get sterilised for a second plot since it is against the regulations to have two plots registered in your name. But if your son motivates you then the plot would not be in your name but in the name of your son. That way, you can get the extra plot.' In such cases, the FP allotment order seemed to provide the possibility of expanding personal property in the colony, but such inter-familial motivations were rare, amounting to no more than 11 of the 486 motivated cases recorded. The vast majority of motivated cases were between people who do not appear to have been related. In one relatively small block, created in 1972, 18 out of the 20 FP allotment orders found record motivated cases, none of which seem to have involved family members of the people concerned. These are mostly regularisation cases, including regularisations of commercial as well as residential property. In some cases, the applicants seem to have 'given two cases' per plot, in others they have given only one. When we tried to question the peon on this, he simply stated 'That block is full of Muslims. Muslims were against sterilisation and so they usually preferred to "give a case".' This did not, however, explain why some had given one case and others two. Neither did it explain why motivated cases also occurred amongst Hindus.

Finally, there are four blocks in the colony which were officially created during the monsoon months of 1976. This, according to the peon was when the DDA had set up a family planning camp in the colony itself. The files relating to these blocks contain a particularly large proportion of FP allotment orders amounting to approximately 80 per cent. Some of the residents in these blocks seem to have been living in other resettlement colonies or in inner city slum areas prior to 1976, but the vast majority appear to have come from Welcome itself where they were either living as tenants in other blocks or else residing in their own 'unauthorised *jhuggis*'. Their FP orders generally read 'allocation of residential plot' rather than 'regularisation' or 'transfer'. Their files also contain affidavits signed or thumb printed by the applicants concerned. Point 4 of the affidavit is worth reproducing. It is a declaration 'That I was residing in a *jhuggi* near block ____ in ____ for the last ____ years and that I have voluntarily demolished my own jhuggi and vacated the Government land.'

There is something very dubious about this declaration. Were people really going around demolishing their own houses, or was 'voluntary demolition' like 'voluntary sterilisation'—a fait accompli? There is always something ominous in the use of that word 'voluntary' in official documents, particularly when they are printed in a language which most of the 'applicants' cannot understand. Again, those thumb prints and shakily written Hindi signatures seem to jar painfully with the formality of the administrative paper. One cannot help but wonder whether anyone had actually bothered to inform the applicants what they were declaring? And even if they had, were homeless *jhuggi* dwellers in a position to refuse to sign?

The problem of how to interpret the phrase, 'voluntary demolition' is, of course, just a fragment of the larger problem of how to interpret the paper truths contained within the files more generally. Going through almost a thousand FP allotment orders spread through every block in the colony undoubtedly provided a clearer sense of the different administrative uses to which this particular document could be put, but it also raised a number of questions. Were people willingly coming forward for sterilisation in order to make the best of the benefits it would bring them? Or was there a structure of intimidation which pushed them into participation? Furthermore, given that the DDA offered two alternative methods for obtaining plots through 'family planning', who were the ones who chose to become 'motivators'? And who were the 'motivated'—the people who got sterilised without getting plots? Added to these questions was the further issue of whether sterilisations recorded actually corresponded to sterilisations performed.

Two conversations with the officials of the Slum Department served, not so much to clarify the answers as to clarify the questions. The first conversation took place in the corridors of the Slum Department, just as the office was closing and after the senior staff had already gone home. The clerks (both lower and higher divisional) approached Rajinder and me with a view to telling us we could spend as much time as we liked going through the files. They did not want us to be put off by the head clerk's less than enthusiastic attitude and seemed to want us to understand how the system worked. When I casually asked about the family planning policy during the Emergency, the upper divisional clerk was immediately forthcoming. 'At first the policy was just to encourage people to get sterilised voluntarily, but since people weren't coming forward voluntarily, Sanjay Gandhi introduced more forceful measures. Looking through the files, you will get the impression that people were voluntarily getting sterilised, but actually that is not the case. It was done by force.' Again officials of the DDA were acknowledging the fragile nature of 'paper truths'. The upper divisional clerk was smudging the boundary between the official and unofficial, this time in the liminal space of the corridor at the liminal time of closing hour. Again, we were in dangerous territory, but I none the less asked, 'forced by whom?'

'By government employees. By people from the Slum Department.' The reply is rather general—an indication that this is a conversation in which names and personal details will not be given:

'They would go around door to door and ask to see people's papers. They were under a lot of pressure. They had been told that they would lose their jobs if they did not fill targets for sterilisation. They were under force. If the residents couldn't provide all the relevant documents, they were threatened with eviction unless they got sterilised or gave a case.'

So that was what was meant by the phrase 'regularisation of residential plot'.

'Take, for example the iron market. It used to be on G.T. Road. It was demolished. At the time of demolition the traders were told that they could not get new plots unless they were sterilised.'

A case of 'voluntary demolition'. But what exactly did the clerk mean when he used the phrase 'By force'? Physical coercion or economic pressure?

'By fear, that's what I mean,' he clarifies, whereupon the lower divisional clerk adds: 'There were some cases of physical force too. There were people bundled into jeeps and taken off for sterilisation at that time too, no?' That uneasy laughter seems to have returned. The upper divisional clerk sticks to his original explanation—'fear'.

He is senior to the lower divisional clerk and was already employed by the DDA at the time of the Emergency. His words sound less like an extract from an oft-repeated narrative and more like a memory which is at once both personal and depersonalised. But unfortunately the conversation has reached its limit. Sensing his defensiveness, I feel unable to ask him directly about his own role. Instead, I ask him what he thinks, in retrospect, about the family planning policy of those days.

'The policy was in the national interest.' He has switched back to an official voice. 'But the government would not have changed were it not for the forcible sterilisation and the demolitions. Those were the two principal things. The fact that the government did change shows the extent to which people were being forced.' An apparently neutral assessment.

This conversation provides us with the missing keys for decoding the language of 'family planning' in which 'family planning' means sterilisation which is defined as 'voluntary'. Government statistics suggest that the word 'family planning' did not always translate thus, but they also show that the slippage in meaning was a gradual process which began back in the 1960s when vasectomy was increasingly advocated over other family planning methods. Literature also suggests that the 'voluntary' nature of the mass vasectomy camps introduced at that time is highly debatable.[14] During the Emergency, the precise nature of the meaning of the term 'voluntary' was clarified. By the time we read of people voluntarily demolishing their own *jhuggis*, we know that we are dealing with the euphemisms of the Emergency when the takeover of meaning has become complete.

We now know that a 'regularisation' takes place under the threat of eviction. In family planning parlance, this is the 'disincentive'. The 'incentive' is the right to remain living in the house one has purchased or built or the right to have an alternative plot after one's home has been 'voluntarily' demolished. An 'eligible' person is a person who

---

[14]In a convincing and thorough analysis of family planning policy in India before the Emergency, Marika Vicziany challenges the myth that India ever had a voluntarist family planning programme. She highlights the implicit coercion built into a system which had always been target-oriented and slanted against the poorer sections of society. See Marika Vicziany, 1982–3, 'Coercion in a Soft State: The Family-Planning Program of India, pt 1: "The Myth of Voluntarism" and pt 2, "The Sources of Coercion"', *Pacific Affairs*, 55, 3, pp. 373–401 and 4, pp. 557–93.

either is sterilised or has 'given a case.' 'Giving a case' means paying someone else to get sterilised. The person who pays for a sterilisation is a 'motivator' while the person who accepts the deal is 'motivated.' An 'ineligible' person is a person who neither gets sterilised nor purchases the sterilisation of another.

Reassessed, in the light of these clarifications, the files of Welcome record the process by which the DDA, caught within a wider structure of sterilisation targets, cast its bureaucratic net over the colony in search of victims for sterilisation. It found its victims in that ambiguous space which had always existed—and which continues to exist— between what is known and what is officially recorded. Just as today the colony contains '*jhuggi* dwellers', 'unauthorised occupants' and illegal purchasers who pay the license fee in the name of the 'original allottee', so in the mid-1970s it was home to a number of people who were living in the loophole between official policies and officially recognised irregularities. During the Emergency, that loophole tightened. Instead of being a space for negotiation, it became a noose which squeezed its victims into participation in family planning— offering them the grim choice either of getting sterilised or of paying someone else to take their place. The rules and regulations of the colony had suddenly lost their flexibility. They now functioned as official levers with which to scoop up sterilisation cases from residents trapped by the finer details of the law.

But does this vertical and totalitarian model of power really correspond to the picture that emerges from the files? Had the system really lost its flexibility, or was it simply that the terms and conditions of negotiation had been redefined? After all, transfers from other colonies and applications for alternative plots could still be negotiated with the officers of the DDA as long as 'evidence' of sterilisation was provided. In such cases, can we be certain that the DDA was 'forcing' sterilisations, or was it rather that some people in the colony were actively exploiting the various possibilities that sterilisation offered? When I questioned the DDA staff of Welcome on this issue, one of the lower divisional clerks responded: 'Some were sterilised by force [*zaberdasti se*] but actually, once it was known that you could get major benefits through sterilisation, then many people chose to get sterilised out of greed [*lalchi se*].'

Greed?

'Well the benefits were high. For example, if you were employed on a contractual basis, you could get your job made permanent through being sterilised. So, of course, people were keen. Permanent work is difficult to find. You take the cleaning woman here, for example. She was just a wage labourer paid on a daily basis before the Emergency. She got sterilised in 1976 and has had a permanent post with the DDA ever since.'

At this point the upper divisional clerk interjected: 'You have to look at the rewards. A plot of land is worth a lot of money. Nowadays those plots sell for lakhs of rupees.'[15]

So what are the incentives today?

'Today they don't offer anything much. Just a clock or a fan, some small thing. That's why today nobody is interested.'

With this second conversation, our brief vision of clarity has begun to blur. Force has somehow transmuted into choice; need has transposed into 'greed'. Our earlier image of innocent victims helplessly trapped in a bureaucratic web gives way to the possibility of pragmatic opportunists, reaching out for benefits and 'rewards'. And yet it is from the fusion of these two pictures that a new perspective emerges from which we can try to capture the diversity of people's experiences of that elusive moment we call 'the Emergency'.

[15]One lakh = 100,000.

4

VOICES FROM THE DUST

Most urgent

MUNICIPAL CORPORATION OF DELHI JJ DEPARTMENT

Dated 7.8.1979

DC(S) [Deputy Commissioner, Slums] has taken a very serious view regarding poor progress of authentication work relating to the allotment of JJ tenements/plots, which was to be taken up on priority basis as decided in a meeting, held in the room of the DC(S) in May 1979. The requisite proformas, after approval of the DC(S), were got cyclostyled and distributed to the rent recovery staff in sufficient quantity. However, it has been reported by the Rent Recovery Officer that the rent recovery staff is neither taking interest in the recovery work nor in the authentication work. To review the situation a meeting has been convened in the room of the DC(S)...and you are therefore requested to make it convenient to attend the same along with figures of authentication work.

signed

Executive Officer (JJ-HQ)

So reads a government circular issued to the executive officers of all the Slum Departments in 1979. The document surfaced when my assistant and I were nearing the end of our study of the files in Welcome. We had gone through the available records relating to almost every plot in the colony when, buried deep, two files of particular interest emerged through the layers of dust. One was called 'Policy file'; the other 'Pending cases'. Both offer snippets of insight into the functioning of the bureaucracy immediately after the Emergency and perhaps explain the Deputy Commissioner's (DC's) concern about authentication work. The post-Emergency period seems to have been a particularly turbulent time for disputes in the colony, with the result

94

that certain files were growing beyond all plausible limits, bursting with papers which, in accordance with the logic of bureaucracies, could only be processed and assessed through the production of further papers. How to make sense of all these papers had clearly become a major preoccupation with those trying to supervise the running of the Slum Department. What can be gained by viewing the Emergency through the period of the late 1970s and early 1980s? The Emergency in the immediate past? Perhaps the greatest advantage is that this is the period before the Emergency could be forgotten. For many journalists, politicians and intellectuals it was a time of compulsory remembering, a time for political exposé, moral remorse and critical reflection. However, for bureaucrats the problem posed itself differently. They were left with the debris of hastily enacted emergency policies, which, in most cases, they themselves had promoted. Transfers may have led to the reshuffling of positions in government departments, but the entire bureaucracy could not be replaced; neither could the policies of the past be wiped out overnight without repercussions.

We begin in the file marked 'Pending cases' which brings to light some of the major issues that resurfaced in the aftermath. The documents bear witness to the fact that by April 1977 the slum wing has been transferred back to the MCD and the old executive officer, K.K. Nayyar, has been replaced by a new executive officer, U.S. Jolly. The files tell us nothing of what happened to the previous executive officer—whether he was dismissed, transferred, or encouraged into early retirement. Yet K.K. Nayyar's name is by no means absent. His signature continues to inhabit almost 1,000 family planning allotment orders for Welcome and possibly many thousands more for the six other colonies under his charge in East Zone B of the Slum Department. What is more, some of those in possession of his allotment orders were, it seems, still awaiting the privilege of receiving their plots.

Two letters in the 'Pending cases' file document the period of transition out of the 'Emergency'. The first is dated 18 February 1977. By this time, Indira Gandhi had already withdrawn a number of Emergency provisions and had accused bureaucrats of being overzealous in their implementation of family planning procedures. The general election was just around the corner and attempts were being made to restore the people's faith in her leadership and, more generally in the Congress Party. None the less, as the first letter demonstrates, the Emergency was not yet over, and those approaching government institutions did so with caution, still speaking in the rhetoric appropriate to the regime.

This letter is addressed to the general secretary of the Congress Committee, but has also been duplicated for the DDA. It reads as follows:

Sub: Appeal of shelterless families

Respected Sir,
    We people were living in *jhuggis* of ____ block Seelampur and were spending our time very uncomfortably and unpeacefully.
    As we heard about the new scheme of our beloved Prime Minister Smt. Indira Gandhi and youth leader, Shri Sanjay Gandhi, for giving new plots to *jhuggi* holders, we became very happy that we will get our new house.
    In September 1976, our *jhuggis* were removed and we were asked to give 4 sterilisation cases for the progress of our nation, and have done so...The Executive officer, DDA, issued us a slip for 4 plots. But when we went there we found that all four plots were pre-occupied [already occupied]. Then we went to him but he did not listen to our appeal. There is no necessity to mention that we have spent the whole winter on the open roads without any shelter.
    In the context of the same I am left with no alternative except to approach your never failing good offices to come to my rescue in this regard and get us the plots for the same.
    May the goddess of prosperity and success keep her constant smile on you for this timely service to the unsheltered poor families, who has none in this world to look after them with the exception of the Almighty himself.

Yours faithfully [four signatures]

Judging by the presence of a second letter from the same four people, the general secretary of the Delhi Pradesh Congress Committee resisted the temptation to play god and to prove the 'never failing' goodness of his offices. The second letter is addressed to prominent individuals of the Janata Party, including the new Prime Minister, Morarji Desai and is dated 11 April 1977. We are now one month into the post-Emergency period when criticism of the Emergency was exuding from almost every direction. The four homeless people have adjusted their language accordingly and now refer to themselves, not as 'shelterless families' but as 'the oppressed dwellers of Seelampur'. Their tale is bitter and resentful. It no longer speaks of 'our beloved Prime Minister' or 'the progress of the nation' but rather of 'hope of redress'

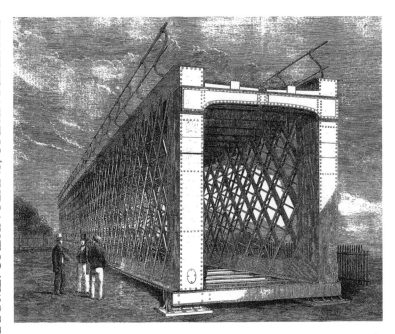

Above 'The Old Bridge' before its assembly and installation across the Yamuna, pictured in the *Illustrated London News*, 9 August 1862.

Below View from the Bridge, December 2000. (Denis Vidal)

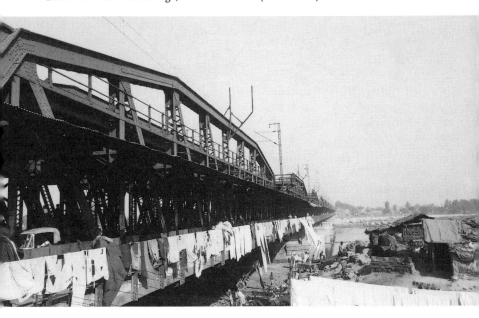

Above Heading Towards the 'other side' of the river, 2000. (Denis Vidal)

Below Cleaning up the city. Map of Delhi indicating the key areas where the residents of Welcome lived before experiencing demolition and displacement.

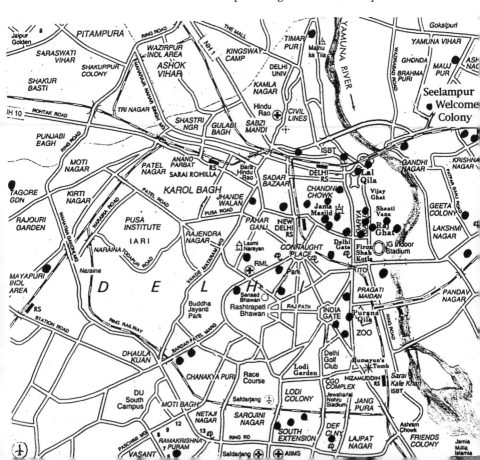

Above A city cleansed. Parkland replaces a segment of one of Delhi's most notorious slums known as Jamuna Bazaar.   *Below* Making do. Dumped with bricks from their demolished homes, women reconstruct their lives in a resettlement colony, 1976. (PD-PIB, New Delhi)

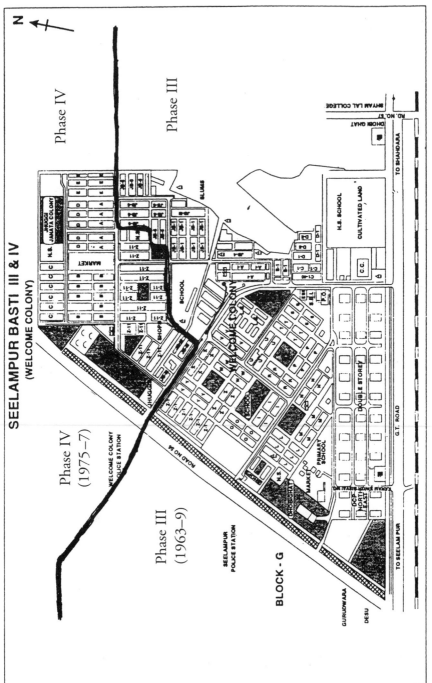

Plan of Welcome Colony. (Delhi Police)

Above Vertical extensions, Welcome, 1997. *Above right* Where paper destinies lie. Location of the Slum and *Jhuggi Jhompri* Department of the MCD, East Zone B, Welcome, 1997. *Right* The Records Room, Welcome 1995. *Far right* Passport to resettlement, 1963: a tenant is registered according to name, father's name, name of block and number of plot. (DDA)

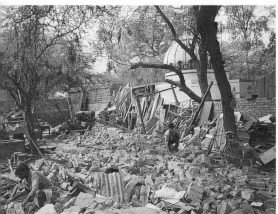

Above left The Janata Colony
– Welcome's unofficial *jhuggi*
area, 1997.   *Left* And so it
goes on. MCD demolishes
jhuggis on the Delhi-Mathura
Highway, March
1997.   *Above* Drip left
hanging where a sick woman
was lying at the time of
demolition, 1997.
Below Jhuggis proliferate in the
riverbed of the Yamuna near
ITO bridge, 1997.

on 'humanitarian ground'. The latent anger of the first letter has burst out in the second:

Sir,

We the oppressed dwellers of Seelampur colony, having lost all hope of redressal from the local administration, have lastly decided to address this petition to you as an SOS.

That we are residents of Seelampur area since 1970. Our houses have been demolished thrice ie. 1973, 1974 and again in 1975. Thus we have incurred huge material losses but have continued to stay here as we were not provided any alternative plot or shelter. Lately the authorities came to demolish our hut in September 1976. Our children entreated them for mercy but to no avail. They demolished them and told us that we should give sterilisation certificates/cases if we wanted no further demolitions. Accordingly, we have since furnished such certificates and then we could build our huts again.

During this cruel demolition, my ailing father, Shri...got hurt and due to inadequate medical care, expired during the exposure to winter. Another girl named...died due to extreme exposure of winter.

Some 500 persons of the colony have been allotted plots in Seelampur block...We approached for the same to all the officers including OSD (JJ) DDA and Shri Jagmohan, Vice Chairman, but to no avail. We have come to learn that some plots are still vacant in...block but we are not aware of why we oppressed people are not being allotted these plots when we have represented to all, including Smt. Indira Gandhi on 11.3.1977 about it and have furnished the necessary sterilisation certificates/cases. We have also got ration cards to prove that we have been residing for so long...

We hope that our above request will receive your earliest attention at least on humanitarian grounds.

Thanking you, Yours faithfully [four signatures]

Unfortunately, like so many cases, this one fades into obscurity before any outcome is given. There is no documentation to tell us whether the new Janata officials proved more attentive than those of the Congress Party did, but the fact that the file ended up buried at the bottom of the shelves in Welcome suggests that a positive outcome was unlikely. Here, then, we encounter the bitter words of four people who despite claiming to have undergone several demolitions and produced the relevant sterilisation documents, have ended up without plots. Are they typical? Probably not. They themselves refer to some 500 others in the colony who did get plots, suggesting they are in the minority. They also sign their names in English, suggesting that they

are perhaps more educated than most in the colony and may even
have composed their appeals without the aid of an intermediary.
Whatever their credentials, they are clearly well informed, addressing
their plea directly to a number of prominent politicians as well as the
housing authorities. So why the lack of response?
There are many possible reasons, of which apathy on the part of
politicians and bureaucrats is perhaps the most likely. It is also possible
that they were quite simply 'unlucky', discovering that their allocated
plots were already occupied whilst others had been given vacant plots.
There is another possible explanation on which I want to focus. By
the time these four homeless people had started appealing to Jagmohan,
Indira Gandhi and various 'high ups' of the Congress Party, the policy
was already in the process of change. Family Planning had transformed
from the national priority of 1976 to the national embarrassment of
1977. With this change, sterilisation certificates had lost much of
their magic cachet; they were already becoming things best-kept
hidden—potential proof of government excesses perhaps? Could it
be that this was just a case of bad timing—of being caught on the
cusp of political change?
In this respect, the 'oppressed people' of Seelampur were not alone.
From April 1977 onwards, more and more cases began to surface of
people with sterilisation certificates but without plots. In most cases,
they had participated in family planning in the last months of 1976
just before the turn in policy. A letter from the *pradhan*[1] of one block
informs the Slum Department that of the 70 families whose *jhuggis*
were demolished in his vicinity, 42 had been sterilised or motivated
cases, but only 36 had been given plots. The letter, which is dated 26
April 1977 ends, 'We, the poor people of *jhuggi jhompris* request you
to allot us plots at your earliest.' With it is a supporting letter written

---

[1] *Pradhan*: self-styled local leader. Welcome has several *pradhans* who exercise power
in different locations of the colony. Powerful *pradhans* act as leaders for several
residential blocks whilst less powerful ones have more limited followings. In most
slums and resettlement colonies *pradhans* act as local big men who offer protection
and access to basic civic amenities such as water and electricity in exchange for
financial and political backing. They also block access to facilities and opportunities
for those who do not support them. Despite the informal nature of their authority
and their reputation for violence, *pradhans* are treated as spokesmen by politicians
and development workers whose access to slum and resettlement populations
generally depends on their friendly relations with the relevant *pradhans*.

on Lok Sabha paper by a member of parliament. It is dated 23 May 1977 and asks the head of the DDA to look into the *pradhan's* request. Another letter, addressed to the new executive officer, U.S. Jolly, reports the existence of a further one hundred people who have sterilisation certificates but are still awaiting allotments. In another file, a man's plea reads: 'I gave a sterilisation case in 1976 but after some time the government changed so I couldn't get a plot. So I request the government to allot me a plot somewhere else.' This last letter is dated 1982 and is accompanied by the FP allotment orders of a further seven people. Their plight bears witness to the fact that many of those unfortunate enough to have participated in family planning near the tail end of 1976 were simply left dangling by the authorities. By 1982, the Slum Department had passed back into the hands of the DDA, suggesting that its brief period under the MCD had not made much difference from the point of view of those who were still awaiting plots.

But the new executive officer of the MCD was not entirely indifferent to the confusing cases that began to emerge the moment he entered office. By mid-May 1977, he was already consulting his superiors about what to do with the people coming to him with family planning documents. His concern was with the vocabulary of the FP allotment orders issued by his predecessor. His memo to the DC expresses a certain disdain for earlier policy and asks for clarification about how to proceed in the future:

Some persons have come with allotment orders issued by Shri K.K. Nayyar, the then executive officer. The allotment order is made provisionally. I find the word 'provisionally' does not bear any material significance in this regard because once a person raises a structure over the plot there is no point in cancelling the same. Therefore once a plot is allotted provisionally or actually, it is difficult to cancel it at a later stage.

He estimates that about 100 such cases have come to light (a number which proves to be grossly underestimated) and asks the deputy commissioner whether such 'provisional' allotment orders are to be honoured or not. To this, the deputy commissioner replies that since the allotment orders were issued by a duly authorised officer of the DDA, 'we have no option but to honour them.' Accordingly, U.S. Jolly sends out a notice instructing his staff that 'those with sterilisation papers should furnish their applications individually' and that 'their cases will be examined on merit.'

Despite this decision no attempt was made to remove the term 'provisionally' from the allotment orders with the result that, over ten years later, the officers who filled up the 1989 DDA survey forms have re-noted the 'provisional' status of the sterilisation allottees. When I raised this issue with the upper divisional clerk, he pointed out the sobering fact that most of the pre-Emergency allotments had also been 'provisional' in the sense that the displaced had only been given 'temporary camping sites'. The government had, according to the clerk, promised to re-house the people in flats which it had never got around to building. To prove his point, he got out an 'MCD Terms and Conditions' form used in the 1960s. Point 5 read: 'The licence can be terminated by either parties by giving at least two weeks notice and, after the expiry of the period of notice, the MCD shall be entitled to re-enter the plot and resume its possession.' This was followed by point 6: 'You shall not be entitled to undertake any permanent construction on the said plot during the period of your occupation...' When I asked him in what year the rules had changed, thereby enabling the 'resettled' to build houses on their plots, he replied, 'Its not that the rules changed as such. Its just that at first people built themselves *jhuggis* of mud, straw, wood, corrugated iron etc. because they couldn't afford anything else and because they'd been told these were only camping sites. Then, after some years, when they saw that nobody came to move them on and nobody demolished their *jhuggis*, they decided to start building *pukka* structures. It was a gradual process. In the 1960s Welcome was nothing but *jhuggis*.' His words were a reminder of the fact that it was not only during and after the Emergency that residents were left dangling in positions of extreme vulnerability. Rather, this was the normal state of affairs in resettlement colonies.

Despite their initial tolerance of post-Emergency sterilisation cases, the officers of the MCD soon seem to have started losing their patience. In response to the request (June 1977) of a Muslim woman who had 'motivated' her husband to have the operation, the executive officer comes out with the curious statement: 'There was no such policy approved by the DDA that those who undergo sterilisation will be allotted plots.' None the less, he passes the case on to the deputy commissioner who again says, 'there is no option but to allot a plot.' Documents suggest that a plot was duly allocated.

By 1979, however, the MCD officials went one step further in trying to wipe out the entire sterilisation episode. Evidence of their attempt is found in a circular, issued from the MCD headquarters on 7 July 1979, and addressed to all executive officers of the Slum Department. The circular refers to a meeting held some four days earlier in which item no. 98 for discussion concerned the 'cancellation of allotment of plots/built up houses made during the Emergency on the basis of sterilisation.' In this meeting, the ad-hoc committee had decided to postpone the issue until provided with concrete examples for discussion. It therefore requested the executive officers to collect within a week 'about 10 to 20 cases for each colony' and to bring them before the committee at the next meeting. It added, 'The cases to be collected should contain information regarding unauthorised occupation, regularisation by way of change of hands, trespassing and fresh allotments on the basis of sterilisation.'

What is revealed in the MCD responses to the sterilisation issue is a gradual progression from tolerance to denial and finally attempted effacement. The MCD was tempted to join the growing national trend, already fairly developed by mid-1979, of forgetting the Emergency. What was to happen to the thousands of people who, only three years earlier, had been forced to adjust to the DDA's demand for sterilisation certificates, we shall never know. One shudders at the thought of their vulnerability as officials casually contemplated a reversal of the entire system. No information is available concerning the outcome of the second meeting. Probably, once the scale of the sterilisation activities was realised,[2] it was decided that cancellation of the family planning allotment orders would cause even more havoc than dealing with the confusion that the sterilisation episode had left behind.

The fact is that the MCD was in a mess. Not only was it inundated with requests from homeless people with sterilisation documents; it was also faced with desperate appeals from 'original allottees', absentee landlords and squabbling tenants, some of whom had lost their plots

---

[2]According to the DDA's own records, one quarter of the plots in Welcome had been allocated or re-allocated on a sterilisation basis and all bore the term 'provisionally' on their allotment orders. I did not study the files for the other six colonies that make up East Zone B of the Slum Department but it is likely that they too contained equivalent numbers. B.N. Sinha, for example, refers to plots being offered on a sterilisation basis in the nearby colony of Nand Nagri (Sinha, 1977, *Operation Emergency*, pp. 169–70).

as a result of the family planning policy. Take for example the case of a woman whose husband had been allotted a plot in Welcome back in 1965. For 12 years the woman lived on the plot, only to discover that whilst she was away visiting relatives for a few days some time in 1976, her house was broken into and re-allocated to a total stranger on the basis of sterilisation. The woman refused to accept U.S. Jolly's declaration, dated 8 June 1977, that 'As per the latest policy we're to accept the claim of the allottee who is in possession of the plot. Accordingly the case of [the sterilised man] stands undisputed.' U.S. Jolly tried to offer the woman an alternative plot but notes in his records that she 'is adamant to get back her own plot since she has already raised a structure on the said plot.' This stilted bureaucratic phrase, 'raised a structure' reminds us somewhat indirectly that the woman has lost not only a small strip of land but also the house which she has built and in which she has lived for the past 12 years. Small wonder that she is reluctant to accept the executive officer's proposal. A note in the file one year later reveals that U.S. Jolly has changed his position. He is now offering the sterilised man an alternative plot in a different colony. The latter, however, was refusing this offer, saying he would only accept another plot if it were in Seelampur itself. What happened to the man is unclear, but papers suggest that the plot was eventually restored to the original allottee.

Others were not so fortunate. One man explains his case thus. He had been allocated a plot in 1976 on a sterilisation basis. He had paid his license fee, dug the foundations of a house, and was busy arranging a loan for the purchase of bricks when he fell ill and had to temporarily abandon the plot. When he returned he found that another man had been allocated the plot on a sterilisation basis and had already built a one-room structure on it. The original allottee supported his request for the restoration of his plot with a number of papers: a DDA FP allotment order to show the original allocation, a receipt to show that he had paid his license fee and medical certificates to prove that he was ill. He also sent copies of his request to the Prime Minister, Home Minister, the Chief Executive Councillor and Vice-chairman of the DDA. Yet despite all of this, the executive officer, U.S. Jolly's response, dated 31 January 1978, is uncompromising. He states that the medical certificates showing that the man was having treatment for chest and diabetes do not show he was suffering enough not to take possession of the plot and build there. He has therefore 'extinguished his right for any alternative allotment'.

Some of these cases had the added complication of landlord tenant relations. A number of landlords found that, by getting sterilised, their tenants had regularised the formers' properties in their own names. In such cases the MCD seems to have been unsympathetic to the protests of the original landlords, even if they had invested considerable money in building houses on their former plots. When I questioned the lower divisional clerk on this issue, he confirmed that it was the sterilised tenants who now had full rights to the plots 'because physical possession is a must, so if the original allottee was not present in 1976 then he couldn't claim any right over his plot at a later date'. This was a case of the normally slack regulation prohibiting the renting out of resettlement properties being redefined as a hard and fast rule which terminated the original allottee's rights to his/her plot. Not only landlords, but also tenants were vulnerable here. One case which reached the attention of U.S. Jolly concerned a plot in which three different tenants were residing. One of them had undergone vasectomy and was now demanding that the plot be regularised in his name. U.S. Jolly clearly recognised that this was a tricky situation, for he records in the file: 'Since there are three different occupants the regularisation in the name of one person will invite dispute.' He none the less decides to regularise the plot in the name of the sterilised man, concluding 'the question of dispossession of the remaining two occupants will have to be sorted out by him at his own level'.

Some cases were so complex that they ended up in court where paper battles waged on from year to year. One such case involved a man whom I shall refer to here as Ram Chandra. According to his solicitor's letters and U.S. Jolly's report issued on behalf of the DDA, this man had been allocated a plot in 1965 in exchange for the demolition of his home in Jamuna Bazaar. In 1968, however, he began to let out one room to a medical practitioner who used it for seeing clients. When some time around 1970, Ram Chandra left Delhi purportedly 'to attend a wedding', his tenant, who had been forced to give up the medical profession owing to various cases against him, grabbed full possession of the plot, throwing out Ram Chandra's possessions. He then put three tenants on the plot, from whom he collected rent. When Ram Chandra appealed to the DDA, they told him that he could reclaim the plot by furnishing a sterilisation certificate. On 24 September 1976, the plot was re-allocated to Ram Chandra by means of an FP allotment order. With the help of the police, he re-entered his newly regularised plot. Nevertheless, two months later, the ex-medical practitioner forced entry and 'with the help of some local persons' recaptured the plot for a second time and continued to rent it out. There is a high level of consistency between the solicitor's letter and U.S. Jolly's report, both of which were written in 1977, but a letter from the Deputy Director (Lease and Liquidation) addressed to the Deputy Vigilance Officer in 1982 reminds us that these are only paper truths, the veracity of which is still in dispute some five years later. He claims that there is no concrete evidence that Ram Chandra was the original allottee in 1965, and that his thumb impression found on a DDA application form must have been made at the later date of 1968 when the slum wing transferred from the MCD to the DDA. Furthermore, his FP allotment order is photocopied and therefore cannot be used as proof of re-allotment. He further points out that the medical practitioner is also claiming rights to the plot on the basis of sterilisation, but that he does not have documents to support the claim. And so the paper battle enfolds, with Ram Chandra's solicitor arguing that the DDA officer who appeared as witness in court was in 'collusion' with the ex-medical practitioner and had therefore removed the original allotment order from Ram Chandra's file. Clearly, once we take into consideration the possibility that certain papers can be removed from the files by officials of the DDA, whilst others can be added at a later date, and yet others forged, we further confirm the malleability of paper truths.

Yet, are there not certain moments when truths seem to transcend the paper on which they are written? This question is raised most poignantly by one particular stray letter written by a woman from a neighbouring colony. It is an accusation of abuse which implicates a number of DDA officials, including U.S. Jolly who, though not active in Welcome during the Emergency, seems to have been active elsewhere. The woman had been allocated a shop plot around 1970 and describes her encounter with the DDA as follows:

That Shri Tara Chand, Patwari, DDA, demanded rent from me which I offered, but he [also] asked for some more money, which I refused to pay his illegal demand. Since then he is bearing a grudge against me and does not accept rent offered by me from time to time.

That during the Emergency, the said Patwari and Shri U.S. Jolly, the then Special Officer on duty at JJ colony No. 1 Nangloi, Delhi, insisted upon me to hand over the allotment slip of my shop no. ____ and undergo an operation for 'Nasbandi' [sterilisation]. I refused to comply with it and then they took hold of my husband, Shri...and forcibly took him away for the operation. No one listened to our hue and cry as we were threatened with tortures of the police, dismissal of my husband from Government service and dispossession of the shop. My husband was forcibly taken away and got examined by various doctors of different hospitals for the operation of 'Nasbandi'. After his examination by the doctors, he was declared to be unfit for 'Nasbandi' operation, as he had already suffered Paralysis, High blood pressure and other diseases. Lastly my husband was taken to Lady Hardinge Hospital, New Delhi, there the doctor under the fear of Government and dismissal from service, operated upon my husband. My husband, as a result of the operation, fell victim to diabetes, body weakness and mental disease. He is still not fully cured and has severe pain and is unable to walk and cannot take up hard work and earn his livelihood and maintain members of the family dependent on him.

Yesterday, the said Patwari Tara Chand, with three or four officers of the DDA, came to my shop no. ____ and asked me to deliver its possession to them. This demand was illegal and I refused to hand over the shop's possession to them. I offered the Patwari rent due from me for the said shop but he did not accept. They did not listen to my entreaties and used unparliamentary language and became harsh with me. I asked for the return of my allotment slip which the said Patwari had got from me some time before. He did not agree...However, he gave me one weeks time to vacate and deliver possession of the shop along with the payment of all dues, failing which, they would forcibly evict me from the shop and recover the money by the sale of my goods and property. This act of theirs is illegal, unwarranted and against the canon of justice. They have no legal right to evict me forcibly from the shop. There was no reason to refuse to accept the rent and return to me my allotment slip.

Under the circumstances I request you to kindly take appropriate action against the said Patwari and Shri U.S. Jolly and other employees of the DDA who are liable for this illegal action and the DDA people be ordered not to interfere in my possession of the shop legally allotted to me.

Thanking you and awaiting an early favour,
Yours faithfully, 4.7.1977

Writing such a letter and daring to be on the wrong side of the DDA requires courage and involves a strong element of risk. It is perhaps this which leads me to believe that the contents are sincerely written on the basis of experience, and that the intimidation faced by her and her husband was something akin to what she describes in the letter.

Interestingly, like the letter from 'the oppressed people of Seelampur', this one appears to have been written by a person of educated status. She signs the letter in Hindi and has a typically Brahman surname. That both letters should be written by comparatively educated people may be a coincidence but it may also suggest that the authors, owing to their educational and social status, are more aware of how to argue their rights through the medium of paper and be less intimidated by high-handedness from government officials.

This is not to suggest that this one letter reveals what other letters conceal, but rather that it is probable that many people in the colony would not have presumed to write an equivalent even if their experiences were similar. What the letter does reveal, however, is the system at its worst; a structure of intimidation which starts long before the Emergency and continues after it. In the woman's lengthy relationship with the DDA, the Emergency features not as a time of sudden violence but as a time when latent violence could be realised; a good opportunity for unscrupulous officials to intensify their already abusive relations with a client against whom they bear a grudge. Thinking back to the conversation with the upper divisional clerk, we know, of course, that DDA officials were 'under pressure' just as the doctor who finally sterilised the woman's husband did so under threat of dismissal from work. We also learn that there were other doctors who dared to resist that pressure by declaring the man unfit for sterilisation, and other DDA officers, who far from acting 'under pressure', seem to have acted 'out of pleasure'. Finally, there are the police who feature, not as agents of justice, but as potential instigators of torture and instruments of fear.

Although this letter cannot be considered representative, it should be noted that the violence it describes is remarkable more for its explicitness than for its presence. We are already aware of the violence concealed by those familiar phrases 'voluntary sterilisation' and 'voluntary demolition'. But we have also encountered more oblique references to violence, both in the words of DDA officers and in the writings of residents and solicitors. What, for example, did U.S. Jolly mean when he decided that the tenant who had outwitted his fellow tenants by getting sterilised, should sort out the problem 'at his own level?' Not an instigation to violence admittedly, but an acknowledgement of its potential use perhaps. And what about the case of Ram Chandra and the medical practitioner? How did the latter capture the plot of the former (if indeed it was the former's plot)? Who were the 'local persons' who assisted him? And what were the techniques employed by the police when they helped Ram Chandra get back the plot in 1976? Clearly, these questions cannot be answered by the production of a single letter which describes the violent networks that existed between certain government officials, doctors and police in a neighbouring colony, and yet the letter can perhaps throw light on some of the possible scenarios hidden beneath the more formal language of other communications.

And so a few more elements are added to our portrait of the Emergency. Looking through the frame of the late 1970s and early 80s, we see the mess left behind by ill-considered policies and begin to hear the muffled voices of those victims who seek justice or who dare to expose violent abuse. In this sense, we return to our earlier image of people trapped in a tightly woven bureaucratic net from which they could not escape. Yet, as always, certain individuals seem to slip through that net. What, for example, should we make of the following letter written in Hindi by a man who describes himself as an 'ex-family planning motivator'?

Dear Sir,
    I beg to state that Shri A. [name not legible] and Shri K.K. Nayyar came to the colony in 1976 with the family planning programme. They assured us those who gave 40–50 cases of sterilisation would be awarded a plot of 25 yards sq. by the government as an incentive. Under that programme, I motivated about 200 people for sterilisation. For that I never accepted even a cup of tea or a glass of water from anyone. Instead I took part in the late Shri Sanjay Gandhi's five-point programme with much enthusiasm. The programme was meant for the poor and dalits.[3] I've been fulfilling my duty to the nation by being an honest social servant for many years now and will continue to do so in times to come. I was promised a certificate and 25 yd. sq. plot by the DDA. After some time my children and I fell ill. In the meanwhile there was also a change in government and the new government in power harassed me a lot for my participation in the programme. Please check your record registers of 1976 and regularise this plot, which is already in my possession, as you have done in the other cases. I shall be much obliged.

Yours etc., 12.7.1980

[3]'*Dalit*', meaning broken, crushed, uprooted, is a self-chosen name uniting various oppressed groups, many of which were stigmatised as 'Untouchables'. The term *dalit* is both a description of their condition and a declaration of pride.

Clearly another case of bad timing. But another victim? Certainly he presents himself as such. This was a man who had poured so much enthusiasm into the family planning scheme that he had apparently motivated an extra 150 cases above what he claims was the requisite number? But why are the numbers so high? The files bear witness to the fact that hundreds of others obtained plots through 'motivating' a single person. And although we do not know the actual cost of 'motivating' a case, we do know that motivating usually means 'paying' and that paying costs money. Who, then, is the man who motivates 200 people? A very rich man or a man who 'motivates' by other means? A man prone to exaggeration or a man who speaks the truth? A self-made tout or a man employed on a commission basis by the family planning authorities? Or perhaps one of those 'local persons' who seem to pop up in situations when residents are under threat or when plots are in need of recapture? A violent man perhaps? At any rate, he seems to be a 'victim' not so much of the Emergency regime as of its withdrawal—a man who has built his identity as a motivator to such an extent that he cannot adjust to the new political climate in which the language of family planning has provisionally sunk to the status of dirty words.

Perhaps if we were to read his letter under different circumstances, we might interpret it more kindly. We might conclude that this was a man with a real enthusiasm for family planning and a genuine concern about India's rapid population growth. We might share his consternation at the fact that after the Emergency he was unjustly punished for his enthusiastic support of a policy which the previous government had so strongly encouraged. We might even believe his innocent assertion that he never accepted even a glass of water, never mind a cup of tea for his 'motivation' work. Yet, we do not approach his letter with neutral eyes for we have already seen too much. We may not know the reality of what happened but we do have some idea of how the system worked—enough to tempt us into doubting this man's innocence just as we are tempted to believe the innocence of the woman who describes how her husband was taken off and sterilised by force. I am reminded of Primo Levi's assertion that 'The distortion of fact is often limited by the objectivity of the facts themselves.'[4]

What were the DDA's responses to such letters? As is so often the case, information is sparse. All we know is that the FP motivator did

[4]See Levi Primo, 1993 (1986), *The Drowned and the Saved*, London: Abacus, p. 17.

get his plot regularised as requested. Perhaps the DDA did have proof of his enthusiastic participation in family planning in their registers. Perhaps certain officers had had close dealings with this man in the recent past and therefore found it difficult to turn him down. These, and many other things, we cannot know. As for the case of the woman who reported the DDA officers' abuses, there is no evidence to tell us whether her case was ever followed up. All we have is a second letter, written by her some nine months later, reminding the DDA of her original letter and asking once more if she can be saved from unnecessary harassment and be allowed to deposit her rent. Some DDA officers have signed the letter to acknowledge its receipt, but whether they took any further action remains unknown. After all, papers filed away, buried or discreetly lost are effective keepers of silence.

The ex-FP motivator's letter has added one more piece to the jigsaw of the Emergency, and yet it is difficult to know where to place it, for this is a puzzle in which not even the edges are clear cut. For, as we have seen, hierarchical and oppressive relations between government officials and residents did not begin and end with the Emergency. Rather, the Emergency served to tighten a structure that was already well in place. Where should we place the FP motivator in this structure? He cannot, like members of the bureaucracy or the police, be classified as an institutionalised 'agent' of the system for he is just a resident of the colony operating on the margins. In fact, his credentials appear to make him a good candidate for being a victim, for, as an 'unauthorised resident', he fits directly within one of the DDA's main target groups for sterilisation. This man has refused to be pushed into the role of victim, and instead of getting sterilised, has 'motivated' others. He seems to belong to that grey and ambiguous category of victims turned agents—a category which challenges the post-Emergency narrative by introducing many shades of grey in a picture that was hitherto black and white.

The reconstruction of the Emergency is further complicated by the fact that many pieces of the puzzle are quite simply missing. How many pieces, we do not know, let alone what they represent. But although we cannot necessarily fill these blanks, we can none the less contemplate them, recognising that some may be invisible partly because of their subtle greyness which makes them difficult to detect and even more difficult to place. Obviously emotions: fear, pain, ambition, rage have little place in this paper archive where communications remain coded, whether they are from residents or officials. These are things which can only be adequately explored when speaking to people in the colony. But what more can we learn from the paper version of the past? So far, most of the cases presented have been written from the viewpoint of the loser who is seeking redress. Yet surely with each loser there must have been a winner in the competition for plots? Such winners are less likely to present their cases to the DDA; they are much more likely to hold on quietly to what they have gained. What do we know, for example, of those tenants who regularised their landlords' plots in their own names? Certainly, they must have been under considerable pressure for, as the clerk has informed us, DDA officers were threatening to evict all those who could not produce proof of an earlier allotment. Perhaps we can argue, then, that their actions were reasonable since they were 'forced' by circumstances to regularise their landlord's plots. But haven't we also come across another category of people described as 'tenants from Seelampur' but whose FP allotment orders show that they got sterilised or gave cases in order to obtain fresh allotments rather than regularising someone else's property? Isn't there a hint of opportunism in the behaviour of the tenants who dispossess their landlords even if we are more used to hearing of the reverse exploitation? Are these tenants, like the FP motivator, characters whose greyness confuses the boundary between victim and agent? At any rate, their presence seems to shift the focus back to that ambiguous terrain in which force is difficult to distinguish from choice, and need from greed. Where should we draw the line? And even if we can draw it, how can we trace the process by which residents of the colony spread themselves along and across such divides? One last case, on which we will focus at some length, seems more than any other to embody the many-faced complexity of the files.

Victims and victimisers: the case of Plot H68[5]

Plot H68 is situated in one of the blocks created in 1975 in the early phase of the Emergency before sterilisation had become a means to

---

[5]As with other cases cited here the number of the plot and the names of the individuals concerned have been changed. Only in the case of officials and other prominent figures like politicians have the original names been retained.

entitlement. It is no different from any other plot except that the documentation pertaining to it is unusually detailed. Consisting of nearly 30 different documents, spread across two files, it represents a small archive unto itself. What can this miniature archive tell us of the Emergency?

The first file opens with a brief summary of the case given by a DDA official in 1981. It reports that a woman named Ganga Lal was allocated the plot on 7 June 1975 after having been evicted from a *jhuggi* in Marj Pur. She paid her first instalment of the licence fee, built a new home on the plot and lived there for some time until her husband became gravely ill. Whilst she went off to look after her husband, she asked a friend, Chameli Chand, to take care of the plot, but the latter regularised it in her own name by giving a motivated case of sterilisation. In 1977, Ganga Lal had approached the DDA, trying to get her plot back on the grounds that her friend had taken advantage of her husband's illness. However, the officer in charge had refused to consider the request on the grounds that since she was not in possession of the plot in 1976, Ganga did not have the right to reclaim it. In 1978 Ganga's husband died.

This summary appears at first to conform to the many other cases in which original allottees lost their plots to people who got sterilised or gave cases. Ganga Lal, whose jhuggi had been demolished only one year earlier and whose husband was gravely ill appears to be the victim of the situation, whilst Chameli Chand, the so called friend, seems to have behaved with calculated opportunism, paying someone else to get sterilised in order to dispossess the already vulnerable Ganga at a time when she was in need of help. The death of Ganga's husband in 1978 serves only to heighten this woman's victim–status, leaving her not only homeless and betrayed, but also widowed.

However, the report goes on to state that in 1980–1, Ganga approached the Panchayat of Biridari [community leaders] and 'with their help' got back the plot which is now in her possession. She is now asking for the license to be put in her son's name because she is scared that if it is in her own name, then Chameli Chand might try to snatch back possession. The report also mentions that in 1976 Ganga had stated that she did not have any further interest in the plot. However, she has decided that she does now require the plot, hence her appeal to the DDA. The officer concerned ends his report by recommending that the licence should be 'mutated' to Ganga's son's name, as requested.

This is a very odd recommendation, given the DDA's usual manner of respecting regularisation cases. Its peculiarity was not missed by the officer's superior who scrawled the somewhat impatient response: 'What a foolish proposal. I don't accept such proposals. Please go through rules of mutation and put up.' To this the original officer replied by saying that the name could not be mutated since the plot has been regularised in Chameli Chand's name which makes Ganga Lal an 'unauthorised occupant'. She should therefore be issued a 'show cause notice'. Whether this officer had originally ignored current policy out of ignorance or for some ulterior motive, we do not know, but whatever the motive, his change of heart transformed Ganga Lal from apparently innocent and wounded applicant to unauthorised occupant almost over night. None the less, by 9 April 1981 Ganga has submitted an affidavit saying that she is a 38-year-old widow with four children, and that she cannot come to the DDA to deposit her licence fee owing to the fact that she works at the other side of Delhi in Safdarjang Hospital. She has therefore given the plot to her eldest son. The document is accompanied by her husband's death certificate and an affidavit from her son in which he declares that he has no other property in Delhi. The affidavits are written on official paper and verified by a subdivisional magistrate.

Why the DDA accepted this affidavit after they had already declared Ganga Lal an unauthorised applicant is not clear. Once we begin to examine other documents in the file, a number of other discrepancies start to emerge. Take, for example, the sterilisation certificate which Chameli Chand cunningly submitted in order to transfer the plot to her own name. According to this, Chameli Chand is a 34-year-old woman with a family of five [i.e. three children and a husband] who underwent a tubectomy operation on 1 September 1976 at Lady Harding Hospital. If this document is to be believed, Chameli did not 'motivate a case' as the officer claimed in his report, but rather underwent the operation herself. With this document is an affidavit, written and signed by Ganga Lal just over two weeks later, stating that she has 'given' the plot to 'her sister out of affection' and that the latter has undergone tubectomy in order to secure it. The affidavit further states, 'I, Ganga Lal, have no interest [or] title in the said plot.' It is signed, dated and verified.

These papers seem to conjure up a somewhat different picture to that implied by the officer's report. In this new picture Chameli Chand emerges, not as a motivator who purchased a case behind Ganga's back, but as a person who underwent tubectomy in order to secure the plot with Ganga's consent. The plot no longer seems to have been 'grabbed', but rather, 'given'. This picture is further transformed by a brief remark written on the back of another document in which a DDA officer mentions that Ganga Lal 'sold' her plot to Chameli Chand who has since regularised it and paid the licence fee. Theft? Trickery? Gift? Sale? As the possibilities increase, so the clarity of the situation diminishes.

Fortunately, however, we have Ganga's version of the story in the form of a potted life-history which she recounts in a third affidavit, submitted to the DDA in August 1981 shortly after she had 'given the plot' to her son. It reads as follows:

I, Ganga Lal, wife of Shri Ram Lal, resident of H68 Seelampur, hereby state that I was a resident of Lahore before partition. After partition I migrated to India and started living in Shahdipur camp on rent. I got married in 1954 to Ram Lal, who was also a resident of Lahore. My family was not given any land by rehabilitation/displacement department. So I built a house in Bhojpur on 200 square yard plot which was demolished by the DDA in 1976. In place of that I was living in this plot in one room. The second room was given to Chameli Chand, wife of Hari Chand. She used to look after my husband and children. She has three children and I have four. I was working in Safdarjang hospital as a Government servant and since my duty was such that I had to be there at all times, I managed to get accommodation over there. When my husband was ill, I took him along. After that Chameli Chand was living alone on my plot. At that time, a rumour was going around that if the original allottee was not in actual possession of the plot, then he would be evicted. Therefore in order to save the plot, I gave an affidavit at the time (19.9.1976) in which it clearly stated that I was giving the plot to my adopted sister, Chameli Chand, out of love and affection. Since she got sterilised, the department also allotted the plot to her. After the death of my husband my family and I started living with Chameli Chand and her husband Hari Chand. But after some time I realised that it was difficult all living together, so I decided to ask Chameli and her husband to leave the house. Since this plot is now in the name of Chameli Chand, I want it to be mutated into the name of my son, Vikram Lal, because I fear that if it remains in my name then Hari Chand and Chameli Chand might capture it by force at any time. This will happen because after my husband's death, I started living with Hari Chand, but now I am no longer concerned with him. At the moment I am living with my family on this plot. Chameli Chand has given an affidavit in my favour which I will produce at a later date. 4.8.1981.

Such a document, cannot, of course, be interpreted in isolation. It is part of a file containing numerous other documents which either confirm, support, add to or detract from its various claims. The demolition slip, for example, seems to confirm that her home was demolished on the 6 June 1975 but casts doubt on her assertion that she was living on a large plot of 200 square yards. The slip records that her previous accommodation consisted of one room only, suggesting that it was probably considerably smaller. We should also be sceptical about the alleged existence of an affidavit written by Chameli Chand in 'in favour of' Ganga Lal. Certainly, such a document is not included in the files.

Although the story given by Ganga coincides to some extent with what we have heard so far, it nevertheless stretches some of the details of the narrative a little further whilst ignoring others. According to this version, Ganga had already left the plot prior to her husband's illness, thereby leaving her husband on the plot with Chameli and Hari Chand. But the DDA documents make no mention of Ganga's husband residing on the plot at all and it is quite possible that he never did. Certainly, his details are not recorded with those of the children on the original allotment slip. This detail is only of minor significance. Of more major significance, however, is the claim that after the death of her husband, Ganga joined the Chands on the plot and started 'living with' Chameli's husband, Hari Chand. This, combined with the statement that she is 'no longer concerned with him' are polite but explicit references to an affair which seems to have taken place under Chameli's nose. In fact, Ganga now cites this affair as the reason why Chameli and her husband will inevitably return to take back the plot 'by force'. To the original story of trickery, betrayal, gift and sale, we can add the further possible elements of love, sex, and revenge.

What sort of picture can we draw of Ganga Lal from this one page affidavit? Evidently, she is a woman who has repeatedly found herself caught up in violent political situations over which she has no control. First she was a victim of Partition, although she must have been only five years old at the time; then a victim of slum clearance and resettlement in 1975. Being resettled about 20 miles from her place of work, she further had to give up her plot to a friend, thereby falling victim to the new family planning regulations of 1976. But if Ganga Lal's life seems plagued by circumstances, she none the less seems to have fought back with considerable skill. She returns to the plot which is no longer legally hers, has an affair with her friend's husband (perhaps as a technique for getting back onto the plot?) and finally throws both husband and wife out onto the streets. A postcard sized black and white photograph of her, surrounded by her grown up and adolescent children, suggests she is more fighter than passive victim. Her face and body are heavy and stalwart; her eyes confrontational. Her hulky sons sit around her looking like bodyguards ready to protect and obey a powerful matriarch. By contrast, Chameli Chand's photograph portrays a thin and wizened woman whose face seems inscribed more with suffering than fighting spirit. But photographs are only photographs—just another form of paper truth, and equally vulnerable to misinterpretation. Is there any written evidence to support the notion that it is really Chameli Chand who is the loser of the case?

Documents concerning Chameli Chand are less numerous than those concerning Ganga Lal. None the less, as we have seen, the files do contain a DDA FP allotment order, a standard affidavit for the plot and a photograph in her name. It is not until July 1983, however, that we get an inkling of her version of the story. This is presented in the form of a letter to the DDA which reads rather like an official statement:

I, Chameli Chand, wife of Hari Chand, resident of H68, was living with my husband on this plot. The plot was regularised in my name after I got sterilised. On producing the receipts of my licence fee payments, the bank had given me a loan to construct a house. But after about three years Ganga Lal came with some people, broke open the door and forcibly entered the house. Then she called her father and son and forced my husband to sign a marriage certificate saying he was married to her. This was obviously done to trick the police so that they could not take any action against her. The police was then shown the marriage certificate and was prevented from acting. After some days, she managed to get the plot transferred into her son's name on the basis that she was a widow, so that the DDA and any potential purchaser could be cheated.

This plot is now being sold for 25,000 rupees as if it were still in the name of the original allottee. This is illegal. I therefore request you to stop this plot from being sold. I am a poor woman and I got this plot by giving my blood. So I beg you to take appropriate action. 24.7.1983.

The DDA seems to have taken a long time to respond to this letter, for the next information we have is in the form of an official note dated 24 July 1984, at the beginning of the second file. In it a DDA officer states that inspection of the site confirms that Ganga Lal, unauthorised occupant is trying to sell the plot and that she has already received 10,000 rupees as an advance on the total of 25,000 rupees. The file also contains a 'Public Notice' issued on the same date which reads as follows:

> It has been reported to me (Assistant Director) that Smt. Ganga Lal is going to sell plot H68 Seelampur which is a Government plot. This is illegal, against allotment rules. It is informed in the public interest that nobody should purchase this plot otherwise he is likely to be evicted from the plot at his own risk and cost.

On the same day, Chameli Chand addressed a letter to the medical superintendent of Safdarjang Hospital, informing him that not only is Ganga Lal renting out the hospital quarters that have been allotted to her with her job, but she also has three other homes, one of which is the plot H68 in Seelampur which she took by force. The letter includes the addresses of each of Ganga's alleged residences and also informs the medical superintendent that Ganga Lal was under arrest under section 1107/153 on 3 June 1977—a fact which she has concealed. The letter continues:

> Please find out:
> 1. Why she hid information of her arrest.
> 2. Why she sublet a government quarter.
> 3. Why she accepted a government quarter when she already had two quarters.
> 4. Sources of income which enabled her to purchase all these quarters.
> 5. Why she encroached on the Seelampur quarter and sold it.
> I earnestly request your honour that the aforesaid case may kindly be investigated thoroughly immediately and if the contentions are found correct, she must be severely punished.

Chameli Chand's version of events adds a number of new dimensions to the tale in which Ganga seems to be emerging less as victim than as opportunist. It alleges that Ganga recaptured the plot 'by force' and that she appears to be wriggling out of the situation by selling it off. It further suggests that Ganga has a criminal record and has been accumulating plots in different parts of the city despite the fact that one of the conditions of resettlement is that you do not own any other property in Delhi. Concerning Ganga's relationship with Chameli's husband, Chameli suggests that this was not an affair but a case of using force to make him sign a marriage certificate as a device for protecting Ganga from the police. It is not clear whether the forged certificate was designed to protect Ganga from being removed from the plot or whether it was to protect her from arrest in relation to the court case that was pending. But whatever the precise meaning, there is little doubt that Chameli Chand feels cheated for, as she simply but evocatively states, she was the one who gave her blood for the plot.

How does the DDA respond to all of this? Belatedly, it seems, for their next communication consists of an eviction notice addressed, not to Ganga Lal, nor Chameli Chand, but to a man of the name of Mohammed Ali. It is dated 6 September 1984 and refers to section 5 of the 'Public Premises (Eviction of Unauthorised Occupants) Act 1971'. The notice declares that Mohammed Ali is an unauthorised occupant of a public premise, and that he is ordered to vacate the premises within 30 days. If he fails to do so he is liable to eviction, if necessary by force.

And so a new victim steps in to inherit the mess, of which he was probably oblivious when he purchased the plot. Instead of quietly paying the licence fee in the name of the original allottee like other illegal purchasers, he finds himself issued an eviction order almost as soon as he takes over the plot. How could he know of the trickery, deceit, 'gifts', 'sales', accusations of violence and bloodshed attached to the home he was purchasing? And more to the point, how can he keep his home? Mohammed Ali tries to deal with the situation by applying to the assistant director of the DDA to ask if he can regularise the plot in his name. He states that he has paid Rs 25,000 for the two-room house and that he is living there with his family. To back up his application, he submits a stack of documents including his photograph, Power of Attorney documents stating the conditions of purchase, a deed of agreement signed by Ganga Lal on 1 August 1984 and a statement of no objection from her son. The DDA turns down Ali's application for regularisation, presumably because, as the clerk originally told us, the license fee must be paid in the name of the original allottee. But the DDA does 'approve' his case and Mohammed Ali agrees to pay damages on the plot. He has saved himself from eviction by entering that ambiguous zone between what is officially known and what is officially recorded—the zone which shelters many in times of calm, but which, as we have seen, offers little refuge in times of crisis. A

survey form, dated 1989, suggests that Mohammed Ali is still living
on the plot some five years later.

The history of plot H68 provides us with a picture of the complex
battle fought over it, waged essentially between two women whose
husbands feature in positions of weakness. In the case of Ganga's
husband, he is ill and later dying. In the case of Chameli's husband, he
appears to have been little more than a pawn in Ganga's manipulations.
At best, he enjoyed an affair with her; at worst, he was forced by her
and her gang to sign a marriage certificate against his will. The precise
nature of their relationship cannot be gauged from the documents in
the files; nor can the details of Ganga's return to the plot because
official housing documents have difficulty coping with the personal
terrains of love, sex, violence and betrayal. And yet it is such human
issues that seem to underlie this case, reminding us of the limitations
of the paper truths contained within the files.

This case also problematises the identification of the victims of the
Emergency, for as the clues accumulate, our image of the participants
undergoes perpetual transformation. Who is the victim? At first it
seems to be Ganga Lal, lately widowed and robbed of her plot whilst
Chameli Chand is betrayer and opportunist. But as the story unfolds,
we learn that Chameli obtained the plot with Ganga's consent and
gave her own blood to secure it. Gradually she transforms from betrayer
to victim as Ganga enters the house by force, transfers the ownership
to her son, claims or possibly has relations with Chameli's husband
and finally throws both husband and wife off the plot. Then, just as
the DDA is catching up with her, she sells it off, leaving the purchaser
to deal with the DDA's threat of eviction. The new victim is clearly
Mohammed Ali, and yet he manages to survive by appeasing the
DDA with appropriate papers accompanied perhaps with other
appeasements—that we do not know. In the final analysis, it is Chameli
Chand, the only person with the legal right to the plot according to
DDA policy, who loses all.

Chameli Chand is a victim, not only of Ganga Lal's behaviour, but
also of the DDA's inadequacy. It is their vacillation, their slowness to
act, and the ambiguity of their policies that stand against her. Having
obtained the FP allotment order which certified her right to the plot,
she then finds that Ganga Lal is still using the original allotment
order to claim ownership of the plot and to transfer ownership first to
her son, and then to a purchaser. The fact that the DDA accepts the

documents of purchase, including an Agreement Deed signed by Ganga and a No Objections Statement from her son, reveals that they are more interested in accumulating relevant papers than in finding out the truth they might conceal.

But if this case highlights the vulnerability of the victim, it also highlights the vulnerability of the bureaucracy itself. For it is from the paper trails left by people like Ganga Lal that we can trace the process by which the very technologies of the state transfer out of the hands of officials and into the hands of apparently marginal citizens who, through their own mimetic performances, reproduce the very artefacts the state requires. Ganga Lal , subaltern producer of paper truths, works, not from the hallowed space of a government department but from some shady corner of a resettlement colony on the outskirts of Delhi where she mobilises local connections—her *biridari*, the police, perhaps an official letter writer to help her phrase her case. She understands the power of official papers which she produces in such number that she ends up outwitting officials at their own game. But she does not rely on paper truths alone. Beyond the yellowing papers that bulge from the files, we learn of other less authorised techniques by which she rides over those around her. For her, paper truths seem to provide a legitimate face for other less sanctified methods of action: violence, seduction and illegal trade. If her case testifies to the reach of the state as its language and technology is reproduced in far off corners of the city, it also testifies to the limitations of that reach. Officials of the DDA seem incapable or unwilling to extend their grasp beyond the manufacture and exchange of paper truths which in this case, and no doubt many others, tell only part of the story.

Where should we place a woman like Ganga Lal in the larger configuration of the Emergency puzzle? If nothing else, her case points to the need to leave space for complexity. We can no longer accept the post–Emergency narrative's simplistic portrayal of the helpless millions rounded up off the streets and herded into resettlement colonies or family planning camps. Yet, neither can we accept the propaganda of the Emergency, for judging from the files of Welcome, sterilisation had much more to do with obtaining or retaining plots than with a national concern about over-population. This is not to deny that the Emergency produced its victims, but rather to argue that it is not always easy to identify who they are, for some victims transform into agents and become victimisers. How many, we do not know.

We end this tour of the post-Emergency documents with a reminder of the limitations of working in an archive where the bureaucracy is more concerned with the maintenance of paper truths than with the realities to which they supposedly refer. Below is a government circular, sent to all the branches of the Slum Department in 1989. It can be read as a statement of the DDA's priorities:

Vice-chairman has been expressing concern about proper paper and file management in DDA and to ensure the same a Circular was issued vide No..., dated 29 October 1988. However, it has been noticed that in spite of this Circular, not much care is being taken for proper up-keep of files and papers. Many times files become so bulky that corners of pages are torn and previous notings become totally illegible. In the majority of files, the correspondence and noting portions are not page numbered, leading to a situation where any paper can be taken out if somebody had malafide intentions...V.C. has therefore desired the instruction for file and paper management must be reiterated...

The case of Chameli Chand and Ganga Lal is, after all, nothing more than a matter of two rather bulky files filled with aging papers. If we want to step beyond its paper truths, we surely have to go elsewhere?

5

TALKING ABOUT THE EMERGENCY
SOME INITIAL CONVERSATIONS

There is nothing natural in talking about the Emergency in a place like Welcome. It is even less natural to be talking about it to a foreign anthropologist and her assistant (a young Indian man)—both of whom are clearly identifiable as 'outsiders'. Why should such outsiders meddle in the potentially traumatic pasts of 'insiders'? Why should 'insiders' feel like revealing their pasts? These and many other questions were foremost in my mind when we first set out to talk with people of the colony about their memories and experiences of the Emergency. I had never intended to work on such a subject. If people did not feel like talking about it, that was fine by me. I would simply return to my earlier project.

The first man we met certainly did not feel like talking about it, nor indeed about anything else. He was sitting on a stone slab in a narrow ally, cradling a baby and it was not long before we realised that he was extremely drunk. He waved us off in the direction of a balding middle-aged man sitting opposite. We began to introduce ourselves, saying that we were interested in different peoples' experiences of living in the colony, and asked if we could talk with him for a while. The man looked nervous and began to shuffle around. He was disturbed by the fact that there wasn't anywhere for us to sit. When he opened his front door, he revealed a home, no more than six feet by six in proportion, with a curious mound of junk piled up to the ceiling. No windows. No light. Seeing an old *charpai* (string bed) on top of the pile, I suggested we could sit on that. There then followed an awkward struggle to clear a space big enough to put the *charpai* legs on the floor. We insisted we could sit outside in the street, but this did not conform to this man's sense of hospitality. He wanted us to be in the shade. So even before conversation began, the meeting had become a complicated affair, highlighting quite painfully the unnatural nature of our sudden appearance in this man's life. Finally, space was cleared for the *charpai* which was jammed up against the front inner wall of the home, so that we sat in semi-darkness with our bottoms inside, our heads, framed by the narrow doorway, and our legs illuminated by the sun as they dangled into the street. The man, who considered it socially inappropriate to join us on the *charpai*, squatted outside on the ground, thereby creating a physical hierarchy in which he was 'down' and we were 'up'. This choreographic arrangement seemed to satisfy our host but it left us feeling awkward and distant. Can one really 'talk' across such divides?

He tried and we tried and things seemed quite promising until the drunk man decided to intervene. Having refused to speak to us initially, he now seemed to feel left out and started shouting across the narrow ally in the universal tongue of alcoholic incomprehensibility. From time to time he would catch phrases and bellow out authoritatively (in Hindi): 'Tell her this! Tell her that!' Then he would point to me and shout, 'Write this! I'm telling you, write this!' But his words were not only repetitive but beyond comprehension. They formed an impossible backdrop to the conversation we were trying to have with our earnest and helpful host.

Although relieved to see the drunken man stagger off after half an hour or so, we were less relieved when he reappeared with reinforcement—a heavily built young man with turmeric matted in his eyebrows. It turned out that he had just undergone a ceremony in preparation for his wedding the following week. He rolled up his sleeves and flexed his forearms as if in preparation for a Hindi film punch up. Then, glowering down at us, he blocked the entrance and our only source of light and demanded to know what the hell we wanted. Would he slam the door shut and leave us marooned in this tiny dark hut full of unidentifiable rubble? I later found out that I had not been alone in my fears. Rajinder, my assistant, had been quietly anticipating how he might defend us both should the worst come to the worst. But the turmeric-smeared man, though clearly ready for a fight, was not drunk. He was willing to listen to an explanation. We told him we were from the university and were writing about the colony. We were not from the government and were not interested in taking down names and addresses. What we wanted rather was to understand something of the experiences that people had undergone since arriving in Welcome. His suspicion began to fade as he listened, sceptically at first, to our conversation with our host, who turned out to be an electrician. The latter had been in his village in Uttar Pradesh 'during that disease' [the Emergency] where people were offered agricultural land for sterilisation. He had had only one child at that time and was not forced, but his brother, who had two children, had undergone the operation in order to get two *bighas* of land. 'Even if you gave me one lakh [rupees] you wouldn't find me getting sterilised,' he added and, before long, the threatening looking stranger with turmeric smears was butting in:

'My father was sterilised to get a plot here in Welcome...Until then we were living in Welcome in *kucha jhuggis* [temporary shacks]. Then the government demolished the *jhuggis* and we were told we could get permanent plots if we got sterilised.'

What do you think of that system?

'I think it was wrong. Of course, some got sterilised out of greed because of all the rewards but it was wrong because it was forced.'

'Forced' in what sense?

'It was a forcible deal on the part of the government even though people went of their own free will because of the benefits. It was not a question of fearing physical attack but a question of plots and advantages. Many thought it was good. Many thought it was bad.'

In this small fragment of a conversation, the turmeric-smeared man had somehow dissolved the false dichotomy between force and choice, need and greed. His simple formulation 'forcible deal' was strangely inclusive. Of course people were 'forced' in the sense that those who had lost their homes were not in a good position to refuse the government offer. But in accepting it, they were accepting a deal which, like any other deal, implied an element of participation. As for the questions of need and greed, weren't they to some extent subjective assessments through which one distinguished those whose motives one respected from those whose motives one suspected? His father had been sterilised out of 'need' for a plot. Others in the same situation had done it out of 'greed'.

The drunken man was irritated that his plan to scare us off seemed to have resulted in our staying even longer. As the turmeric man was talking, his inebriated companion demanded a piece of paper from us, then settled back on his stone slab and began to write. Some 15 minutes later, he approached Rajinder with an air of self-importance and handed him the paper. On it were written letters from the Hindi alphabet strewn apparently randomly across the page—no attempt to formulate words. There was much ambiguity in this gesture but the message seemed to be something like this—Who did we think we were coming here with our fancy notepads? Did we think we were the only ones who could write? And what kind of gibberish were we writing anyway with such apparent seriousness? Rajinder kept the paper since it had been handed over with such reverence, but its drunken author was soon back to reclaim it. When we left an hour or so later, he was still bent over the stone slab, furiously writing letters all over the page.

The drunken man had, in effect, provided a wonderful parody of the researcher at work, as well as a reminder that what I was writing was just one more form of paper truth. Conversation, alive and interactive; experience, rich, emotional, personal, cultural—transformed into mere scribbling across a page. Strangely gripped by the act of writing, this man had taken on the role of a Shakespearean fool whose very foolishness revealed a terrible intelligence. How can you reduce a person's life to a series of squiggles, and that in a language the person doesn't even understand? Why should anyone trust yet another paper version of the truth? But like most comic figures, this man also breathed a certain sadness—drunk and probably unemployed, cradling a dirty and neglected-looking baby, and resurrecting his writing skills almost as if he had forgotten that he even had them. Perhaps this was the first time he had tried to write since leaving school?

Apart from parodying my research with great alacrity, the drunken man had, of course, introduced that age-old anthropological problem of interpretation. Who knows what he really meant? I choose to interpret his gesture as a reminder that all written knowledge is an artefact which invites reflection, not only on its content but also on its form. What is presented here is a series of approximations: memories self-consciously elicited and transformed into words; words rearranged to make an argument; a portrait of an era built through reconstructions which transform the era as they reconstruct it. And yet, through the different voices that inform this text, I believe we do gain insights both into how things were, and how they are re-membered,[1] and since memory is itself a form of experience, its unreliability as a barometer of fact does not invalidate its capacity to tell us about people's lives. After all, humans *are* selective—we all choose to reveal or conceal, distort or exaggerate, remember or forget, and so these very qualities of memory capture something of the complexity of our relationships to one another and to the larger events of history of which we are a part.[2]

And so began a long and open-ended conversation with people in Welcome—auspiciously or inauspiciously—I'm not sure which. Like most fieldwork encounters, this was an unnatural one in that it took place between people who, in the normal course of events, would not think of sitting down together and talking hour after hour, week after week on and off over a period of two years. This is not to say that 'people like us' do not interact with 'people like them', but that the interaction is usually mediated by services and/or money. I might have ridden in the rickshaws of men from Welcome several times for all I knew; I might have purchased fruit from the fruit seller who lugs his wares to Connaught Place or had my roads swept by a woman sweeper who happened to come from Welcome, but it is highly unlikely that we would have really talked. Similarly many of them were familiar with foreigners as people who frequent tourist spots and from whom one could extract extra money for goods and services. It was foreigners like me who often paid double for a rickshaw ride or who did not know the local price of an orange. But they were not familiar with a foreigner in their colony, let alone one who was interested in what they had to say. Such things needed getting used to, and before each conversation with a new person, explanations were both desirable and necessary.

Not surprisingly, people wanted to fit us into the existing categories familiar to them. If I was not a tourist, then who was I? The fact that we were asking questions and writing things down inevitably associated

---

[1]Judith Zur splits the word 'remember' to make 're-member', thereby emphasising the fact that memory is put together and constructed in the present. It is a re-assembling of elements from the past. See Judith Zur, 2000, *Violent Memories: Mayan War Widows in Guatemala*, Boulder, CO: Westview Press.

[2]For further discussion of this, see Beth Roy, 1994, *Some Trouble with Cows*, Berkeley: University of California Press, pp. 3–9.

us with government officials in people's minds. This often led to one of two interpretations: either we were sent from some official body like the DDA to check up on housing irregularities, or else we were doing a 'survey' in which case we were expected to pose set questions with one word answers. It was therefore particularly important to convince people that we had nothing to do with the government and that we were not interested in taking down names and addresses, but rather in what people felt about life in the colony. For some, this itself was a cause of panic, eliciting the response: 'But I don't know anything. I'm not educated. You'll have to speak to someone else...' This type of response, more common with women than men owing to the unequal distribution of education, could usually be overcome by just chatting which made people feel more relaxed and, before long, they usually found themselves talking and often found it difficult to stop. More common still was the inevitable request: 'So tell, me, what are we going to get out of this?' To this question, which came up near the beginning of almost every conversation, we gave what became some sort of standard reply: 'Look, we are not from the government, so we are not going to pretend to you that you will get something from us, and then not give it. The truth is that you won't gain anything directly out of talking to us. What we are doing is writing a book about the history of the colony and we would like to include your opinions and experiences in it. We can also hope that if some influential people read the book, they might better understand the sort of things you have gone through. But we cannot say that what we write will lead to a change in government policy. We can only hope that influential people who make the rules might read the book and might think a little more about the effects of what they do on people's lives.'

This little speech became horribly repetitive, like a recitation from an oft-repeated play. The predictability of it made me uncomfortable as if it somehow detracted from its sincerity. It seemed to underline the fact that fieldwork often involves a considerable amount of persuasion, if not psychological manipulation. What to us was a rehearsed retort was to them a fresh and unexpected response. Most people voiced explicit approval at the bit about not making empty promises like politicians and government officials. In fact, I would argue that this one statement was crucial in defining people's attitudes to us. It revealed an element of humour and cynicism—both of which were abundant in the colony—and showed that we considered them worthy of knowing the truth—that they would not in fact get anything in material terms. This created a space for a new kind of encounter. It was a sign that this was going to be a different type of conversation to what you might expect from people with pens and paper. It also acted as a license to speak freely—demonstrating that we were not interested in dolling out 'official versions', and did not expect them in return. Of course every place has its sceptics and silent types just as it has its enthusiasts and avid talkers. There was one sweeper who was rude and hostile; an astrologer who talked mainly in sexual innuendo as he tried to persuade me to have my fortune told, and, of course the drunken man whose non-co-operation introduced this chapter. But those who chose not to speak to us were so few that even one year later, I can remember them distinctly. The vast majority of people we approached not only talked with us, but did so at considerable length for several hours at a stretch. The question is, why?

Nowadays, social anthropology has become an unfashionable discipline among some sectors of the 'politically correct'. Some argue that it is on the verge of extinction partly because it can never free itself of its initial imperialist connections and partly because its fantasy object (the exotic other) is no longer willing to play the part. Other critics insist that unless anthropology is used directly to improve people's conditions of existence, it is nothing more than an exercise in narcissistic reflection. One of the major targets of these various criticisms is the 'fieldworker' who is accused of 'taking from people' without giving anything 'in return'; of objectifying and reducing; of appropriating the voice of the other whilst simultaneously claiming to represent it. These critiques are even more accentuated in cases where the anthropologist is from a so-called 'developed country' and is working amongst the so-called 'developing'.

Such criticisms have been healthy in making anthropologists reflect about their position as both researchers and writers, but some of the presuppositions that underlie these arguments can be misleading. In particular, they often impose a materialist model on the fieldwork encounter as if words are quantifiable commodities that should be repaid in sewage systems and water pumps. Sewage systems and water pumps are, of course, essential. Anyone who has worked in inner city slums or poor colonies like Welcome would hardly deny it. But assuming that poverty obliterates the desire to express opinions and perceptions is like claiming that only we,[3] 'the enlightened', are capable

[3]This 'we' includes educated Indians as much as foreign anthropologists.

of 'giving value' to something as transient and intangible as conversation. Yet I can think of no other reason why most people were willing to talk at such length except that they too gained something from the experience of talking and, more importantly, of being listened to by people who inhabited the other side of the socio-economic divide. We greeted them, not as digits of the 'slum problem', 'the water problem', 'the housing problem',[4] but as people whose experiences and opinions we wanted to understand, whilst they came to accept us as chroniclers of their pasts.[5] In particular, it was when an old Muslim woman with fading sight charged me to write about sterilisation during the Emergency that I finally decided that I would write, not a short article, but a book on the subject. She had turned my inquiry into a responsibility of sorts. This feeling of responsibility was accentuated when I encountered the stylised and totalising narratives both of the Emergency and of the immediate post-Emergency period, and became aware of the extent to which the entire episode had been edited out of contemporary Indian history. The need to recover the voices of both 'victims' and 'agents' and to re-inscribe them into the history of events seemed even more apparent.[6]

Veena Das has emphasised the importance of listening in the

[4]The literature about Delhi's 'urban poor' reads rather like a collective catalogue of misery and deprivation, of dirt, disease and impoverishment. Most books focus almost entirely on statistical evaluations of economic and environmental conditions: How many water pumps are there? How many toilets? How much electricity? Behind these statistics, there often lurks the implication that the 'slum population' poses a terrible threat to the honest well-bred middle-class citizen despite the fact that the latter employs the former as cheap labour. This means that people in colonies like Welcome get used to being perceived by outsiders as embodiments of 'a problem' and as suppliers of 'problem statistics'. Since they do indeed have many problems, the role is not difficult to fulfill.

[5]Nancy Scheper-Hughes elaborates on John Berger's description of the country doctor as the 'clerk of the records', suggesting that this is also a suitable idiom for the anthropologist who is often distanced from the local people by class and upbringing, but who none the less keeps the records and offers some understanding. Her account of working in a Brazilian shanty town bears witness to the humane side of being an anthropologist as well as its frustrations and limitations. See Scheper-Hughes, 1992, *Death without Weeping: The Violence of Everyday Life in Brazil*, Berkeley: University of California Press, esp. pp. 29–30.

[6]In this sense ethnographic writing can, as Das argues, be an act of resistance against various forms of totalising discourse, including those initiated by the academy or resistance groups as well as those initiated by the state. V. Das, 1995, *Critical Events*.

fieldwork process. She talks of how survivors of the Sikh massacre of 1984 'eagerly accepted the opportunity to simply talk...to construct the events as they remembered what had happened, and to help in the writing of these events. All this signified the fact that their lives had a meaning, and that their suffering would not go untold.'[7] Elsewhere, she draws out the relationship between the victim's suffering and the anthropologist's role more explicitly when she states: 'To be the scribe of the human experience of suffering creates a special responsibility towards those who suffer.'[8] This sharing of pain, she argues, has the potential to make anthropology 'a healing force' in people's lives.[9] Whilst I do not subscribe to the view that anthropology should become a new form of therapy, I do feel that such insights are more adequate for explaining people's willingness, and in some cases desire, to confide in strangers than the model of the voracious anthropologist mercilessly extracting information out of professional greed. This is not to suggest that we should exaggerate the value of simply listening, talking and writing which all too often feels inadequate. Neither should we restrict ourselves to listening only to the victims of violence, for every violent situation has its participants and aggressors whose voices we cannot afford to exclude if we want to understand the totality of events. This point is poignantly illustrated in Urvashi Butalia's compilation of Partition narratives, the value of which would be greatly diminished had she not included the narratives of the 'perpetrators' of violence along with those of the victims as well as exposing the grey area where the two converge.[10] She also reminds us that there may be times when it is better to accept silence rather than run the risk of causing further pain by unearthing uncomfortable or intolerable pasts. Whether historians, writers or anthropologists, it seems worth taking heed of Nancy Scheper-Hughes's observation that 'the reading, reflecting and writing are nothing in comparison with the cost to those who have lived the stories...'[11] And to this we might add one more reminder: there are many other things which are shared in the fieldwork encounter.

[7]Veena Das, 1990a, 'Our Work to Cry: Your Work to Listen' in V. Das ed., *Mirrors of Violence: Communities, Riots and Survivors in South Asia*, Delhi: OUP, p. 395.

[8]V. Das, 1990a, 'Introduction: Communities, Riots and Survivors—The South Asian Experience' in V. Das, ed., *Mirrors of Violence*, p. 33.

[9]V. Das, 1995, 'The Anthropology of Pain' in V. Das, *Critical Events*, pp. 195–6.

[10]Urvashi Butalia, 1998, *The Other Side of Silence*, Delhi: Viking.

[11]Scheper-Hughes, 1992, *Death Without Weeping*, p. xiii.

Trust is perhaps the most essential but irony and laughter also play an important part.

Locating the Emergency

Some 25 years have passed since the Emergency, and a further 12 years since the first wave of resettlement in Welcome. In this stretch of nearly four decades governments have come and gone, policies have been transformed, wars lost and won—all of which have left their mark in Welcome. The experience of past events, along with future fears and aspirations, form an invisible framework through which people's memories of the Emergency are assembled and recounted. These other events, like the Emergency, have also left their physical imprint on the morphology of the colony. Just as a lake, a temple or a tree in the Indian landscape often embodies a mythological story, so particular blocks, markets, and streets in Welcome physically recall a whole series of violent moments in recent Indian history. Welcome is not so much scarred by disruptive events like the Emergency, as structured by them—as we soon discovered when we talked to the residents of different blocks. Their memories of other violent moments are important for locating the Emergency in people's lives and for comprehending the nature and tone of their narratives.

An extract from a conversation with a demolition man who had been living under the old iron bridge before being shifted to Welcome in 1965 is revealing:

Do you remember the Emergency?

'Yes. Of course. That was when there was a war going on with Pakistan. That is how we ended up living here.'

How come?

'We were living in *jhuggis* in Jamuna Bridge at the time. There were lots of blackouts. The government was worried that the Pakistan forces would drop a bomb on the bridge. They instructed us to remain in darkness, but someone lit a fire, so the police told us we were a threat to security and would have to be moved. Then they came and demolished our *jhuggis* and dumped us here. It was in September 1965.'

Were you given plots?

'No. Because it was an Emergency situation. We were just thrown here so we built ourselves *kucha jhuggis*. There was nothing here in those days. It was just a jungle full of serpents and roaming with *goondas* [ruffians]. Later they demolished our *jhuggis* here as well and tried to give us plots in Seemapuri. There had been some fighting between Hindus and Muslims and that was why they said we had to move. Most people went, but some 40 families stayed on. We just rebuilt ourselves new *jhuggis* in Welcome.'

So how did you finally get this plot?

'That was during "*nasbundi ka vakt*" [the sterilisation time]. They were going about demolishing *jhuggis*, but they said we could stay in Welcome if we got sterilised. So I got sterilised to get this plot.'

Would you say you were forced?

'No. I wasn't pressurised at all. I got sterilised because I wanted the plot...[*and later*]: It was impossible to live here without getting sterilised because you would be evicted. Nobody liked the idea of sterilisation. But people didn't have any choice.'

In this brief extract, the demolition man reminds us that his relationship to the city is intrinsically bound up with a series of violent events. Quite apart from the fact that he earns his living by demolishing the *jhuggis* of others on behalf of the Municipal Corporation, he himself has had his home demolished three times: first during the external Emergency at the time of the Indo-Pakistan war, secondly as a consequence of local communal riots and thirdly during the internal Emergency which he refers to as '*nasbundi ka vakt*'. His story is at once individual and collective. Although its main features relate only to the members of his block of 36 plots, residents of other blocks often made their debuts in Welcome at similarly violent moments—whether as a result of slum fires or other external factors.[12] Newspaper reports

[12] *Jhuggi* clusters are notoriously inflammable. Houses are poorly constructed; electric wiring haphazardly rigged; cooking generally performed on kerosene stoves, earthenware *chulas* or with gas cylinders. A small accident has only to occur in one home, and an entire *jhuggi* cluster is at risk. But this does not mean that all slum fires are 'accidents', or at least that all 'accidents' are accidental. There are moments when it is the interests of certain individuals and groups to stage-manage the burning of a slum as a cheap and easy way of clearing the area. Just as it is often impossible to know whether a young married woman accidentally burned to death or was burnt by her in-laws, so it is often impossible to know if a slum fire was accidental or deliberate.

of June 1967 bear witness to the fact that the demolition of *jhuggis* in Jamuna Bazaar—the first slum clearance to be carried out in Delhi on a massive scale—was also a product of Emergency regulations which enabled tight security and the arrest of opposition forces.[13] The slum was later re-tackled by the municipality on several occasions. Six blocks containing over 700 plots in Welcome bear the prefix JB, acting as physical and mnemonic reminders of the government's successive attempts to wipe out this famous slum from the banks of the Yamuna.[14]

If the above account gives some idea of the different manifestations of state-initiated violence in people's lives before the Emergency, other accounts are formed in relation to violence that has happened since. In particular, Welcome had played a major role in the 'communal riots' which spread throughout many parts of north India in December 1992. The 'riots' were a reaction to the destruction of an ancient mosque at Ayodhya in Uttar Pradesh. The mosque was literally pulverized by right wing Hindu extremists, following an intensive political campaign by Hindu nationalist parties and organisations. This campaign was built around the notion that Ayodhya was the sacred birthplace of Lord Rama; that there had previously been a Hindu temple there; and that it was the duty of contemporary Hindus to rebuild that temple. The destruction of the mosque was the culmination of a long-term political strategy and rhetoric which some Hindus interpreted as a license to attack Muslims just as Muslims interpreted it as a call for active defence. Through television and newspaper coverage, news of the demolition spread rapidly throughout India where it provided fuel for further violence between Hindus and Muslims. Welcome with its large Muslim population became one of the key sites in Delhi where communal tensions were enacted. The events of 1992 have left their trail not only in the mutilation of bodies and buildings in the colony, but also in the re-organisation of residence patterns:

A HINDU WOMAN
'There used to be some Muslim families living in our block. But after the fighting, they sold up and left.'

---

[13]'Emergency here to Stay', *Hindustan Times*, 23 June 1967.

[14]For a more detailed account of how policies and events are inscribed within the spatial structure and architecture of the colony, see Tarlo, 2000, 'Welcome to History' in Dupont, Tarlo and Vidal, eds, *Delhi*.

ANOTHER HINDU WOMAN

'There were five Hindu families living in this *gali* [alley] before the fighting. They all left during the riots and didn't come back. Now we are the only one.'

A MUSLIM WOMAN

'I don't feel safe living here any more. I'm alone in the house all day long. We are the only Muslims in this street. I have told my husband we cannot stay here. We have started looking for somewhere else to move but he says this place is cheaper.'

Although the violence and the curfew that followed had spread fear throughout the colony, much of the 'action' had been located in the north side of the colony in areas which already had a high concentration of Muslims. Here houses and businesses had been looted, markets burned and mosques attacked. The police arrested over 300 people, some of whom were reportedly tortured and killed.[15] The accounts of men and women who live in this area reveal that for many residents in the colony, the distinction between 'spontaneous' and 'organised' violence is by no means clear cut. They spoke of fleets of jeeps of armed men descending upon the colony from outside, of policemen operating in conjunction with locals 'to target Muslims'[16] and of the government's deliberately slow attempt to restore law and order. These accounts are of course highly subjective, making it impossible to distinguish individual and collective fear and anger from fact. They are formulated, not only in relation to the past, but also in relation to

[15]According to the authors of a report for a well-known secular organisation whose members conducted research in Welcome just one week after the violence, Welcome experienced some of the worse 'anti-Muslim riots' to have happened in Delhi in recent years. The report reveals that 87 per cent of the 343 people arrested in the colony were Muslims and alleges that the 32 Hindus arrested were not part of the violent mob of Hindus and policemen, but were mostly labourers employed by Muslim families. The authors go on to suggest: 'The accused Hindus were actually rounded up along with their Muslim co-workers and employers, during arrests at the timber market [in Welcome]. To our knowledge it was impossible for the police at that juncture to realise that they were not Muslims and it was only at the police station that they were conveniently segregated and charged on community lines, in a crude attempt to cover up an error made.' See *Seelampur 1992: A Report on the Communal Violence in Seelampur*, 1992, New Delhi: Sampradayikta Virodhi Andolan or People's Movement for Secularism.

[16]There is a striking contrast between Hindu descriptions of the violence in which the police feature as saviours and protectors, and Muslim descriptions in which they feature as protagonists, aggressors and torturers.

a projected future produced by the growing feeling of insecurity that the violence had engendered. As one young Muslim man put it: 'We are, after all, living in a country which is governed by others. Whatever they want to do to us; they do it whether we want it or not.' This was in fact a reference to the sterilisation of Muslims in 1976. As such, it is a statement about the Emergency, but it followed on from a discussion the previous day in which a group of men had been telling us about government and police participation in the riots and about how almost all Muslims of the colony had been excluded from the electoral roll in the recent local elections.[17] Furthermore, these discussions were taking place in a space which was far from neutral. We were sitting in the wood market, most of which had been burned to the ground during the 'riots' and many of the men who joined the discussion were wood merchants. To what extent the young man's statement about sterilisation was shaped by these other experiences and narrations, it is impossible to judge, but to see his statement purely in terms of the Emergency would seem misleading in view of the context. Just as the *chaudhuri* of the Turkman Gate Committee had used the Emergency experience as a platform for voicing future 'rights' and electoral issues, so people in Welcome remembered the Emergency through a mixture of personal, political and communal discourses and agendas. Sitting in the wood market, a space charged with the memory of recent violence perceived as 'anti-Muslim violence' no doubt encouraged this young man, who must have been no more than an infant during the Emergency, to give a communal interpretation of the past.

The same circumstances can, however, encourage the opposite interpretation. Such was the case when we talked to a Muslim dye-manufacturer whose office was located at the entrance to the wood market. His property had been damaged during the riots but he was not a wood merchant, and had not been either sterilised or resettled during the Emergency. He had, in fact, purchased a property in Welcome at a later date. The air-conditioner in his office marked him

[17]Like Muslims in Bombay and other major cities, Muslims in Welcome had found themselves classified as 'Bangladeshis' unless proved otherwise. Most could prove otherwise by providing a number of official documents relating to their birth and to previous census lists, but not in time to vote in the local elections of 1993. According to one newspaper report, over 1,500 names were deleted from the electoral role in Seelampur alone. (*Amrita Bazaar Patrika,* 22 December 1993)

out as a man considerably more prosperous than the average Welcome resident. All of these factors no doubt combined with this man's personality, to produce a very different portrait of the Emergency:

'I wish they would impose another Emergency so that the government can do its work properly and efficiently.'

What do you mean?

'Well, in an Emergency, everything becomes strict. If you have an Emergency, you can control riots. The only people who suffered during the Emergency were corrupt businessmen and corrupt officials. Ordinary people do not suffer from it.'

What about those who had to get sterilised? Many of your neighbours in the wood market tell us it was a very difficult time?

'The only people who were forcibly sterilised were government servants [*pause*], and maybe some hangers on. But listen, I was a young man during the Emergency and no one forced me to get sterilised. If there had been forcible sterilisation then the younger generation would not have produced all the children they have [*laughter all around*].

So you would say an Emergency is a good thing?

'Look, people of both communities were living here in perfect harmony in 1991 before the fighting, and even afterwards in 1993, 1994, 1995 and so on. The real threat is not from the people of other communities. It is from the ones who are supposed to be the protectors of people's lives and properties. If they become the destroyers then the threat is with us for ever.'

Here again the interpretation of the Emergency is framed by not only the memory and experience of the violence of 1992 but also by the anticipation of future strife. Fear of the larger 'threat' posed by 'protectors' (the police) turning 'destroyers', and the fact that this particular man had not suffered directly in the years 1975–7, led him to paint a favourable picture of the Emergency as a time of discipline and order. As such his interpretation is much closer to the common interpretation offered by the educated middle classes than to those offered by the majority of Welcome residents. With the exception of government servants, most middle-class citizens had not suffered particularly during the Emergency and many remember it as the era 'when trains ran on time', when 'people worked hard', when 'corruption was rooted out and discipline maintained'. Such interpretations are rare in Welcome where the majority of inhabitants were directly at the receiving end of aggressive government policies. This is not to argue that some did not use these policies to their advantage; the example of Ganga Lal in the previous chapter has already made that clear, but rather to suggest that they rarely perceived the Emergency as a time of order and reduced corruption. More often, they remembered it as a period of chaos when the terms and conditions of their existence in the city were once more thrown into a state of confusion from which some suffered but others gained.

Given the extraordinary range of interpretations possible, how can we locate the role of the Emergency in the lives of the people of Welcome? One factor which needs to be considered when assessing people's narratives is the particular combination of experiences that they underwent during the Emergency itself. These experiences varied considerably. Some, like the demolition man, had suffered demolition and sterilisation but had gained a plot; others had been sterilised but had not got plots or been resettled without getting sterilised. Yet others, like the dye merchant, had successfully avoided both housing and family planning pressures and was not even in Welcome at the time. These different circumstances inevitably impinged upon people's perceptions of the Emergency and influenced their ways of talking about it. But, as we have seen, the Emergency was not an isolated disruptive force in people's lives. It was located after and before other critical events. For some, these other events made the Emergency seem little more than just one in a long series of violent disruptions. For others, more recent losses had encouraged the elaboration of a narrative of oppression which formed a contiguous chain of suffering linking the past to the future. Yet others had improved their circumstances considerably during the 20 odd years which separated the Emergency from the present, and this too was reflected in their narratives. Some, for example, now consider themselves fortunate to have 'gained a plot' in Welcome which is not ill-placed by contemporary standards; others are pleased to have had less children than they originally intended, even though they had bitterly resented sterilisation at the time. In short, remembered pasts, present conditions and projected futures fed our conversations, no doubt transforming the Emergency into an era quite different from how it would have been remembered in the immediate aftermath when wounds were still at their freshest and political will was on the side of the victim, however briefly. Since time has intervened to recreate the Emergency, one might ask whether it makes sense to isolate the period as an object of reflection at all. I would argue that it does make sense owing to the specificity of the Emergency both at the level of memory and at the level of experience although these two levels of specificity often coincide in unpredictable ways. To highlight the problem, let us begin with the accounts of people who were resettled from Dujana House in 1975. By comparing their memories of the resettlement experience with those of people resettled before the Emergency, we can gain a clearer sense both of the specificity of the Emergency and of its continuity with other events.

Narratives of resettlement

Four months before the opening of the most notorious family planning camp of the Emergency, a demolition squad descended on Dujana House in the hub of the Muslim dominated quarter of the old city and destroyed unauthorised homes there. It was 20 December 1975; a cold grey morning by all accounts. Before long, the residents found themselves herded into trucks and dumped in some unknown wasteland across the river. A carpenter's wife who was among the 30 odd families who were carted off to Welcome described the events as follows:

'I had six children at the time they came to sweep away our houses. There was no warning of any demolition. Sanjay Gandhi appeared in the area that morning and everyone began to celebrate by flying pigeons and balloons.'

Did you see him?

'Yes. I was standing on a rooftop. He was wearing a white *kurta pyjama*. Everybody was shouting, "Sanjay Gandhi has come, Sanjay Gandhi has come!" I had no idea what he looked like but I could tell which one he was because he had a whole neck full of garlands. At first, we thought, "He has come to see what conditions we live in." We thought, "He is going to offer us some help." We had no idea that he was going to wipe out the whole area. He went off in the direction of the Jama Masjid and immediately after that, just some 15 to 20 minutes later, we heard the bulldozers coming. We didn't even have time to eat or collect our belongings. We just ran out of the house and saved what we could...There were no men around since they had all gone to work so we women had to manage everything.'

While most women recall feeling stranded without their husbands, many men expressed a feeling of helplessness about their inability to protect their women, children and homes. A baker recalls his feeling of devastation when he returned to find that their home had already been levelled to the ground before he even knew what was happening:

'I used to do night shifts [in the bakery] at that time, after which I would go to Turkman Gate to learn embroidery in the morning. It was when I arrived there that I heard about the demolition at Dujana House, so I rushed back. It was about 11 o'clock in the morning. The whole place had already been destroyed...I had no idea where everyone had gone. Then I found my children sitting together in one place and crying. I felt terrible and helpless. Trucks were standing by. They had dumped our belongings in the trucks. My wife had been able to save our cooking vessels but other things got crushed. We had no idea where they were going to take us. The whole thing happened so suddenly.'

The gendered nature of such accounts was not unique to the Emergency; nor were the events described. Even before the Emergency, demolitions were usually carried out during the day when men were at work, leaving the women to fend for themselves. Many of the women resettled back in the 1960s claim not to have been given any advance warning. For them the arrival of the demolition squad followed by bulldozers was equally disturbing. An old Hindu woman who was resettled from Jamuna Bazaar in 1967 recalls:

'Nobody knew anything about the demolition. We didn't have any warning. Suddenly the bulldozers came and people ran out of their houses. Some were in the middle of making *rotis* [bread]. Others were doing this and that. No one had a clue what was going on. It was as if foreigners had come from nowhere and just destroyed everything.'

Conversation with the old woman's nephew revealed that there had in fact been some advance warning but that people had not taken it seriously at the time. He recalls a meeting, attended almost exclusively by men, some three days before the demolition. None of the women we spoke to remembered such a meeting. Perhaps the fact that they had not attended it encouraged them to forget it, or perhaps the trauma of the demolition wiped out the significance of the meeting from people's minds. It is also possible that women did not remember it because their husbands and fathers had not bothered to inform them at the time. At any rate, meetings about the fate of the slum were common place and usually came to nothing, as one old man explained:

'The government had in fact been trying to get rid of us [from Jamuna Bazaar] for some time, but the issue had always got relegated to the back seat because of the vote factor. This must have gone on for about 15 years. Every time an election came, the leaders of the main parties would come and explain that they would not allow us to be removed. This was so that they would get votes and seats from us. Then, after winning the elections, they would change their stance and say, 'This area must be cleaned up. These people must be removed...' When the actual time came [in 1967], it happened all of a sudden. They made an announcement over loudspeakers. People clambered to collect their things. Government trucks carried away the stuff and took us to this wilderness.'

The feeling of disorientation about being taken off to an unknown place outside Delhi was common to all resettlement narratives, as was the perception of Welcome as an uninhabitable place, characterised by the presence of all that was uncivilised: snakes, wild animals, excrement, skeletons and hoodlums:

A HINDU WOMAN FROM JAMUNA BAZAAR, RESETTLED 1967
'The land was a total wilderness with long grass everywhere. It was very marshy and full of snakes. Some of the people already there were using this area for defecation so it was full of excreta. And we had to cook in the middle of all this!'

A MUSLIM WOMAN FROM DUJANA HOUSE, RESETTLED 1975
'It was a wilderness. There were animals everywhere: snakes, scorpions, skeletons of humans, dead dogs and cats. It must have been a graveyard.'

While death, excreta and wild animals seem to symbolise the hostility of the environment in these accounts, the absence of shelter and other basic necessities symbolised the impossibility of taming and transforming such an uninhabitable place. In particular, the absence of milk, a symbol of purity, nourishment and nurture, features in many accounts:

A MUSLIM WOMAN FROM DUJANA HOUSE, RESETTLED 1975
'By the time we arrived, it was evening. There wasn't a single shop. You couldn't find milk for the children. We had no idea where we were and didn't dare to sleep at night for fear of *goondas* and animals.'

A HINDU WOMAN RESETTLED 1965

'The place was so wild that even though there were Gujars[18] living nearby, they didn't dare to stop here to sell their milk. People were afraid to come near this place after twilight. Life was very difficult.'

While women's memories tend to centre on the problems of re-establishing domestic activities—how to cook, where to get milk, where to sleep—men's memories centre on the drastic issue of employment and the feeling of economic stress. Most now found themselves several miles from their places of work. Since employment opportunities were more or less non-existent in Welcome, and bus services extremely sparse, many found themselves walking or cycling for several hours each day. From this point of view, the situation was no doubt worse for the very earliest resettlers. Records in the Slum Department reveal that most of the people resettled in 1963 when Welcome was first conceived, had left within a year. By contrast, many of those resettled from the late 1960s onwards have remained in Welcome, although statistics do vary considerably from block to block.

The above extracts reveal a number of continuities between pre-Emergency and Emergency accounts of resettlement. Viewed from the perspective of the person whose home was demolished, there seems little reason why post-Emergency authors should have been so outraged by slum clearance during the Emergency since such activities had been going on for several years. True, the scale of activities was different as was the speed of execution. Whilst there were less than 60,000 families resettled in the 15 years leading up to the Emergency, there were at least 140,000 families resettled in a mere 18 months during the Emergency.[19] But from the point of view of the person whose home was being demolished, such statistical differences have little meaning. Those displaced in the 1960s had also seen their homes reduced to rubble, experienced the panic of being taken off in trucks and the horror of being dumped in inhuman conditions without shelter. In fact, it could be argued that conditions were worse for the original resettlers since they were not given any permanent rights to the land. Instead, as we have seen, they were just given provisional

---

[18]A community whose dominant occupation is rearing livestock and selling milk.

[19]For details of the history of resettlement policy, see Misra and Gupta, 1981, *Resettlement Policies in Delhi.*

allotments known as 'temporary camping sites' and warned that they may be removed again in the near future. That future never came and they remained uncertain of their destiny until the Emergency of 1975–7 when the permanence of Welcome as a colony became assured even if allotments made on a sterilisation basis remained provisional. Assessing the scheme through which he was displaced from Rajghat in 1964, an old Hindu man told us, 'They always said that they wanted to remove poverty, but in actual fact their intention was not to remove poverty but to remove the poor. They just wanted to throw us out of the city.'

Yet although everyone resented being 'thrown out of the city', the people from Dujana House tended to speak about it with a greater sense of devastation and injustice than did most others. This can partly be explained by the circumstances; the fact that the demolition of Dujana House was probably carried out more speedily and with greater professionalism than earlier demolitions, but also the fact that the people living there were not recent migrants living in *jhuggis*, but long-term residents of the Old City. For them, what were being demolished were not just their houses and neighbourhood, but also their sense of locality and related cultural traditions. One of the most vivid portrayals of this aspect came from the wife a rickshaw driver who equated the demolition of Dujana House and the subsequent resettlement with the cessation of the tradition of wearing the *burqa* (veil worn by Muslim women). In her account, women were quite literally ripped out of their traditional security:

'We were very *purdah*-abiding people in those days [before the Emergency]. We would not even have been able to sit and talk to you as we are doing now. We wore *burqas* then, but once we came here, that stopped.'

How was this?

'It was like this; when we were removed from the area, everything happened so rapidly that we did not even know whether we were wearing sandals or not, never mind *burqas*. We were too busy saving our children and our things to think of anything else. We were Delhi people and had never even seen anything outside our own houses so we had no idea where we were being taken or what would become of us...It was only when we got here that we found out that this place even existed. At that time, we were just wearing *salwar kurtas* [tunic and trouser combination]. There was no time for *burqas*. Our men weren't even around to help us.'

So what happened when you arrived?

'We were given slips of paper. There were some boundaries marked out for plots. Later they gave us numbers. It was cold and we had no shelter. All we could do was put two *charpais* together and cover them with cloth...After that most of our men were unemployed, so we women had to manage everything alone. The men would go out searching for jobs during the day and we used to stay here looking after things. There was no one here. Everything had to be managed by us and that is how we became *burqa*-less.'

Here the *burqa* has become a metaphor, for the protection not just of bodies but also of home, neighbourhood, locality, community and culture. Once exposed to the outside world, it no longer made sense for women to conform to their age-old traditions. They now had to fend for themselves and mix with people of other communities:

A SECOND WOMAN FROM DUJANA HOUSE

'Who is yours in an area like this? It was just a wilderness. There wasn't anyone to tell you "Wear the *burqa*! Wear the *burqa*!" When we go into Delhi [Old Delhi, i.e. Shahjahanabad], then we put it on.'

A THIRD WOMAN FROM DUJANA HOUSE

'We stopped wearing the *burqa* here because it was said that Hindus and Muslims were like brothers. But actually, that never happened.'

In this sense the demolition of homes in Dujana House was qualitatively different from the demolition of haphazard *jhuggi* clusters which contained a relatively mixed and unsettled population of Hindu and Muslim migrants. Jagmohan, backed by Sanjay Gandhi, used the Emergency to demolish a number of ancient areas in the Old City which had long been classified as 'notified slums' and scheduled for demolition as part of a larger project of gentrification. Further probing into the narratives of the people from Dujana House reveals that here too there is more continuity with the pre-Emergency period than it first appears. What the DDA demolished in Dujana House in 1975 were not ancient *havelis* (historic houses), but relatively newly constructed *jhuggis*. The original architecture and the two ancient gateways of Dujana House Fatak and Azizabadi Fatak had already been destroyed by the DDA back in the 1960s. Most of the residents had been temporarily displaced and later relodged back in the area in four storey concrete blocks built by the DDA. Only some fifty families had not been able to get quarters and had built new *jhuggis* in the Dujana House area. This surplus population experienced the second round of demolition during the Emergency and ended up in Welcome. What these people lost in 1975 was not so much their ancient homes, which they had already lost, but rather their location in the heart of the Muslim community of the Old City. It was a loss of locality.[20] Loss of community and locality is different from loss of space. In fact, a number of people from Dujana House say that they now find Old Delhi crowded and are quite glad to live in Welcome. Two issues converge here. Welcome, though hardly spacious, is less congested than Shahjahanabad and, since the people of Dujana House have on the whole been successful in setting up craft industries here, many have been able to build two or three storeys, thereby giving themselves a space of 50 or 75 square yards on their 25 square yard plots. Secondly, in the past 10 to 15 years, something of a new Muslim community has developed in Welcome which draws in many Muslim families who choose to leave the old city of their own accord as well as new migrant families. This Islamisation of the area has increased since the violent events of 1992 with the result that this part of Welcome now has a well-established Muslim majority and is considered a desirable location by many Delhi Muslims. It is also the most prosperous part of the colony and is noticeably more developed than Phase Three which was resettled back in the 1960s.

Why then, in view of the fact that things have turned out not so badly for the people displaced from Dujana House, do they speak of the Emergency with such particular hostility? To answer this, we need to consider the various ways in which memory and experience feed into one another and to trace the inter-weaving of local and national narratives. What is particular in the case of the people from Dujana House is that they come from an area which became one of the key locations of tension during the Emergency. It was here that Ruksana Sultana set up her infamous family planning clinic. Although those resettled in Welcome were displaced before the clinic was established, many describe it as if they had been there all along. They speak of

[20]Arjun Appadurai, *Modernity at Large*, ch. 9.

people being grabbed by force off the streets, of some who went in and never came out, as if they were watching the entire proceedings day by day from their windows. One old woman even gave a graphic description of Ruksana Sultana's visits, claiming that the latter had forced her to get sterilised in the clinic. But although some of the resettled may have been staying with relatives in Dujana House during the brief few weeks of the clinic's existence, it is unlikely that many of them would have participated in the sterilisation activities there. These were in fact the people most able to escape sterilisation since they left Dujana House before the clinic opened and were allocated plots in Welcome before sterilisation became a prerequisite for DDA housing. What they seem to have imbibed, then, is the narrative version of an event which has entered collective memory and been further elaborated after the event when Dujana House, along with Turkman Gate became central symbols of oppression and resistance in the post-Emergency narrative we have already encountered. Through their relationship to the lieu and to the local and national narratives that developed around it, those resettled from Dujana House are legitimate heirs to the collective memory of the Emergency as an oppressive event above all others. Furthermore, since they were expelled from the Old City at that time, they tend to perceive the resettlement process as a product of the Emergency even though they had already experienced the demolition of their homes before the Emergency.

Ironically, it was the ahistorical nature of post-Emergency critiques that so infuriated Jagmohan when he found himself depicted as one of the key villains of the Emergency after the event. His defence centred around the fact that he was simply carrying out housing policies which had been formulated long before the Emergency. Carefully concealing the DDA's role in the family planning drive, Jagmohan claims that there was nothing abnormal about the way he directed the slum clearance policy at the time. In a way, he was right. It had become 'normal' for poor people living in slums to be treated with callousness and indifference by the authorities. Jagmohan's point was that usually the educated classes remained uninterested and un-perturbed by such activities, so why this sudden outrage and concern over Emergency resettlement?

Part of the specificity of the Emergency lies, then, in the way it has entered the collective memory of certain individuals and groups as a particular moment in recent Indian history. However, many of those resettled in Welcome do not frame the period either as clearly or as collectively as the people resettled from Dujana House. For them, the specificity of the period lay not so much in the resettlement issue as in the threat of sterilisation which, by September 1976, pervaded the structures of everyday life in the colony. A common means of referring to the Emergency in Welcome is through the use of the phrase '*nasbundi ka vakt*'. This was the era when many of the things one normally took for granted became redefined in terms of sterilisation—so much so that one woman even thought that the word Emergency meant sterilisation. But if the pervasiveness of the sterilisation threat characterised the period, it was the nature of that threat which surely captured its ethos? Unlike the demolition drive which was forced and un-negotiable, the sterilisation drive operated, less through physical coercion, than through inviting participation in a particular kind of deal in which human infertility was traded off against a whole range of basic amenities.

Of course, sterilisation, like resettlement, became an important symbol of Emergency abuses in Delhi. In fact, it is almost universally perceived as the most significant reason for Indira Gandhi's defeat in the 1977 elections. These abuses were not restricted to the capital. Rather, they radiated out from the capital, affecting most of the northern states as different chief ministers competed to fill and exceed their sterilisation targets. As such, it might be expected that people's accounts of how they were trapped into sterilisation in Welcome might share the same level of predictability as their accounts of the resettlement process. Yet this is not the case. When discussing the issue of sterilisation, not only do we find considerable diversity in people's memories and experiences, but we also find that many of their accounts depart widely from the collective critique of family planning found in the post-Emergency narrative. Theirs is a story untold.

Why, when there is a clear homology between public critiques and individual perceptions of slum clearance, should there be such discrepancy when it comes to the issue of sterilisation? It is here that we need to return to the words of the turmeric-smeared man at the beginning of this chapter: He had described the family planning policy, not in terms of physical violence, but in terms of a 'forcible deal on the part of the government'. As a deal, the sterilisation policy implied an element of choice that was entirely lacking when it came to the issues of demolition and resettlement. With this element of 'choice', however forced it may have been, came the possibilities of temptation and judgement. While the post-Emergency narrative sides almost unanimously with the victims of sterilisation, the people of Welcome, many of whom were victims, are not always so generous in their assessments. Rather through their accounts, we get an idea of the nature of the deal, the tensions it caused and the criticisms it evoked.

6

THE 'FORCIBLE DEAL'

A UNIVERSITY PROFESSOR, NEW DELHI

'That sterilisation threat was everywhere. You take my village. My brother is a teacher there. In the Emergency, the pressure was on all teachers to get operated and produce cases from their students. The government was offering increments and forcing to withdraw their salaries if they did not agree.'

So did your brother get sterilised?

'Look, we are Brahmans. And my brother is in the respected profession of teacher. We are important people in the village. Who could make him do anything? [*Laughing*] You just can't force a Brahman like that!'

Was his salary withdrawn?

'You know, people could generally get around it somehow by giving cases or whatever, that sort of thing.'

A FAMILY WELFARE ADMINISTRATOR, NEW DELHI

'There was a lot of pressure on government servants in all departments. If you had more than two children you couldn't escape the operation.'

But would you say it really affected everyone?

'Yes, everyone! We had so many teachers coming to us in distress, asking for our help and support, saying they needed certificates. They thought we must have some influence or other. It was a very difficult time.' [*Laughing*]

Did you yourself get sterilised?

'No. I had only one child then.'

What about those above you? Your boss, for example? Did people like him actually get sterilised?

'Probably you could avoid the operation if you were a high-up employee. You could give some cases or what not to keep them happy. That's how it seemed to work.'

AN MCD PEON, WELCOME

'In schools they used to make announcements that those whose parents did not get sterilised would not pass their exams...I was studying in ninth grade at Chameli Chand School near Chandni Chowk in Old Delhi. The Sanskrit master went to my father and told him to go for the operation or else he would fail me and my studies would be ruined.'

What did your father do?

'At first he refused, but then he started worrying that I would fail my exams. He was worried about his son's future so eventually he decided to go for it. The teacher got a case out of it; my father got a plot.'

What did your mother think?

'She didn't think anything since my father was about 60 at that time!' [*Laughter*]

Wasn't he a bit old for sterilisation?

'Look, it was the time of cases. The teacher wanted a case. He had to give four or five cases to get promotion. So that was his main concern. Nobody bothered about my father's age.'

And what did you think about his having the operation?

'I tried to persuade him not to go for it. I was very scared. I was frightened he would die. I thought he would go in and never come back.'

And did you pass the exams?

'Yes. All those whose parents had got sterilised were passed and all those whose parents had refused were failed.'

Three short extracts from conversations with three different people all of whom were living in Delhi during the Emergency. Taken individually the tales tell us something of how the family planning drive was in fact negotiable, but taken together they reveal something else. The government had struck a deal—a 'forcible deal' in which all government servants with more than two children were penalised if they failed to get sterilised. In theory, everyone was under pressure. In practice, that pressure accumulated downwards in such a way that

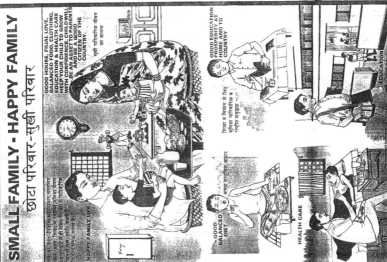

FAMILY
PLANNING:
AN ONGOING
SAGA

Contemporary posters, 1997.
(Vidhya Chitr Prakashan)

Top right 'The family planning movement aims at restricting the size of the family to two and not more than three. Yes, a family with two small children is a happy family.' (PD-PIB, New Delhi). *Right* Puppets of the policy. A mischief-making ghost threatens large unplanned family in a government-sponsored puppet show (1960s). *Below* In the days before mass vasectomy. Women testing condoms at the Hindustan Latex factory in Trivandrum (1960s). (All by PD-PIB, New Delhi)

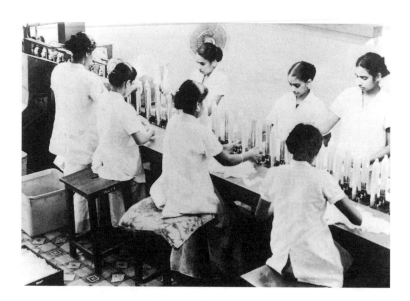

Above A Mass vasectomy camp in Kerala creates a world record by performing 62,913 operations in one month. Cochin, July 1971.   *Below* 'Gift packets' for the sterilised, Cochin, July 1971. (Both by PD-PIB, New Delhi)

Vasectomy – the answer, 1976.   Era of targets, 1976.

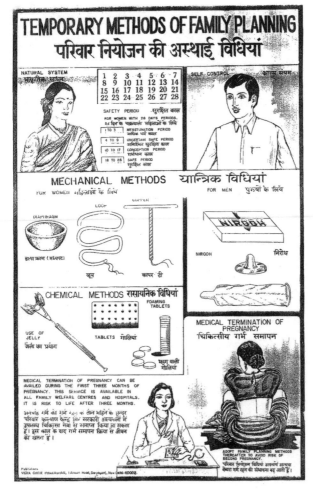

Contemporary poster (Vidya Chitr Prakashan), 1997.

it is only the young boy's father, a sweeper with the MCD, who actually gets sterilised in these accounts. In other words, how that deal presented itself, the choices it offered, depended very largely on where one was placed in the social system. For those near the top, there was always the possibility of deferral—of finding someone else to get sterilised, of trying to obtain a certificate through influential friends. For those at the bottom the options were more limited. In this particular case, the choice was simple: get sterilised or your son will fail his exams.

The young boy's father was illiterate. He had invested time and effort in trying to ensure that his son would get an education—a better chance in life. Presenting himself to the surgeon's knife was a way of protecting his son's future—at least that is the version given by the son.

There is much more we could say about these three conversations; the techniques of evasiveness employed, the role of laughter, the question of location, but I want instead to explore how these responses relate to the oft-repeated claim in family planning literature that the sterilisation statistics of the Emergency were grossly exaggerated and that, in reality, very few people were actually forced into having the operation. These two claims take as evidence firstly the fact that the fertility rate did not drop as dramatically as it should have done given that 70 lakh (7 million) people had purportedly been sterilised and secondly the fact that only 600 people came before the Shah Commission claiming that they had been forcibly sterilised. The family planning administrator, who after all is well placed to know, gives us a clue to the rationale behind such explanations. When he speaks of people approaching him for certificates, he is quite clearly suggesting the possibility, if not the actuality, of forgery on the part of government officials. That statistics were fiddled to some extent seems inevitable, given the target-oriented structure of the programme and most researchers argue that the actual figures for sterilisation must have been considerably lower than claimed. The professor's account further corroborates the notion that there were ways and means of getting around sterilisation—that although in theory government servants were 'forced', in practice high caste men in 'respectable' positions were not. All of this seems to suggest that statistics are deceptive and that things were not quite as bad as they seemed. The personal experiences of men in high places, the sort of men who write about family planning statistics, adds further confirmation to this comforting view.

However, the young man's account of how his father got sterilised suggests some different possible interpretations. It reminds us that some of the people who were sterilised were already at the end of their fertile life and would not have contributed much to the drop in birth rates anyway (a point recognised but little emphasised in family planning literature). Secondly, it reminds us of the much-neglected point that coercion does not have to be physical to be coercion.[1] As for the question of why so few people presented themselves before the Shah Commission, it hardly seems worth asking. Emergency abuses were embedded in social relationships of power which functioned not only before and during the Emergency but also after it. We have only to remember the symbolic potency of official papers in the Slum Department, the language of deference appropriate to the displaced, the layers of distance which separated them from the hallowed realm of officials. How and why should the victims of sterilisation present themselves before an official commission? In what language should they speak? With what papers should they come? In which officials should they trust when yesterday's officials were the actual perpetrators?

The sterilisation statistics of the Emergency *are* deceptive—of that there seems little doubt. Frightened and/or ambitious officials are well known to have boosted numbers and it was certainly in their interests to do so at the time. But suppose we framed the problem a little differently? Suppose, instead of emphasising the forged statistics, we drew up a sample based on such factors as wealth, social status and geographic location? Suppose we took a resettlement colony, a marginal space on the outskirts of Delhi containing the 'social dregs' of the population and asked quite bluntly what proportion of them were sterilised during the Emergency? Suddenly that phrase 'statistics are deceptive' would take on a different meaning. It would no longer re-assure us that things were not as bad as they seemed. It would probably tell us that things were at least as bad and in some ways worse. But I am not a statistician and do not have the data. All I have is the knowledge that when the files in the Slum Department tell us that 28 per cent of the plots in Welcome were legalised on a sterilisation basis, they refer to only a fragment of the sterilisations performed on or motivated by people in Welcome. After all, the housing department was just one amongst a whole range of government institutions that needed some genuine cases amongst which they could conceal their false ones.

---

[1]For detailed discussion of this issue in relation to family planning in India, see Vicziany, 1982–3, 'Coercion in a Soft State.'

What better place to find those cases than amongst the bodies of displaced slum dwellers: sweepers, rickshawwallas, labourers and craftspeople? Their accounts may not provide us with the statistics but they do provide an ethnography of how the 'forcible deal' of sterilisation operated on the ground, of how it entered the structures of everyday life, invading social relationships and spreading from the public to the private domain.

The right to work

A government job is generally considered highly desirable in India. It offers the security of a salary and employment to last throughout a person's working life. Welcome has its fair share of government employees—more than its fair share some would argue. The large proportion of people from scheduled caste backgrounds are well placed for getting low level government employment and it is not surprising to find that Welcome contains employees of the MCD, the DDA, DESU, the Indian Railways and so forth.

During the Emergency, having a permanent government job seems to have taken on a new dimension as this conversation with a sweeper and a bus driver illustrates:

MCD SWEEPER

'I was working for the MCD in those days. They told me that unless I went for the operation they wouldn't allow me to continue my job. So I went.'

Did you have any children?

Yes, six.

Did you go immediately, or did you hesitate?

'They made me sit at home for 15 days first. So after that I decided I had to save my job. My wife also works in the cleaning department and she was also made to sit at home.'

Did any people in your department leave their jobs as a result of this?

'No. In my department everyone got sterilised.'

BUS DRIVER

'What would a poor man eat if he left his job?...People are only realising the benefits of that sterilisation today. In those days we felt bad because only we Hindus were being pressurised and not the

Muslims. This country is ours so why should it be we who are forced?'

What makes you think Muslims were not forced?

'The fact that they have as many as 16 children each today is surely proof enough that they were not forced!' [*Laughter all round*]

If the Municipal Corporation was tough about forcing sterilisation on its sweepers, the centralised DDA was even tougher. Whilst the former introduced compulsory sterilisation for all those with three or more children, the latter set the limit at two. Neither did it allow the 'luxury' of a fifteen-day waiting period:

DDA SWEEPER
'The officers said you can keep your job only if you get sterilised.'

What did you think of that?

'Think? I didn't have time to think. When I reached my duty we were told this. The transport had already been arranged and we were immediately taken off for the operation. I agreed to it because I had to save my job and bring up my family.'

SWEEPER'S SON
'Whatever laws in India are enforced, it is the poor people who face the problems; not the rich. And even then, it was only Hindus. Muslims were not forced. Don't they have more children than us? That's the law in India for you.'

There is nothing very valiant in these accounts—steeped as they are in the discourse of necessity intertwined with that of communalism. In both cases it is the younger men, the ones who were not sterilised (the bus driver and the sweeper's son) who reconstruct the period as a time of religious discrimination, thereby transforming the past into suitable ammunition for present and future communal conflicts. This is not to say that the family planning drive was devoid of communalist interpretations during the Emergency but rather to argue that some of the new generation of scheduled caste youth in Welcome have appropriated the past to suit their current political orientation. Their discourse echoes that of the right wing BJP which actively propagates the notion that Hindus must protect themselves from the rapidly expanding Muslim population. It is a theory based on the notion of the danger of the small minority to the vulnerable majority—a theory which has many historic and contemporary parallels all over the world.[2] Needless to say, young Muslim men can offer a different explanation as to why so few Muslims were sterilised through the channel of government employment:

AN ENGINEER
'You will notice that we here [in the Muslim-dominated section of Welcome] are mostly self-employed. We work from home. That is because it is impossible to get government employment if you are a Muslim. Even if you were to get a government job you would face so many problems that you would not be able to keep it.'

Whatever the truth of this man's claim, it is noticeable that in Welcome, nearly all the government employees we met were Hindus, mostly from scheduled caste backgrounds. With the exception of packers and coolies in the railway department and one part-time electrician, all had been 'forced' to produce or *become* sterilisation cases under threat of dismissal. They included sweepers, gardeners, carpenters, coolies, demolition men, peons and water carriers. Collectively their infertile bodies contributed to the statistics of each department, acting as evidence of the dedication of individual officers and forming a basis for the increments and promotions of those above them in the (in)human chain. Individually, each case represented a different story providing subtle variations on a singularly repetitive tune. There was the sock-factory worker who had got sterilised on his wife's behalf in order to save not only her job as a sweeper but also her unborn child. She had been pregnant at the time and had been told at work that the foetus would be forcibly removed if her husband did not get sterilised. There were also the exceptions; the two railway coolies who had the good fortune to have an employer who was bold enough to refuse to carry out the order to get his staff sterilised. However, in most cases, what people recounted was a straightforward deal with the government; surgical infertility was the currency with which they had purchased the right to retain their jobs.

Nevertheless, this is not to say that Muslims could avoid sterilisation simply by dint of their social disadvantage when it came to the question

[2]For a particularly extreme and paranoid example of right-wing Hindu discourse on family planning see Sudhir Laxman Hendre, 1971, *Hindus and Family Planning*, Bombay: Supraja. He refers to the Government of India's early attempts at family planning as 'an undeclared war on Hinduism' and as 'nothing short of the genocide of Hindus...' (pp. 10–11).

of getting government employment. The forcible deal did not limit itself to government departments any more than government departments limited themselves to their staff in the search for bodies to be sterilised. Whether an employee in the private sector 'escaped' sterilisation or not ultimately depended on the nature and circumstances of his employer. Some workers were what you could call 'fortunate' given that amongst the urban poor, this was a period when remaining fertile became the 'privilege' of the few.

RETIRED FACTORY WORKER
'In those days they would take you to the camp, ask how many children you had, then ignore it and sterilise you anyway...I knew exactly what was going on, So, I didn't stir out of my house unless absolutely necessary. I was doing a private job in a factory. That factory was not on the main road. This sort of thing happened mostly in crowded places and main roads. In fact my employer even advised me to stay indoors as much as possible.'

Others were not so 'fortunate'. One factory worker gave a particularly detailed explanation of how the 'forcible deal' of sterilisation entered and spread in the small private cooler and geyser factory where he worked:

FACTORY WORKER
'The policeman came up to my employer. He told him: "Listen, you want a license? I'll tell you how. Get your workers sterilised. Four cases should be enough." '

What did the policeman get out of it?

'The police were under pressure from above and so they used to put pressure on all around...There were eight of us employed in the factory at the time: four skilled craftsmen and four labourers. Since I was a labourer, it was I who was forced. My boss told me I had to get sterilised so that he could get the licence. But once I had got sterilised I was immediately sacked. My boss argued that now that I was sterilised I was no longer any use to him. He said I was unfit for heavy work. From that day onwards I have been facing many difficulties.'

What about the other labourers?

I was the only one who had the operation, but the others were also under pressure. Two of them were accused of stealing things from the factory and were handed over to the police. They ended up in jail. The other left and went to Pakistan. He was also sacked without any pay even though he had been working there for 40 years.

But how could the boss sack you when it was he who made you get sterilised?

'Because I refused to hand over my certificate. I had heard they were allocating plots in Seelampur for sterilisation. I was homeless at that time. My *jhuggi* in Mata Sundari Road had been demolished some months earlier and I had been given a plot in Mangolpuri [another resettlement colony], but I couldn't live there because it took me three hours to get to work. So I left that place and started living in my sister's house on rent but that too was demolished. I needed a place to live so I used my certificate to get a transfer from Mangolpuri and got this plot. Then I reasoned that if I gave my certificate to my boss for his licence, he might take advantage and start claiming that the plot was his since he would have all the documents. That is why I kept my own certificate to prove that the plot is mine. I still have that certificate. Shall I show it?'

In Slum Department terminology, this is a 'transfer case' subsumed in that simple phrase 'Transfer to Seelampur—vasectomy'. One more number added to the statistics of the DDA as it set about fulfilling its target. In human terms, however, the cost of such a transfer was high. Not only did the man lose his reproductive capacity at the age of twenty-six (he had three children at the time) but he also lost the job he had held for the past seven years. His account bears witness to the extent to which individuals found themselves caught between conflicting pressures and demands. His home had been demolished in the slum clearance scheme and he had found himself 'resettled' so many miles away from his workplace that it had made life impossible. By staying with his sister he found a means of continuing his job but then her home was also demolished. It was in order to have a plot not far from work that he got himself sterilised, only to find that he was dismissed from work for not handing over his certificate. The story ends with a bitter twist. After presenting himself for a number of jobs, this man returned to his original employer and has been working for him ever since as a contract labourer on poorer pay and with less security. 'I am not qualified for any other type of work and cannot get permanent employment' was his explanation. His home, limited to a single room and small courtyard, bore witness to the fact that although he had gained a plot, he lacked the means with which to develop it. As a contract labourer, his income was unstable, varying between Rs. 800–900 per month in the summer to nothing at all during the rainy season. His son who also contributed to the family income worked as an apprentice tailor in a jeans workshop. Paid on a piecework basis, his income was also unstable.

The factory labourer's account gives only a fragment of a much larger picture. We have his voice, his reconstruction of how things were, but we also encounter a number of blanks. Though he gave me the name and address of his employer in Old Delhi, I did not try to meet him, fearing it would only add to this man's troubles. But there are other silences. What, for example, was the fate of the other labourers who were dismissed under apparently 'false' accusations? Did they succeed in avoiding sterilisation or did they instead get caught up in the police search for cases? From what others tell us, it was not uncommon for those under arrest to be offered release from jail if they 'agreed' to get sterilised. I use the word 'agreed' in inverted comas for this was, after all a 'forcible' deal.

The factory workers, the policeman and the factory owners in both of the above accounts were Muslims—a fact which is both relevant and irrelevant. It is irrelevant to the wider picture of how individuals found themselves caught up in the sterilisation net that had spread itself across Delhi and most of the northern states. It is equally irrelevant for introducing those who squeezed sterilisation cases out of their employees. Government servants or private sector employers, both 'agreed' to participate in the forcible deal through which they would benefit by getting those beneath them sterilised. But to paint a picture of human behaviour without providing the details as to who is Hindu and who is Muslim in contemporary north India is unfortunately to invite further communalist re-interpretations of the past. And so it becomes necessary to state that these men were Muslims and that they too were 'forced' into participating in the government-initiated deal even if not directly forced through the channel of government employment. There are many other cases I could cite—the accounts of two Muslim women, for example, who described how their rickshaw-driver husbands were denied access to the rickshaws they rented on a daily basis until they submitted evidence of having been vasectomised. There is no shortage of examples from either community just as, during the Emergency, there had been no shortage of human material on which operations could be, and were, performed.

The right to civic amenities

RETIRED MUSLIM EMBROIDERER

'The time was such that you had to produce that sterilisation certificate wherever you went if you wanted any work of yours to be done. If you went to the hospital for some treatment, they wouldn't treat you unless you had that *nasbandi* card. It was exactly like it is now with Seshan's identity card. That *nasbandi* card was needed at every place and in all government offices.'

The man who said these words spoke as someone intimately familiar with the value of official papers. Like most Muslims in the colony, he had recently experienced exclusion from the voting list in the 1993 local elections because, along with thousands of others (mostly Muslims), he had officially *become* 'Bangladeshi'. He first learned of his new identity when he went to vote and discovered that his name had been wiped off the voting list. Later he received official notification of the fact in the form of a letter in which he was informed that unless he produced evidence to the contrary he would be deported to Bangladesh. It is, of course, useful to know when you have 'become Bangladeshi' in India. It would have been even more useful had people known some time before the elections so that they could have prepared 'evidence' to the contrary in time to submit their votes. It was the suspicion that certain political parties had deliberately created fake Bangladeshis as a means of suppressing the Muslim vote which led T.N. Seshan, the Election Commissioner, to introduce a new system of identity cards. When the embroiderer compared the sterilisation certificate with Seshan's new identity card, he was informing us that during the Emergency this small piece of card had acted as an essential passport to the basic amenities of every day life in a so called civic society.

We have already learned something of how sterilisations were extracted from the parents of children studying in government schools. Production of a sterilisation certificate had apparently become a prerequisite for all those who wanted to pass their examinations in Chameli Chand School in Old Delhi at least. Another kind of deal. In practice, the precise nature of the deal varied from school to school. Some teachers apparently refused to teach pupils whose parents had not been sterilised; others refused admission to children unless they could produce those magic cards. But schools were not alone in putting moral responsibility aside in the effort to fulfil sterilisation targets. As the embroiderer has suggested, hospitals were no better.

IRON MONGER
'During the Emergency I was working in Calcutta. I received a message saying that my wife was very ill and had been taken to hospital. So I immediately rushed back to Delhi, but by the time I reached the hospital they had already sterilised her. They gave me the certificate and said that the operation was compulsory for everybody.'

Had they asked her consent?

'No, she didn't even know that it had been done. She thought she had been operated for her illness.'

So who told her?

'They never told her. And how could I tell her when she was ill at the time? I waited until a month or so later and then told her.'

How did she feel?

'How would anyone feel if someone tortured them?'

It is, of course, possible that a tubectomy had been necessary for this woman's health, but it seems unlikely given the doctor's supposed explanation that sterilisation was compulsory for everybody. Others who tried to seek hospital treatment at the time lend weight to the view that such treatment had become conditional on the production of a sterilisation certificate—something also recorded by Dayal and Bose who documented Emergency abuses nearer the time.

MIDDLE-AGED WOMAN
'When you went for treatment, they asked you how many children you had. Suppose you said 'two', and then some neighbour came nearby, they would ask them in order to confirm the number. Later, they told you to bring your ration card to check the details again. If you had two or more children they told you that you could only get treatment after getting sterilised and showing the certificate.'

According to official policy the government deal was not sterilisation for treatment but sterilisation for free treatment. Officially, there was a third option: that of avoiding sterilisation by paying for hospital treatment. It is quite possible that many of the residents of Welcome would not have been able to afford to pay, but it is also possible that they were totally unaware of this third option. At any rate to them the deal has been remembered as a straightforward bargain through which treatment was purchasable only through sterilisation. This formula does not seem to have been limited to government run hospitals. According to one man, his expectant wife received similar treatment in a private nursing home:

'They would make people go for it [sterilisation] by delaying the delivery until they did. This happened to my wife. They delayed the delivery for three days...I took her there [to a private nursing home] because her condition was critical and it was easier to get quick treatment in a private clinic. For two days they were after me, trying to get me to go for the operation, so I told them I was ill. So then they made me sign a form and sterilised my wife.'

What did they get out of it?

'They could show the government how well the nursing home was working and could get some government recognition. My wife has never fully recovered. She still gets a problem with swelling.'

However, one should not assume from such accounts that the Emergency was unique in transforming the relationship between doctors and patients. The target-oriented focus of the family planning scheme was initiated long before the Emergency[3] and continued to function after it when women rather than men became the main 'target group.' One woman, after listening to her neighbour's description of Emergency abuses, suddenly interjected: 'You are talking about *then*. What about *now*? I was forced just four years back.' This woman's high-pitched voice and wide-open eyes spoke of indignation and contempt as she recounted her experience:

'I had gone to the hospital to deliver my daughter but when the time came they wouldn't admit me unless I agreed to get sterilised first. My family members were standing outside the hospital. The hospital staff went to them and told them to sign a paper. They asked *them*, not *me*. I was not even unwilling to have the operation. I said I would come back to have it after a few days. They said: "No one comes back after a few days. Sign now!" My husband signed. We had four children and wanted to do it anyway but it should not have been done like this. They don't consider anyone's feelings or circumstances. They just make them sign. Later I saw a nurse hit a woman because she wouldn't agree to the operation—and that was inside the hospital.'

Doctors, nurses and schoolteachers are by definition in a position

---

[3]Vicziany, 1982–3, 'Coercion in a Soft State'.

of power in relation to their patients and pupils. Like any relationship of power, it is open to abuse. Perhaps the only difference between now and then was that during the Emergency, abuse of power was not only sanctioned but actively encouraged by the extreme nature of the 'incentives' and 'disincentives' offered to those in positions of responsibility. Dayal and Bose record how, in government hospitals, 'staff set up their own motivation offices and their scouts roamed the dispensary and out-patient queues hunting for someone who looked remotely virile'.[4] Many seemed to perform their task with zeal, motivated by the fact that they could earn an extra two rupees with each person sterilised. Describing their activities a doctor from Hindu Rao Hospital is said to have told Dayal and Bose: 'These people have gone absolutely crazy. They have forgotten that they too have been placed under so many restrictions. They are busy hunting more victims.'

Of course some of the urban poor were 'eligible' for free hospital treatment during the Emergency because they had already been sterilised through their work, but for those who had escaped the sterilisation net, hospitals, schools and government offices were places to be avoided. What emerges in people's accounts is a sense of a shrinking environment as all civic institutions and public spaces in the city came to be perceived as places of danger:

AN EMBROIDERER
'You didn't even dare to sit in a park at that time for fear that they would pick you up under one pretence or another.'

A MOULDER
'The pressure was everywhere. The roads used to be empty during the daytime as there was fear of being picked up from the street.'

It is impossible to draw an ethnography of the fear that spread amongst the capital's poor, fed by a combination of rumour, reality, imagination and experience. We can only encounter fragments of that fear—in verbal reconstructions and on people's faces as they re-member their experiences. I take the liberty of 'reading' faces, separating out the ones who clearly love to exaggerate from the ones whose faces still bear the shadow of what seems to me 'genuine fear'. I also register gestures—in particular that horizontal slicing motion through

[4]Dayal and Bose, 1977, *For Reasons*, p. 135.

which those who dared not breathe the dreaded word none the less conveyed its meaning. I also try to relate the fear to the actual danger, recognising all the while that the fear was no less great even if and when the danger was imagined. I note, for example, that the embroiderer and moulder cited above both succeeded in avoiding sterilisation. I also note that none of the people we met spoke in the first person when they talked of people being lifted out of the parks and off the street. Putting together the collective experiences of different people in Welcome I deduce that direct physical force was probably extremely rare in Delhi where people were not so much captured as cornered into submitting themselves for the operation.

But although I cannot chart the ethnography of fear, I can nonetheless plot the progress of the danger as it spread from government offices to private enterprises and public institutions. Until August 1976, it seems to have been a danger which was primarily 'out there' in the public domain. By the beginning of September 1976, two things had changed. First, the DDA had launched its family planning centre allotment scheme and secondly it established special family planning motivation camps in different corners of the city including Welcome. With these two factors, the danger had moved not only to the neighbourhood but also to the doorstep. The state was making direct inroads into people's homes in the form of DDA officials who were moving about door to door in search of 'cases'. For some residents the only option seems to have been to run away. But to where?

FIRST MAN

'Many had [already] started running away, giving up their work. They were mostly casual labourers. They left the city for their villages. But the threat was in the villages too and many villagers ran to the cities trying to escape.'

SECOND MAN

'Yes, my brother-in-law escaped from his village [in U.P.] and came here.'

FIRST MAN

'Not long after the camp came to Welcome I went into hiding. My parents sent me away to stay with relatives. I was just 20 at the time and we were very scared that they might come and take me. We had heard that they sometimes even captured grooms from marriages. We were so scared that we couldn't even sleep at night.'

So where did you go?

'No place was safe at that time but I hid with my relatives in a *jhuggi* on the banks of the Jamuna, near the Central Power House. This wasn't safe either, so whenever people came, we would run towards the river and save ourselves by hiding behind the shrubs.'

When did you come back?

'I stayed there some 20 days, until they had closed the camp in Welcome.'

The right to a home

The arrival of a DDA officer on the doorstep had never been something to celebrate, even before the Emergency. It generally signified the need to pay money. How much and to whom depended on the circumstances and the officers concerned. Occasionally officers would come in search of the monthly licence fee to which the government was entitled. But this was rare. Just as the licence fee was set at a low rate, so the motivation for collecting seems to have been minimal. Even today it is common to find people who haven't paid their licence fee for over 20 years. The reason they give is that no one is ever interested in collecting it. From this we might surmise that when a DDA officer bothered to step outside his office he was generally in search of something a little more substantial.

A brief sidetrack to the Slum Department might clarify the issue. Rajinder had returned there one day in the hope of finding some information on local industries and found instead a new official willing to discuss illegalities:

SLUM DEPARTMENT OFFICIAL
'It is very easy to manipulate the laws here. It is so easy that whenever a law comes in your way, all you have to do is bribe the officer responsible or entrusted with protecting that particular law. Then all your obstacles are removed. Give money to a politician, the police or to us and you can do whatever you like—coolly and smoothly.'

When a Slum Department officer turned up on the door step it was generally because he was expecting, not an official payment but an unofficial payment in exchange for which he would agree to turn a blind eye to 'irregularities'. This would appear to be the system through which Slum Department officials posted in 'god-forsaken' spots like Welcome boosted their feeble incomes. It must have been a relatively lucrative pursuit since the rules governing resettlement colonies were so restrictive that the rate of irregularities was bound to be high. Quite apart from the rule stating that allottees were not allowed to sell, transfer, sub-let or vacate their plots under any circumstances (other than the death of the original allottee), there were also rules prohibiting the use of residential plots for commercial activities or for keeping livestock. Every allottee who had been granted a plot on a demolition basis had signed or thumb-printed a complexly worded affidavit agreeing to abide by these rules (whether or not they comprehended them). This meant that the range of 'irregularities' was varied and the rate was high.

By September 1976, Slum Department officials were no longer willing to accept their usual payoffs. They too 'were under pressure from above' and had been threatened with the withdrawal of their salaries if they did not accumulate sterilisation cases. Of course some cases came 'naturally' to them in the form of people who perceived the new DDA offer of plots as a good deal:

A VARK[5] MAKER FROM OLD DELHI
'I first came to know of the *nasbundi* thing from a person who was selling lottery tickets. He told me that I could get 85 rupees and a plot if I got myself sterilised. So I thought, why not? Who dislikes money?' [*Chuckles*]

The *vark* maker, who incidentally had nine children at the time and whose wife became pregnant for a tenth time *after* he had undergone the operation, was not the only person we met who had come forward for the operation of his own accord. There were a few families who had been living on rent in other colonies who saw the DDA's offer of a plot as a vital opportunity. There were also others who had got sterilised as a means of 'transferring to Welcome'—some, like the man from the cooler factory had done so under pressure; others of their own accord. Then there were the people with sufficient means to 'motivate' others of whom we shall learn more in the following chapter. They too were applying for plots. Welcome being one of the oldest resettlement colonies in Delhi, its location in the city was relatively 'desirable' compared to that of many other colonies. It was not as far out of town as some of the new colonies and was not quite as lacking in facilities as those which consisted of nothing

[5]Beaten silver film used in the preparation of sweetmeats.

but an empty field. But the DDA's scope for accumulating sterilisation cases in Welcome was limited by the same factors that made Welcome a desirable place. Being a relatively established colony, founded back in the 1960s Welcome had very little space for developing new plots. The south side of the colony was already choc-a-block with the semi-built up *jhuggis* of the first resettlers and the northern side was packed with people who had recently been dumped there under the new wave of slum clearance initiated in 1975. Meanwhile, the so-called recreation areas had been taken over by squatters who had built unauthorised *jhuggis* in the available space. All of this meant that if the DDA officers were to gather large numbers of sterilisation cases in Welcome, they had to accumulate them, not just from outsiders, but also from those already resident in the colony. As Slum Department files testify, they found their victims amongst those living in Welcome on an 'irregular' basis. This was the time when those who had succeeded in avoiding the sterilisation threat at work suddenly found that it had followed them home.

MIDDLE-AGED WOMAN
'My husband was working in Old Delhi Railway Station as a coolie and the pressure was on in the railway department. The officer in charge called a meeting and announced that he would not allow his employees to be sterilised since it would affect their ability to lift heavy loads. So my husband was spared. Then the pressure came on us here and since we had four children, we couldn't escape. Nayyar Sahib along with the *pradhan* told us if we didn't get sterilised or give a case then our homes would be demolished and we wouldn't be able to get [official] plots. If we wanted to save ourselves, we had to have the operation. So I decided that since my husband did heavy work, I would have to be the one to have the operation...I was very scared. I went there [to Lady Hardinge Hospital] with the idea that I would never come back. If my life could be saved, then well and good but suppose it couldn't?'

A FORMER RICKSHAW DRIVER
'They used to come round to your house and demand to see your allotment slip...They wanted to see if people were authorised occupants or not. If they were unauthorised then they threatened to throw them out of their homes unless they got sterilised or gave a case. Although I had an allotment slip we were also told we had to get sterilised.

On what grounds?

'To us they said: "Either get sterilised, give a case or pay damages! If not we will throw you out." We couldn't afford to pay for a case so my wife had to get sterilised.'

The damages to which he was referring went right back to 1960 when the government had conducted a census of squatters and decided to collect 'damages' from all those trespassing on government land. For many, the payment of damages had been a pre-requisite to resettlement in Welcome, but this man seemed to have slipped through the net—provisionally that is. In September 1976 his past misdemeanours or inconsistencies came back to haunt him in the form of the threat of sterilisation, the burden of which he transferred to his wife. The coolie's wife cited above had been in a different situation. She was not in possession of an allotment slip since she was living in an 'unauthorised *jhuggi*' rather than an allotted plot owing to the fact that, like the demolition man, she had had her home at Jamuna Bridge destroyed during the Indo-Pakistan war and had never been granted official papers. Others who faced the threat of sterilisation were purchasers and tenants who were living in official plots but were not identifiable as 'original allottees'. The desperate urge to retain their homes led to a number of practices which, though they contributed to sterilisation targets, did nothing to reduce the national birth rate:

A YOUNG MAN

'The pressure was everywhere. They were looking for one or other excuse. Those who didn't have slips were pressurised on that account; those who had not paid their rent were threatened on that account; those who had purchased plots were threatened on that account; those who had already had the operation had to have it again.'

What do you mean?

'My father had already had the operation some 15 years back but he had to go a second time to save his plot.'

Couldn't he have used his old certificate to save his plot?

'Had we shown that certificate then they would have forced us to give a second case because they had started saying you had to give two purchased cases to regularise a plot in our block. How could we have done that? Giving cases was very expensive. [*At this point the father comes out of his house and joins us sitting on the stone slab which covered the gutter in their gali and I ask him about his experience directly. He is mildly embarrassed but nonetheless willing to talk.*]

HIS FATHER
'There was a doctor of about your age examining me before the operation. She took one look and realised the situation immediately. I denied it giving the pretext that I had once fallen off a ladder and cut myself right there, but she said: "Don't give me your excuses. I'm a doctor and I know perfectly well that you have already been sterilised!" [*We all laugh*] But later she allowed me to go for it again. They just gave a cut in the right place and stitched it up then gave me the certificate...That is how I saved this plot.'

A COUPLE IN THE BUILT-UP TENEMENTS
Husband: 'People did it under compulsion. Naturally! What would you do if you were being evicted from your house?'

What about those without children?

Wife: 'Those people gave cases. They were asking four cases for a tenement. It was a lot of money...First we thought we would rather vacate the house but then we realised that it would make life impossible since we didn't have any place to live in. So then we decided we would have to go in for "self-sterilisation" to save the flat. The police had also started coming to the door.'

How did you decide which of you would have the operation?

Husband (smiling sheepishly): 'I had already got myself sterilised some years earlier so I couldn't go. There were quite a few women going for it so my wife went along with them.'

Wife: 'It was totally pointless since my husband was already sterilised, but what could we do?'

This last couple belong to the privileged minority in Welcome. They live in one of the 415 built-up tenements rather than one of the 4,009 official plots or the innumerable unauthorised *jhuggis* found in the Janata Colony area. The tenements had been built by the DDA for those displaced families who could afford to pay a regular rent on top of the license fee. Like elsewhere in the colony, some of the original allottees had sold up and left so it was the purchasers who faced the threat of sterilisation. A tenement flat consists of 37 square yards of space, usually divided into one square shaped room and a separate kitchen, bathroom and toilet. Though far from luxurious, these quarters represent the prime spot of the colony—not only because they are *pakka* (solid and permanent) DDA constructions in concrete but also because they are situated in the more sparsely populated part of the colony away from the 'masses' and to some extent protected by trees. In the 1970s this distinction would have been more marked than it is today since most people living in the plotted area had not yet been able to build *pakka* houses. It is no doubt for this reason that the price for regularising quarters in the tenement area seems to have been set high, at not one or two motivated cases, but four per apartment. The alternative, as the couple indicate, was one case of self-sterilisation regardless of its appropriateness to the family circumstances.

The accounts of those who got sterilised to save their homes reveal that the messengers of sterilisation were multiple and varied. The couple from the tenements talk in terms of the police pounding at the door. The rickshaw driver spoke of DDA officers, but when pressed further, said they were accompanied by local ruffian types from the colony. Meanwhile the coolie's wife described the threat as a direct message which came through K.K. Nayyar and the local *pradhan*. The fact is that the DDA officers were not alone when they went about the colony levering cases. Rather, they operated through existing informal networks which linked government officers, policemen, *pradhans* and their hangers on. Just as certain officers of the DDA customarily collected payments for irregularities in the colony, so the police regularly collected their due. It was therefore natural that the police should be the ones to back up the threat when the DDA was on the doorstep. As for the *pradhans*, they were the self-styled local leaders who had always acted as the linkmen between politicians, government officials and the people at a local level. For these informally elected 'big-men' the Emergency seems to have offered a good opportunity for proving themselves both to the government and to their supporters. It was a time for building and consolidating local networks and expanding spheres of influence as our encounter with the *pradhan* of QW2 block made clear.

The *pradhan* of QW2 was not entirely new to us when Rajinder and I finally met him. We had first encountered his activities in a letter in the file marked 'Pending cases' in the records room of the Slum Department. The letter, dated 26 April 1977, revealed that the people of QW2 had been living in unauthorised *jhuggis* in Welcome before the Emergency; that their homes had been demolished; that 42 out of the 70 families had furnished sterilisation certificates in order to obtain official plots, but that only 36 plots had been allocated. The *pradhan* was writing on behalf of the six families who had not been granted plots in spite of having all the relevant documents. A letter from a member of parliament, written on Lok Sabha paper, supporting the *pradhan*'s request bore witness to the fact that this man had connections in high places.

We next encountered him through the incidental references of people living in his block: the coolie's wife who referred to the *pradhan*'s close connection with 'Nayyar Sahib' by whom she meant the DDA executive officer, K.K. Nayyar, who had signed all the family planning allotment orders found in the files. From an MCD labourer we learned further details: that the *pradhan* went around first persuading people that their homes would be demolished if they didn't comply, then allocating numbers to those who agreed to have the operation and who went as called. The demolition man we had interviewed at the beginning of our research was also from this block where sterilisation had clearly been an organised activity and the man at the centre of it was undoubtedly the *pradhan*.

It was a dark evening when we finally got to meet him—a thickset burly man bristling with muscle. He was standing outside his home, a concrete multi-storey house, painted in what seemed an incongruous sugary pink. The house occupied two plots and was noticeably bigger and more luxurious than any other in the block. Bulging out of his white vest and checked blue *lungi* (waist cloth), the *pradhan* eyed us with undisguised hostility. He looked like a man who was used to getting his way by physical means. We humbled and ingratiated ourselves, stressing both our innocence and our ignorance, until he eventually agreed to talk. As we sat outside in the street, he demonstrated the nature of his authority—bellowing orders to his wife, blasting instructions to hangers on and threatening local children with a ferocious growl whenever they came too close. This was a man anxious to convey his power, if not his potential for violence.

Nonetheless, he agreed to give us a brief résumé of his career, combined with a potted history of the block since the two were indivisible. He told us how he had originally come to prominence with local people in the famous slum of Jamuna Bazaar; how in 1965, during the Indo-Pakistan war, their homes had been demolished and they had been shifted to Welcome. The government had promised them plots at the time but did not allocate the space officially since the country was in a state of external Emergency. The result was that people built themselves homes without having the official permission to do so—something the demolition man had already described. This meant that in 1976 their homes were targeted for demolition and they were told they could only get official plots by means of sterilisation. The *pradhan* was the man who had taken personal responsibility for persuading the people to get sterilised, thereby securing them the right to rebuild their houses in the same spot. In Slum Department terminology, these were cases of 'voluntary demolition'. This was the year in which he expanded his authority to cover four residential blocks in the colony. He spoke of the period as a difficult time but ultimately a good one:

Pradhan: 'The pressure was on all of us. We had to get sterilised in order to get the plots. No one was happy with that but no one had any choice either...Initially I had a lot of difficulty persuading people to get sterilised but then I told them that I myself had had the operation and that I had not suffered any problems, physical or otherwise. After that people gradually started following.

What do you think of such a scheme?

'It was a very good scheme. Poor people benefited a lot from it. They got relief and a plot. We used to live in *jhuggis* and now we live in proper houses.'

Tentatively we ask him about those people who had been sterilised but never received plots. He frowns and explains that there had only been space for 36 plots to be cut and that although he had tried to negotiate with the relevant officials on several occasions they had never ratified the outstanding cases. Undaunted, the *pradhan* ended his account with a reaffirmation of his power: 'If the government ever wants to start causing trouble [over this], they will have to seek my permission first.' Somehow, his threat did not sound empty. The *pradhan* has the power to mobilise human resources as his ability to galvanise people into sterilisation clearly showed.

Did local residents resent his role or did they admire it? It was difficult to tell. Certainly there were some who were quick to point out that the *pradhan* had had vested interests in the sterilisation drive. An MCD labourer, for example, suggested that the *pradhan* had been promised a car and that this was why he had been so keen to get other people sterilised. Others pointed out that the *pradhan* had been rewarded two plots for his work despite the fact that there were some families who had not yet been granted a single plot. At least one man felt that the *pradhan* could have resolved the problem if he had really made an effort since he was 'the one with all the connections around here'. We also managed to trace a woman whose husband had 'motivated' a case of sterilisation but who had never been granted an official plot. But her bitterness was more directed against the system than against the *pradhan* who had accompanied her to the Slum Department and apparently succeeded in gaining verbal reassurance from officials that they would not destroy her *jhuggi* again if she simply rebuilt it in the same place as before. All of the six families which had not got plots in spite of having sterilisation certificates had in fact remained in the immediate area under the protection of the *pradhan*. That his 'protection' only extended to those who had complied with the sterilisation drive is suggested by the fact that the remaining 28 families had all moved elsewhere. This highlights the ambiguous role that such local big men play in mediating between the people and the state. *Pradhans* have contacts and get things done but the means by which they attain their goals are often dubious and the fine line that exists between a *pradhan's* 'protection' and his 'threat' is something well recognised by his supporters.

Family and community negotiations

Once the government's forcible deal had entered individual homes there seemed to be no corner of life, no relationship exempt from the burgeoning threat of sterilisation. With the deal there came a series of choices, each unpleasant in its own way. Should a family try to 'obtain' or 'regularise' a plot by paying someone else to get sterilised or should it rather submit one of its own members to the operating table? Those who could not afford the former option had little choice but to settle for the latter. For them the option narrowed down to the question of who from amongst the various family members should shoulder the responsibility of sterilisation. We have already encountered a young man's memory of the fear he felt as a child when his father got sterilised in order that the boy should pass his exams. Later when we spoke to the young man's uncle (the father's brother—the father himself being dead) we learned that the father's primary motivation had been to obtain a plot in Welcome and that his son's exams had been only a secondary incentive to sterilisation. The family had been living near

Chandni Chowk in Shahjahanabad (Old Delhi) at the time and their inner-city rented room had been targeted for demolition. They had heard that plots were being offered for sterilisation in various colonies and chose Welcome because of its relative proximity to Old Delhi where the men of the family worked. Getting sterilised had been the means by which the head of the household had been able to secure a plot in Welcome, plus the added guarantee of his son's success in the forthcoming exams. Weighing up the alternatives—a plot even further out of Delhi or perhaps no plot at all plus his son's failed education— he had decided to come forward to accept the government's deal. Looking back, this family considers itself fortunate to have secured a plot in Welcome which, though far from luxurious, is less cramped than their previous rented accommodation in Shahjahanabad.

At one level, this story can be taken as a good example of how a false statistic comes into being. The same sterilisation case was registered in two different government departments, thereby counting as two cases in the national figures. But at another level this story lends insight into how the government's sterilisation deal was negotiated within individual families and how various family members perceived their responsibilities differently. The young man's account of how as a child he had tried to prevent his father from having the operation was particularly moving because it revealed how even children could be brought to feel the burden of responsibility for their parents' fate. The fact that the father would probably have had the operation regardless of his son's circumstances is irrelevant to the level of stress and anxiety experienced and remembered by the son. The point is that as the threat of sterilisation spread it planted tensions at the very heart of the family structure, engendering a whole range of feelings from guilt to remorse.

In some families, it was the men who came forward for the operation—sometimes because the alternatives were too painful—as in the case of the sock factory worker who had got sterilised to prevent his wife from being forced to abort. At other times, it was women who had the operation, either because their husbands were unwilling or, as in the case of the coolie's wife, because they wanted to preserve the strength of the family breadwinner. Sometimes the question of who should get sterilised was a matter of familial debate; at other times it was treated as a private matter of shame that could not even be shared with one's marital partner. Several women informed us that their husbands had got sterilised without informing them until after the event—something that is not all that surprising given that this is a culture where sexual relations are rarely openly discussed between marital partners. Not only were men easier to catch through the work place but also vasectomies were easier to perform than tubectomies. It is not therefore surprising to learn that 75 per cent of those sterilised during the Emergency were men.

Discussion or no discussion, sterilisation and its threat placed a pressure on marital relationships, not least because of the effects (real or imagined) that it was thought to have on the body. Whilst women's fear seems to have focused principally on the operation itself, men's fear was concentrated around the notion of lost virility and the idea that they would no longer be able satisfy their wives.

A MUSLIM MAN
'Initially the problem came up between husbands and wives as to who should go for the operation. Those wives who did not care for their husbands preferred their husbands to go. Those wives who loved their husbands went of their own accord...The sterilised man's wife has difficulty reaching orgasm.'

A HINDU MAN
'Women didn't want their husbands to be sterilised because they thought their husbands would be weakened and become impotent. If you cut a vein unnecessarily there are bound to be problems.'

A MUSLIM WOMAN
'To tell you the truth it's not quite the same after [the man has had] the operation.'

This feeling that sexual life could never be the same again was reinforced by the popular assertion that vasectomy metaphorically transformed men into women.

OLD WOMAN
'Women used to mock men who had been sterilised saying, "Look! Our men have been converted into women."'

YOUNG MAN
'A man is considered a woman after being sterilised. In fact, he becomes half-man and half-woman.'

This theme of emasculation seems to have featured in a number of popular rumours and jokes of the time. Hence many told us of the men who sat in the women's section of the bus and who, when asked to move, said 'We too have become women now'. So common was the association of vasectomy with castration that many actually referred to it by the term '*khassi*' (castration). Hence certain residential blocks in Welcome were sometimes referred to as 'castration blocks'. Later we learnt of the existence of an entire colony on the U.P. border where all the plots had been allocated on a vasectomy basis after the Emergency in the early 1980s. When we visited the colony, we found to our surprise that the place was commonly referred to as 'Castration Colony' not only by outsiders but also by its own inhabitants.

According to one man, the desire to avoid the horrors of 'castration' sometimes led to curious practices. It is not unlikely that the man was describing his own behaviour when he commented:

'There were some men who although they had not been sterilised pretended that they had in order to save themselves from being carted off for the operation. Then, in order to strengthen their claim, they began accusing their wives of infidelity if they got pregnant. They seemed to have got certificates from somewhere. I don't know where. They did it in order to save themselves. When people started accusing them of causing problems for their wives, they just claimed incomprehension.'

There was also the opposite problem of women getting pregnant after their husbands really had been sterilised. Statistics relating to the period reveal that the number of unsuccessful vasectomies was high— a fact which can be partly explained by the poor conditions and extreme pressure under which doctors were working at the time. According to the gossip of the day, such instances often led to accusations of adultery and sometimes to marital splits. However, we met only one old man who had personally experienced the problem of his wife conceiving a child after he had been operated. He had resolved the issue by interpreting the post-vasectomy conception not as a sign of his wife's infidelity but as a gift from Allah and as living proof that man cannot intervene in the affairs of God. The old man who recounted this was in fact embarrassed to admit that he had been sterilised, emphasising that it was against his religion and that for this reason he had always kept it secret from others in the colony.

That there was an added edge to the tensions surrounding the issue of sterilisation among Muslims is indisputable. The head *Imam* (cleric) of the Jama Masjid in Shahjahanabad had taken a vehement stance against sterilisation, instructing all Muslims to avoid it and denying them last rites if they underwent the operation. At the same time the government was particularly anxious to ensure the participation of Muslims precisely because of their generally negative attitude to family planning.

A MUSLIM MAN
'The *nasbandi* drive was originally directed at Muslims because they thought that Muslims had the largest number of children. But once it actually got going the pressure was on both communities. In fact in the end larger numbers of Hindus were sterilised than Muslims.'

ANOTHER MUSLIM MAN
'The pressure was equal on Hindus and Muslims, rich and poor alike. But the rich could get away with it by paying for cases. The pressure was hardest on Muslims because sterilisation was forbidden in their religion, and the *Imam* Sahib had already made an announcement concerning this. This meant that Muslims resisted more and so they started pressurising them more. Hindus felt less pressure because there were no religious objections for them so they could more easily be persuaded.'

It is no doubt the effects of these dual pressures from within the community and without that has resulted in the Muslim narrative being on average more extreme and divided than the Hindu narrative when it comes to discussion of the issues of force and choice, need and greed. Those Muslim families who had been shifted to Welcome from Dujana House gave a particularly violent account of innocent victims being dragged off the streets and sterilised under conditions of physical force—an account which coincided with and was not untainted by the post-Emergency narrative in which Ruksana Sultana's family planning camp at Dujana House had played an important role. However, when probed further, it became clear that the Dujana House families who had come to Welcome had actually been resettled four months before the opening of the clinic at Dujana House. In effect the timing of their resettlement meant that they had been able to escape family planning harassment at Dujana House and at the same time were able to avoid harassment from the DDA in Welcome since they had only just been allocated plots on a demolition basis and therefore had all the relevant official paperwork. Some of the men from Dujana House had, of course, like men everywhere been cornered into sterilisation to save their jobs but those women who had got sterilised seem to have done so for the financial incentives. One old woman, for example, spoke of how she had been persuaded into having the operation by Ruksana's workers whilst she was visiting relatives back in Dujana House some months after she had been allocated a plot in Welcome.

OLD MUSLIM WOMAN

'Let me tell you how I was forced...Initially we women were prevented from going for sterilisation by the men of the family who were immediately opposed to the idea. But then Ruksana's workers would come to the house when all the men were out. They tried to entice us by offering various things like money, blankets and ghee. We women got tempted by such offers and gave our names for sterilisation...I was promised a blanket and Rs 500, but all they actually gave me was Rs 70. I was forced.'

At the same time, some of the Muslims who had been able to avoid the operation were particularly severe in their criticism of those of the community who had got sterilised, accusing them of having gone purely out of greed. This meant that although the most brutal accounts of forced sterilisation generally came from Muslims, so too did the interpretations which placed most emphasis on choice and greed rather than force and need. These were moral assessments which left little concession to circumstance:

OLD MUSLIM MAN

'Every religion has its own strict rules, whether Muslim, Hindu or whatever, but it is ultimately up to the individual to choose his own path...Sterilisation is strictly prohibited in our religion, but in the end, it is up to the person to decide whether he wants to please Allah or himself. Many people got themselves sterilised or gave cases basically because they wanted to reap the benefits. And what did they get? [*He laughs sardonically*]—a kilo of ghee and Rs 125!'

ANOTHER OLD MUSLIM MAN

'Yes it is considered a very grave sin...The *Musla* says that whatever nature has to produce, it will, whether from the soil, the stomach or the sky. No one can interfere with that...But people will do anything out of greed...One of my friends suggested I should go for the operation since I had many children. But I refused to oblige and told him: 'I don't have any property so I don't have any fear of it being taken away. You are a rich man. So you can consider having the operation.'

MIDDLE-AGED MUSLIM MAN
'Sterilisation is against our religion, but some people even tried to outdo that. The argument they used was that the consumption of liquor is also prohibited in Islam but some people still drink. And these people drink of their own free will; no one forces them to do it. And that was also how it worked with sterilisation. You cannot prevent people going for it of their own free will...I would argue that the government can't force people in spite of the fact that it wants to contain the population. We argue that if god sends someone to this earth then he also arranges everything for him. Only government employees were actually forced. The rest were not.'

Towards an ethnography of the sterilised

What do the personal narratives of the sterilised add to our knowledge of the way the family planning drive operated in Delhi during the Emergency? Perhaps the most striking feature of their accounts is the total absence of reference to the question of whether or not they wanted more children. In all our conversations we never came across a single person who claimed to have got sterilised during the Emergency because they had wanted to curtail the growth of their family. In fact, sterilisation and family planning seem to have become entirely disconnected as if the latter were just an unfortunate by-product of the former.

On the other hand, the accounts of the sterilised rarely conform to the dramatic tales of physical force recorded in the post-Emergency narrative. The only individuals whose accounts coincided with this established version of the past came from Dujana House—a location saturated with the dominant narrative. In general, accounts of how the family planning scheme had operated in Welcome revealed that people had not in fact been rounded up in the streets and forced like cattle into camps. Rather, they had submitted their own bodies for sterilisation, not out of choice nor, on the whole, for financial incentives, but rather in order to gain or retain access to basic civic amenities such as work, housing, hospital treatment and education. For many of those at the bottom end of the socio-economic heap, life in Delhi without a sterilisation certificate became untenable, if not impossible.

Though less sensational than the post-Emergency narrative, the accounts of the sterilised are in many ways more chilling for they demonstrate the ease with which the threat of sterilisation was enforced through the routine structures of the state which played on existing hierarchies between employers and employees, doctors and patients, officials and residents, rich and poor. All public institutions theoretically designed for the benefit of the people had in the late monsoon months of 1976 functioned as little more than levers for gathering sterilisation cases. At the same time the threat spread well beyond the structures of the state as it was taken up by local opportunists like *pradhans* who perceived it as a means of self-aggrandisement. Caught between official and unofficial pressures, ordinary citizens had found themselves having to weigh up the drastic consequences of not getting sterilised against the relative benefits of doing so. Ultimately the pressure was reworked in such a way that it invaded basic relationships, igniting tensions between parents and children, husbands and wives, humans and gods. Within the Muslim community, it encouraged and exacerbated internal divisions as people split along moral grounds according to whether or not they had had the operation.

By demonstrating the extent to which the sterilisation drive entered everyday social relationships, the voices of the sterilised in Welcome may de-dramatise the Emergency[6] but they do nothing to diminish the coercive nature of the family planning programme. What they demonstrate is how the notions of force and choice did not so much contradict as reinforce each other. In effect what people faced were 'forced choices' in which they were proposed something which most were not in a position to refuse. A poor family threatened with the prospect of homelessness or unemployment was unlikely to reject the government's deal. And yet that deal was formulated in such a way that although most people felt they had no choice, few felt able to argue that they had been forced, for ultimately they retained a sense of how they themselves had participated in the deal in order to safeguard their own futures. In Slum Department terminology, these were the cases of 'self-sterilisation'—the ones who did not, and in many cases could not, take up the third option of avoiding sterilisation by 'motivating' someone else.

[6]The tales of amputation and literal castration that occur in Rohinton Mistry's novel are noticeably lacking. See Mistry, 1995, *A Fine Balance*.

7

THE VICTIMS TURNED AGENTS

'The time has come to explore the space which separates the victims from the persecutors...It is the grey zone, with ill-defined outlines which both separate and join the two camps...It possesses an incredibly complicated internal structure, and contains within itself enough to confuse our need to judge.' (Primo Levi, *The Drowned and the Saved*, London: Abacus, 1988 edn, pp. 25–6)

The voices of the sterilised have helped us read beyond the phrase, 'self-sterilisation', found in the Slum Department files. But they have done nothing to explain the other side of the equation, the so-called 'motivated cases'. Out of the 1,098 operations recorded by the DDA in Welcome, as many as 486 fitted this other category. Only in 11 cases did the motivator and motivated appear to come from the same family, suggesting that love, loyalty and shared interests may have been the motivating factor. If the peon's explanation was to be believed these were largely instances of families obtaining or regularising extra plots by motivating their own members. Usually it was juniors motivating seniors in which case young men and women could retain their fertility whilst at the same time securing a plot by persuading an older member of the family to have the operation. The older member (usually the father) would not have been able to register for self-sterilisation if he already had a plot registered in his name. The motivation system therefore provided a means by which families could pool together their resources and maximise their interests in land in Welcome. Like many other sterilisations performed during the Emergency, operations on these older generation of motivated people would not have had much effect on the national birth rate since they were probably nearing, or perhaps at the end, of their fertile life. But the Emergency was a time of targets; a time when government officers were anxious to accumulate numbers. What these numbers actually signified in demographic terms was not their concern.

The Slum Department peon had also given an explanation for the remaining motivated cases, the 475 instances which had not involved family members. Here, he suggested, the motivating factor had been, not loyalty but cash. How then did motivators set about finding people willing to accept sterilisation for cash? What were the terms of negotiation and techniques of persuasion they employed? An ethnography of the motivation structure is essential to our understanding of the Emergency for it reveals the process by which those at the bottom end of the socio-economic scale were brought into collaboration with the authorities at the top. By passing the burden of sterilisation on to others whilst avoiding the operation themselves, these motivators set in motion a process of co-victimisation whereby members of the main target group turned against each other as many chose to become agents of the state regime—hunting the streets and by-lanes of Delhi in search of victims whose sterilisation would enable the motivators to obtain or retain plots. Though initiated by the DDA, the motivation structure seems to have developed a logic of its own, functioning more in accordance with market forces than demographic imperatives. It is through the actions of the motivator that we can trace the process by which the DDA Family Planning Allotment Scheme ultimately degenerated into little more than a market for surgical infertility in which the infertile bodies of the poor became a currency through which other poor and less poor citizens purchased their right to live in the much-neglected margins of the capital.

Meeting the motivators in Welcome was no more difficult than meeting the sterilised. We never searched them out; nor indeed would we have recognised them had we so desired. There was nothing distinctive about them; their homes, jobs, incomes varied little from those of others in the colony. It was only through their conversation that their role as motivators surfaced and even then, they never used the term. Their terminology was altogether different from the official language of the Slum Department. They spoke not of 'motivating' people for sterilisation, but of 'purchasing' and 'giving' cases. This language is a reminder, if reminders are needed, that 'motivating' someone had nothing to do with convincing them of the benefits of family planning just as sterilisation had nothing to do with wanting a smaller family. Nor should it be assumed for a moment that those who underwent self-sterilisation would not have chosen this third option had they had the choice. Such a choice was simply never offered to the sweepers, peons, gardeners and electricians working in government departments who would have lost their jobs if they had not got sterilised themselves. It was only the DDA which offered this unique third option and it was only those capable of finding the money with which to pay someone else to get sterilised who were able to take it up. An old man seemed to voice the opinion of many when he stated, 'We would not have got sterilised ourselves if we had had the money to purchase cases.'

This is not to argue that the purchasers of cases were necessarily rich. The majority were themselves evicted slum dwellers trying to regularise or obtain a humble 25-square-yard plot. To purchase a case of sterilisation, they needed two things: a person (usually a man) willing to get sterilised and the money with which to pay him. The government was already offering a variety of sterilisation incentives from tins of ghee, radios and electric clocks to cash to the value of Rs 75–95. It was additional cash that the motivator offered. In this way the transaction could be of interest to both parties. We begin with the account of a retired rickshaw driver whose brother had purchased a plot in Welcome after failing to get one officially allocated following the demolition of his previous home in Jamuna Bazaar in 1967. During the Emergency, he had 'regularised' his unauthorised plot in Welcome by 'purchasing a case'.

RETIRED RICKSHAW DRIVER
'Although my brother had been living in Jamuna Bazaar before [the demolition], he was never given a plot here in Welcome. There were many others like him. On the one hand, there were people who genuinely deserved a plot; on the other hand, there were people who, by paying a bribe, had purchased demolition slips and got plots. That was the only document that gave you entitlement. Of course, this always happens. There is nothing new in it. People employ false means to get the benefits they don't deserve. This is what India is all about...So we also had to pay for a case in order to get this plot registered in our name. At that time people were demanding huge sums of money for the operation, but we were lucky. We found someone who already had seven children and who suggested his own name. We did not even have to persuade him; he readily agreed to give his own case

Left 'Nowadays we don't want so many children. Two boys and one girl are enough.'
Above 'This serves as our kitchen and our bathroom too ...'
Below 'The pipeline was put in some six years back but the water only comes for an hour in the morning.'

Left 'These plots are so narrow. But those who can afford it, keep on building up.' *Above* 'Some have managed to get more than one plot. Those houses are worth lakhs.' (Photos by Denis Vidal) *Below* 'They tried to burn only Muslim houses [in 1992], but in this area everyone is muddled up so no one could control the fire.'

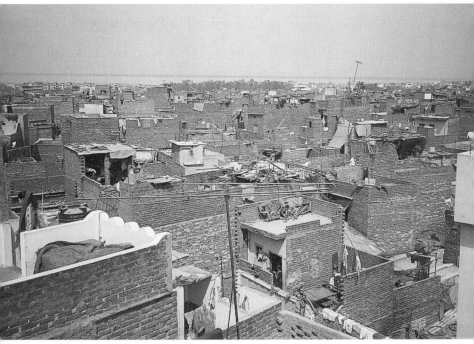

Left 'The wood market is run by Muslims. That is why it was burnt to ashes.' *Above* 'I don't feel safe living here any more. I am here on my own all day long.' *Below* 'A strong body is essential.' (Photos by Denis Vidal)

Above 'Nowadays we have many of our own community in this part of the colony.'
Below 'My party is called the Ali Sena [army]. We formed it as a
result of the demolition of the Babri Masjid...Our sole motive is to rebuild the
mosque in the place it stood before.' M.A. Chand, President of the Ali Sena.

Left 'For me both the Ali Sena and the Shiv Sena are the same. In my election campaign I argued, "Why are these two armies [*senas*] fighting here? Why not send them to the border if they are armies?"' Hasin Ahmed Pradhan.

Below 'The police have accused me of many things, but basically I am a social worker who lives among the people and knows their problems closely.' Cheena, *pradhan* of Janata Colony.

Left 'Some Delhi people came here and commissioned that statue of Ambedkar, but they never came to collect it and I have no room to store it on my plot.'

Left 'If you want cheap jeans then you can find them here in Welcome where they are made.' *Below left* 'Everything is made here; even the tailor's scissors.' *Below right* 'The municipality pays the sweepers but they just sit idle while the pigs do the work!'
Bottom 'Our colony is like a factory that keeps the city running.'

even though he had seen that we had no money to spend on purchasing cases. Out of sympathy, he did not demand anything but we gave him Rs 100; that was the maximum we could afford.'

To confirm the 'voluntary' nature of this man's offer, one would need to speak to him in person but the 'motivated' man is no longer around, leaving only the motivator to recount the story. The ease with which he and his brother had found someone for sterilisation contrasted strongly with the difficulty experienced by many others. An ironing man who found that his authorised 1960s plot had been regularised in the name of a squatter who had taken it by force during his absence, told us of the many difficulties he had faced in trying to find someone to motivate. Having three small children and full financial responsibility for his family, he was frightened of getting sterilised himself lest he should be weakened by the operation. On the other hand he needed a plot to replace the one that had been seized from him by force and regularised through sterilisation. Scanning the colony, he was, he claims, unable to find anyone willing to be motivated for less than one thousand rupees which was way beyond his meagre capacity (probably at least four times his monthly income). In the end he had been forced to abandon the search altogether and has been living on rent ever since whilst his original plot has remained in the hands of the impostor who had had a vasectomy in order to transfer the leasehold into his own name.

Both accounts lend insight into the underside of life in Welcome: people bribing officials for demolition slips; squatters getting sterilised in order to appropriate other people's property; men scouring the colony in search of others who might be willing to take their place on the operating table for some extra cash. That people in Welcome were as ready to exploit their neighbours as anyone else is suggested by the fact that those few merchants who were in a position to employ labourers in the colony had regularised their plots by getting their labourers sterilised. Whether these labourers were ever paid or whether, like the factory man from Old Delhi, they had 'given' their 'cases' under threat of dismissal is not clear. Yet again, it is only the motivator who remains to tell the tale.

According to most motivators' accounts, it was extremely difficult to find local people to 'motivate' in Welcome unless one already happened to have some sort of hold over them. Furthermore, it was awkward and embarrassing going about trying to entice one's neighbours to face a knife you yourself were trying to avoid. The fact that plots were also on offer on a self-sterilisation basis meant that most of those willing to get sterilised in Welcome did so in order to get a plot for themselves. Only a few residents who were more in need of money than land were willing to contemplate getting sterilised for money and even then, striking a bargain was no easy task.

There was, however, a simple way of avoiding the embarrassment of having to scour the colony in search of 'cases'. A much simpler and more common option was to obtain a potential candidate for sterilisation indirectly through a *dalal* (broker). Such *dalals* were easy to find since they hung around in droves outside the family planning camp, and sometimes even came door-to-door offering their services. They found their victims mainly from outside the colony amongst pavement-dwellers, beggars, unemployed men, wage-labourers and villagers who had come to the city. Once outside the vicinity they were in a good position to obtain cheap sterilisations and to sell them at competitive rates back in colonies like Welcome. For motivators, not only were the cases purchased through *dalals* as cheap if not cheaper than direct motivated cases, but they had the added advantage of reducing the human contact since all the arrangements and financial transactions were done by the *dalal* who was an experienced negotiator. All the motivator had to do was accompany the stranger to the hospital in order to ensure he did not escape or try to run off with the sterilisation certificate before it was registered in the motivator's name.

In order to comprehend the circumstances that led people to approach *dalals*, let us examine the predicament of a *kabadi* (second-hand/junk) wood merchant in the colony. He had been allocated a plot in 1972 after the demolition of his *jhuggi* in Matka Pir—an area which was cleared of slums to make way for the international trade-fair complex of Pragati Maidan. Since being shifted to Welcome he, like other wood merchants, had purchased a second plot, enabling him to live on one plot and trade on the other. During the Emergency, government officials accompanied by local *goondas* came to his door and presented him with an ultimatum: either he was to hand over the documents of purchase pertaining to his second plot, or else he was to get sterilised or 'give a case'. As a practising Muslim he considered sterilisation a sin against God and was also convinced of its negative effects on the body. This left him with two options: either he was to hand over his documents, thereby losing both the plot and the warehouse he had built on it, or else he could pay a *dalal* the sum of around Rs 500 in order for the latter to purchase a case on his behalf. Had he himself been faced with the direct task of finding a person for sterilisation, the *kabadiwala* may well have hesitated or perhaps even chosen to renounce his plot. But with a *dalal* to do all the intermediary work, it made sense to pay for a case and save his property. Like many other 'motivated' people, the *kabadi* man's victim was a villager who had fled to Delhi to escape sterilisation in his village.

THE *KABADIWALA*

'The person who got sterilised for me had escaped from a village called Mehwad [in Uttar Pradesh]. His buffaloes had been captured by the *patwari* and *amin* [land officers] with the help of the local police, and he was threatened that, if he didn't get sterilised, his land and house would be confiscated too. So he ran away from his village and came to Delhi thinking that if he had to get sterilised then he would rather do it here where the doctors were better and where he could earn some money for having the operation.'

Asked about the victim's age and whether he had children, the *kabadi* man answered: 'He was a young man…I think he must have had children, but I can't say for sure.' Then, with an ironic laugh, as if suddenly struck by the brutality of his own vagueness, he added: 'You only thought of yourself at that time!' The money he had paid went directly into the hands of the *dalal*, and the *kabadi* man never knew how much of it was seen by the person who got sterilised. Neither did he need to think too much about it. The victim had disappeared out of his life on the same day he had entered it, and the *kabadi* man did not have to see or hear of him again. There are many people in Welcome who, like the *kabadi* man, accepted the services of *dalals* either to save their purchased or rented plots or to obtain a plot to replace their demolished *jhuggis*.

However, if the victims of the sterilisation trade were often strangers, so too were the *dalals* who had entered the business to make a fast buck and who showed no particular fidelity to their clients. An auto-mechanic's account of how both the motivated person and the *dalal* had tried to trick him reveals the perils of entering this new trade:

AUTO-MECHANIC

'In my family nobody was in a position to go for the operation so obviously we had no choice but to look for a case outside. To do that we caught hold of a *dalal* and gave him Rs 400 for his services. He brought a person from a place called Fuaara in Old Delhi. They [*dalals*] could easily find such people either outside the railway station or at Kaudia Pul. Everything was finalised—the papers were prepared and we took the man to Lady Hardinge Hospital where he was to be operated. But whilst examining him, the doctor discovered that he had already been sterilised and outrightly refused to operate. By this stage we also came to know of it and we protested to the *dalal*. He was apologetic, but only on the surface. In fact, he had known about it all along and had just been trying to trick us. He then took us along with him to Fuaara to find another person. At least, that was the pretext. Actually he was trying to get rid of us. His intentions were clear enough to us by then so we demanded our money back. Coincidentally, a man from the navy happened to overhear our dispute and agreed to give his own case. He came back to our house and stayed the night. The next day we went through the whole process of registration again and then took him to the hospital. The moment he came out of the operating theatre, he was swarmed by a whole gang of *dalals* making offer after offer of more and more cash. But he ignored the lot of them and came straight back to us. He handed us the certificate without even asking for money, although he himself was in great need.'

Asked why he had agreed to have the operation, the mechanic replied:

'We later found out that he had been dismissed from the navy and was unemployed. So maybe it was the need for money that drove him. He was so honest and modest that he did not even have the courage to ask for money directly. When we insisted that he should state his price, he hesitatingly said he would leave the decision to us, pleading that we should not pay more than our capacity. As it was, we couldn't afford to give him much since we weren't any better off than him. However, we did give him some money along with dried fruits and ghee. He stayed with us for a few more days and then left. When he was leaving, we told him that from now on he was like a member of our family and that he could come here any time in his life. But he never came.'

There is something disconcerting in this man's attempt to humanise what was ultimately a cruel financial transaction by stressing the heroic nature of the victim and by describing his own attempts to incorporate the unemployed navy man into his family despite having just denied him the right to produce a family of his own. There are also many questions left unanswered in such accounts. Why had the ex-navy man been dismissed? Might he perhaps have been under threat of sterilisation in the navy? Had he merely chanced upon the motivator or had he deliberately hung around in an area, known to be a hunting ground for sterilisation cases? Had he agreed to get sterilised out of sheer financial desperation, in which case why had he seemed so reluctant to state his price? Or had he reasoned that by possessing proof of sterilisation, he might be able to use his certificate to get other benefits, for the DDA only required the registration and sterilisation number of the 'motivated' person, not the actual certificate. This might explain why the villager from Mehwad had apparently come to Delhi with the specific aim of having the operation there. That way he could not avoid the inevitable but he could at least get some financial benefit from it, returning to his village not only with a sterilisation certificate but also with a little extra cash. How much, we do not know, for the *kabadi* merchant had paid the *dalal*, not the villager.

It is through these accounts that we enter a space where the desperate meet the desperate, where human fertility has been reduced to a bargaining point and where one poor person purchases his right to live in Delhi by denying the other the right to reproduce. It is the grey zone, described by Primo Levi as a space with ill-defined outlines which both separate and join the victims from the persecutors.[1] Where does victimhood end and persecution begin within an overall structure of coercion? How can different interests be disentangled, when, two decades later, only one set of actors remains to tell the tale? And yet there is one figure who seems both to feed off that greyness and to reproduce it, who not only inhabits the intermediary space but who makes his profit out of blurring the point of intersection where the two camps meet. He is the *dalal*—only too willing to ease the process by which a painful imperative became a lucrative trade.

By finding candidates for sterilisation and delivering them directly to the doorsteps of motivators, *dalals* effectively reduced the contact

[1]Levi, 1988 edn, *The Drowned and the Saved*.

between the two. But there was still that awkward moment when the motivator had to meet the motivated and accompany the latter to the hospital, a moment when the boundary separating the victim from the persecutor had to be acknowledged. Whether dried fruits and ghee could ever disguise the cruelty of that moment remains debatable in a culture where fertility was, and still is, highly valued and where the very concept of family planning was alien to most of the people entering this new trade. The fact that motivators are still able to recall the details of those who, more than 20 years earlier, had 'given their cases', suggests that they were not entirely oblivious to the plight of the motivated.

But some *dalals* developed a solution to the problem of the potential awkwardness of this relationship. By obtaining sterilisation certificates directly from the sterilised and selling them in the open market, they succeeded in eliminating the contact between the motivator and the motivated altogether. In this way, awkward factors such as the age, identity and circumstances of the sterilised person were reduced to nothing more than a few details on a slip of paper. Motivators no longer needed to worry whether their victims were married or unmarried, willing or forced; they were simply purchasing pieces of paper for which they would bargain as best they could. This left *dalals* free to obtain the valuable certificates by whatever means possible. The elimination of the human element was therefore liberating both for the motivator and for the *dalal*, making the sterilisation certificate just one more commodity on the black market. At the same time, it deprived the sterilised person of what had become a vital document through which he or she might have gained access to land, loans, hospital treatment, school admissions and so forth.

Like all black market products, sterilisation certificates had clandestine histories. These were sometimes cruel and violent tales, involving whole chains of collaborators through which the plight of the victim became directly linked to the profit of others. To learn more of these networks we return to the account of the sterilised factory worker who has already informed us of how, during the Emergency, he had lost his job in Old Delhi for failing to hand over his sterilisation certificate to his employer who had wanted to use it to secure a factory licence. From the sterilised man's account of the practices prevalent at the time, we can better understand why he had been so reluctant to part with his own certificate.

DISMISSED FACTORY WORKER

'It happened like this; the shopkeepers would give information to the police concerning local labourers, telling them who were the ones who were homeless or slept outside in the streets since these were the easiest targets. The police would then arrest these people and keep them in the police station over night. The next day, the shopkeepers would go to the station and offer to bail the labourers out if they agreed to get sterilised. Once there, it was not difficult to make them get sterilised since they wanted to escape from the police and were frightened of going to jail...For every 40 cases bailed out by the shopkeepers, the police could keep 10 sterilisation slips for themselves.'

Obviously victims trapped in such tenacious sterilisation networks were not in a position to ask for money. Rather, they had to be grateful to the shopkeepers for bailing them out. Meanwhile their certificates were siphoned off, entering local markets where they were purchased by *dalal*s who sold them to individual clients. Divorced of the circumstances under which they were obtained, these certificates appeared to their purchasers, not as evidence of blackmail but as passports to security in the struggle over DDA plots. Concentrating more on their own plight than on that of the people they 'motivated', these purchasers were apt to believe the *dalals* when the latter told them the certificates had been obtained without any use of force.

Whilst it is easy to be critical of the position of the purchaser, it must also be recognised that such purchasers, trapped at the intersection between family planning and housing policies, were often in desperate positions themselves.[2] Take for example the DESU worker who managed to escape sterilisation at work on the grounds that he had only one child, but who then found his *jhuggi* demolished only to learn that he could not get a new plot without producing a sterilisation certificate. Technically a couple with only one child was 'eligible' for a DDA plot without a certificate, but since priority always went to

[2]By focusing on the dilemmas of the urban poor, I do not wish to imply that the process of co-victimisation was specific to them. Rather, I would argue that it characterised the structure of the family planning policy in general. Teachers, for example, were told to produce five sterilisation certificates and threatened with the withdrawal of their salaries if they failed to comply. Many motivated their pupils' parents with reluctance, whilst others purchased certificates from *dalals*. They too were co-victims of the system, but for those with neither power, education, money nor influence, the situation was inevitably harsher.

people with certificates, those without (which included the childless, some widows, the aged and people with only one or two children) stood little chance. For this reason quite a number of people who produced 'motivated' cases rather than self-sterilisations in Welcome were those with less than three children. Feeling themselves unable to have the operation on the grounds that they desperately wanted more children, they considered themselves obliged to purchase cases. A notable example is that of a young woman labourer who was working on a building site and living on rent in a *jhuggi* at the time of the Emergency. Despite being only 17 and having only one child, she had initially decided to get sterilised herself in a desperate attempt to save her family from the burden of paying rent. But her husband and mother had forbidden her to have the operation and even pulled her out of a government jeep that was heading for the hospital. Poor though they were, they decided that their only option if they wanted a plot was to motivate others. When they contacted a relevant official, they were told to produce five sterilisation certificates, a figure which was later reduced to three. In the desperation of the moment, the couple's attention was focused more on how to raise the money than on whose certificates to purchase. Selling all her wedding jewellery the woman was able to raise enough to purchase three cases for the cheap price of Rs 150 each. After much difficulty, including sexual harassment from a dubious agent, she was able to register her cases and obtain a plot. Speaking nearly 20 years later, the couple are adamant that there was no force used in the family planning programme in Delhi (even though they claimed that one of their own relatives had died following the operation in U.P.). They claim that the people who got sterilised and sold their certificates to *dalals* did so because they wanted the monetary benefits. This may be true of some of the 'motivated', but in this particular instance the couple had paid only Rs 150 per case to the *dalal*. One wonders, then, what possible benefits the victims could have enjoyed. Perhaps they got only the official Rs 75–90, or an electric clock, or some ghee from the government. Or perhaps, like the labourers duped by the police and shopkeepers in Old Delhi, they did not receive even this. The point is that when people purchased sterilisation certificates in the open market, they did not know the history of the 'motivated' and it is no doubt this very ignorance that enabled them to ignore the more sordid aspects of the trade. Some even inverted their potential guilt by turning against the invisible victims, accusing the latter of abnormal levels of greed. Such reasoning left some motivators free to look back on the Emergency as a positive time of opportunity for all. The woman above even stated that she wished another such opportunity would arise so that other poor *jhuggi* dwellers and homeless people could obtain a plot, although she did qualify her statement by saying that the sterilisation should not be forced.

The functioning of the market

How is it that the cost of sterilisation certificates seems to have varied so dramatically with some people claiming to have paid as little as Rs 100 per case; others as much as Rs 1,000 and the vast majority somewhere around Rs 400? Time has intervened to make it impossible to gauge the accuracy of these figures. Being black-market transactions they were never officially recorded and do not appear in the Slum Department records any more than they appear in the family planning literature. Post-Emergency political exposés speak in terms of tiny sums of Rs 2 being paid to family planning 'touts' who earned a living out of motivating large numbers of people outside hospitals and camps. The *dalals* in the narratives cited by the residents of Welcome clearly earned considerably more than this. The fact that so many residents independently quoted the same figure (around Rs 400 for a case) suggests that either this really was the price or else that this is today's equivalent of it in terms of relative value. In the mid-1970s low-level government employees were, according to Slum Department files, earning between Rs 100 and 400 per month, with the majority earning around Rs 200. This would have meant that if they had to pay a *dalal* Rs 400 for a case, they were paying the equivalent of two months' salary. This seems a huge amount for people living on or near the bread line. Today people in equivalent jobs earn around Rs 1,000 per month. It may well be that when people said they had paid a *dalal* Rs 400, they were trying to tell us that certificates cost the equivalent of half a month's salary.

Whatever the actual amount, there were clearly fluctuations in the market which seemed to rise and fall according to the ease with which *dalals* could obtain certificates; the number of cases required per plot; the number of plots available from the DDA at a given time and whether the *dalal's* profit was made on the proportion of cases per plot turned over to the DDA or on the sale of a single case to a client. The price also seems to have depended on the victim's willingness to sell and the purchaser's capacity to buy. Since some victims came more expensively than others, the *dalals* may well have sold the most expensive certificates to the wealthier purchasers whilst reserving the certificates they had obtained for nothing for their poorer clients. There must also have been some forged certificates in circulation, although it is difficult to know their proportion and number. One of the post-Emergency authors recalls the arrest of a gang of forgers in Delhi who claimed they had recently switched from forging university certificates to forging sterilisation certificates.[3] But it must also be remembered that the Emergency was a time when policing was at its strictest and a culture of fear made people scared to be caught on the wrong side of the law. Certainly, of all the people we interviewed in Welcome, none confessed any knowledge of the trade and only one person ever mentioned someone having obtained what he thought must have been a false certificate. This apparent 'ignorance' of the market for forged certificates could perhaps be partly explained by the fact that since motivators were anxious to secure legitimate rights to land through the certificates they purchased, it was in their best interests to assume that they were genuine. On the other hand, we found that people in Welcome were usually extremely open about discussing all manner of irregularities from illegal electricity connections to bribes to the police. Perhaps a more plausible explanation is that the people of Welcome had little reason to suppose that certificates might be forged since they were surrounded by cold-blooded evidence of the reality of sterilisation. Some motivators, as we have seen, had accompanied their victims to the hospital in person; many in the colony had been sterilised themselves and probably most residents of Welcome had close relatives who had faced the knife. Sterilisation for such people was not a matter of rumour and forged certificates but a cold fact of everyday life.[4]

[3]Vinod Mehta, 1978, *The Sanjay Story*, Bombay: Jaico Publishing House, pp. 123–4.
    [4]There is an interesting discrepancy here between the attitudes of the poor and those of the educated middle classes. The latter, when discussing this issue, tend to place emphasis both on the production of forged certificates and on the trumped up nature of figures quoted for sterilisation achievements. The most plausible explanation for this discrepancy is that it was the educated classes and, in particular, high and

Another element that influenced the price of certificates was the decreasing availability of people to be sterilised. As one man put it: 'As time went on it became more and more difficult to find people who had not already been sterilised. So the rate increased and some people paid up to Rs 1,000–1,200 for a case. Before that the price had depended on how easily the people could be persuaded. Now it depended on how difficult it was to find someone still eligible for the operation.' All of these factors help to explain why some residents in Welcome seem to have paid considerably less than others, but they do not explain why some residents gave two or three cases for a single plot whilst others gave only one.

Three factors seem to have been influential here: timing, the nature and location of the plot and the identity of the motivator. As far as timing was concerned, plots got increasingly difficult to obtain once the number of people applying began to exceed the amount of space left available. As we have already learned, Welcome was by no means the worst placed of Delhi's resettlement colonies, many of which were situated further out of the city and some of which were located in flood-prone areas. Also, being an older colony, it was more developed than those colonies which had sprung up from scratch during the Emergency itself. All of this meant that Welcome was pretty desirable as resettlement colonies went with the result that the DDA was inundated with requests for plots. According to Slum Department files, there were at least one hundred people who failed to get plots even after having submitted the relevant sterilisation papers. With such a rush on plots, it seems plausible that the DDA should have raised the premium as time went on.

That location was also relevant is suggested by the fact that the number of cases required per plot seemed to vary partly in relation to where a plot was situated and what it was perceived to be worth. In Welcome there were various types of DDA land: the 25-square-

---

middle-ranking government servants including doctors and teachers who relied on purchasing forged certificates and who had access to the forgers who were probably mainly located within government institutions. One disturbing consequence of the elite emphasis on corrupt practices in family planning during the Emergency is the implication that not that many people actually were sterilised. This notion is blatantly false as the experiences of the people of Welcome show. If reproductive rates did not decrease as much as expected after the Emergency, this was partly due to the fact that many of the people sterilised were those reaching the end of their fertile life.

yard residential plot, the 12-square-yard shop plot, the 60-square-yard commercial plot (unique to the scrap iron market) and the 40-square-yard built-up tenement. The advantage of having a tenement lay not just in its size but also in the fact that it consisted of a building rather than simply a piece of land. It is therefore not surprising to discover that the price of regularising a tenement was usually higher than that of regularising a plot. According to Slum Department files, residents of the built up tenements generally paid between three and five cases to regularise their positions. Next in value were the 60-square-yard commercial plots which had been allocated to the *kabadi* iron merchants who, as we shall later find out, were asked to give three cases per plot. Finally, there were the 25-square-yard residential plots where one sterilisation case was normally enough to regularise one plot, although in some cases officials seem to have raised the premium.

More difficult to assess is the extent to which the cost of a plot varied in relation to the identity of the applicant. Examining the personal files in Welcome, it appears that a high proportion of the givers of two or three cases were either young couples with one, two or no children or else they were Muslims (occasionally they were both). What childless couples and Muslims shared in common was their violent opposition to self-sterilisation, the former on reproductive grounds and the latter on religious grounds. This raises the possibility that the DDA and/or individual officers within it were deliberately exploiting the reluctance of these groups to get sterilised by using them as agents to extract the maximum number of certificates from others. If such a hypothesis were true, it would certainly help to explain why the labourer who had only one child and her neighbour, who was childless, were both expected to produce three cases for a simple 25-square-yard plot. It would also suggest another possible explanation as to why so many motivated cases were extracted in the *kabadi* markets for iron and wood. What the two markets had in common was not the size of their plots, but the fact that they were both run entirely by Muslims, most of whom were vehemently opposed to getting sterilised. This probably made them a particularly good target for extracting motivated cases from others.

How officials justified their extraction of extra cases varied according to context. In some instances they simply claimed that the cost of a plot was high from the start. The Hindu labourer and her neighbour cited above had initially been told to produce five certificates until the number was later reduced to three. Since they were from outside the colony, they did not know that others had obtained plots with only one certificate. While the former had to sell her jewellery to raise the money, the latter, who had no jewellery, had to resort to selling every cooking vessel she possessed. Their accounts seem to suggest that a person's wealth was not the criterion for establishing the number of cases they had to give. In other instances, the DDA officials would begin by demanding one case but later raise the demands to two or three by producing some convenient excuse. This was the technique employed in the wood market. In situations where a wood merchant produced a sterilisation certificate by motivating his craftsman, he would be told by intermediaries that only sterilisations within the family could be accepted. But in situations where a family member did get sterilised, the merchant was sometimes informed that his first certificate had been mislaid and he would have to produce another. How many of these extra certificates went into the pockets of *dalals* and how many were used for official purposes is not clear but at least nine files concerning plots in the wood market contain evidence of two motivated cases submitted per plot.

The accumulation of cases through the scrap iron merchants was even more systematic and excessive—partly no doubt because these were larger plots. Unlike the wood merchants, the scrap iron merchants were trying to enter the colony for the first time owing to the fact that their existing *kabadi* market on GT Road was due for demolition. The fact that the existing market of 30 shops had been authorised by the DDA gave the merchants the bargaining the power to negotiate for 50-square-yard plots in Welcome. Initially they were told that allotment slips would be issued at the time of demolition, but as time went on, the executive officer, K.K. Nayyar, told them it was impossible to allocate the plots without their producing one sterilisation certificate per plot. This was agreed to by the *pradhan* of the Market Association who took personal responsibility for finding the cases. Taking on the role of *dalal*, it was he, accompanied by 'assistants', who scanned the streets and railway stations at night in search of possible candidates for sterilisation. When he found them, he brought them back to the traders, each of whom paid to have a case registered in his name. But by the time they had accompanied 30 men to the hospital for sterilisation, the DDA premium had increased. The *pradhan* recalled: 'At first they demanded 30 cases. But then they kept on increasing the amount.

When we gave 30 cases, they said: 'What are 30 cases?' That's nothing! Give us 30 more! And when we gave them 60 cases, they said, we want another 30!' The *pradhan* laughed heartily as he recalled the tale. The DDA executive officer had justified these demands on the grounds that his superiors were trying to get the market moved to a less convenient location. Only by producing more certificates could the *kabadi* merchants be shifted to Welcome which was the colony they most favoured. Just what personal rewards the *pradhan* reaped from organising the 90 sterilisations is not clear but it is certain that, like the *pradhan* of QW2, he would have benefited for his labours.

By trying to extract the maximum density of cases out of Muslims, the government was, it seems, hoping to compensate for the general reluctance of Muslims to participate in the family planning scheme. The fact that the head *Imam* of the Jama Masjid had announced the denial of last rites to all Muslims who got sterilised had boosted the common Islamic view that sterilisation was a sin against god. Trapped between threats from the government if they did not get sterilised and threats from their own religious leaders if they did, Muslims were presented with a particularly difficult dilemma. Giving a motivated case, though also considered a sin by some, was the only way of minimising potential losses on both sides. Where cases were found from outside the community this at least saved Muslims from having to lead their own people down the path of sin. But at times the government did not even allow this option, specifying instead that only Muslim sterilisation certificates would be accepted from Muslim applicants. This had the effect of inviting people, not only to turn against their own religious doctrine, but also against their community in the struggle for survival. A Muslim toolmaker found himself faced with just such an invitation when the government demolished his shop near the Jama Masjid and allocated him a commercial plot in Welcome. Since his home was still in Old Delhi and most other toolmakers were obtaining plots in the newly constructed Meena Bazaar near the Jama Masjid in Shahjahanabad, this toolmaker tried to get a transfer. But a senior government officer told him he could only transfer if he produced ten cases and not just any old cases:

TOOLMAKER
'He told me: "Give me Muslim cases! I don't want any purchased cases from you; I want only the cases of your own close relatives." I

continued to say that I didn't have any possible relatives, but he was very stern. He said, "I just want an answer, Yes or no."'

Unable to promise to betray his own relatives into committing the sin of sterilisation, and unwilling to get sterilised himself, the toolmaker had to resign himself to remaining in Welcome. His plight seems to confirm the notion that it was a combination of identity and location that affected the number of sterilisations demanded per plot. A commercial plot in the heart of Shahjahanabad was worth far more sterilisation cases than the average plot in a peripheral resettlement colony like Welcome, and when the person demanding the plot was Muslim, the price was likely to be even higher.

There were, however, plenty of Muslims who were willing to impose the operation on other poorer members of their community and Muslims in Welcome were often quick to condemn those 'traitors' who had done 'anti-religious work' in order to reap the benefits. Ruksana Sultana's infamous family planning camp at Dujana House had after all been run by Muslims and there had been no absence of local *goondas* ready to assist her. Similarly the *pradhan* of the iron market had been responsible for finding some 90 people for sterilisation, most of whom he claims were Muslim villagers. A brief extract from our conversation with him demonstrates both his awareness of their fear and his ultimate lack of concern:

PRADHAN
'Most of them [the people we got sterilised] came from a village in the Muzaffarnagar area where people were being forced into sterilisation by the police. They were very scared and used to hide in the sugarcane fields and forests. Some had even stayed there for many days, living just on sugarcane since they didn't dare to return to their village. After some time they came to learn that the operations were also taking place in Delhi and that people there were paid for having the operation and that the doctors were better. So many ran away and came to Delhi. We used to catch such types in the railway station at night. We would bring them back, pay them, give them food, and then take them the next day to Lady Hardinge Hospital for the operation...Since I was the President of the Iron Traders Association, it was up to me to find all the cases and make sure that the traders got their shops.'

How long did it take?

'It took a full two or three months. It was a very difficult task. You might only find two people a night. Some of course would take themselves to hospitals directly. Then there were so many people hanging about the station looking for cases at that time...We had to pay between Rs 400 and 700 per case.'

Wasn't that a lot of money?

'Some said, "What is Rs 400? We wouldn't even go if you offered me Rs 4,000." Muslims especially thought like that.'

So were they mainly Hindu people you paid?

'No. They were mainly Muslims because Muzaffarnagar is mainly a Muslim area. They were trying to avoid having the operation there because of the risks.'

Did you ever contemplate having the operation yourself?

No...In our religion its considered a sin to disturb nature. God will send whatever number of children he has to send...'

Asked his opinion about the implementation of the family planning scheme as a whole, the *pradhan* concluded: 'Had force not been used it would have been impossible to make that programme successful because people were not willing to go for it of their own accord. So the government had no choice but to use force.' Like the *pradhan* of QW2, he had been reluctant to speak to us at first but had ended up getting carried away by memories which seemed to invoke, not guilt but a sense of pride in his own power and efficiency at organising so many cases. Recounting his exploits to an anthropologist in front of a motley band of local courtiers seemed to prove a good opportunity for demonstrating his importance and authority as *pradhan*.

These last examples raise the question of whether the family planning policy developed into a vehicle for systematic religious discrimination against what was already a minority—an accusation which was often raised in the literature published immediately after the Emergency. However, as we have already seen, Muslims in Welcome do not on the whole subscribe to such an interpretation.[5] They

[5]This is perhaps surprising given the communalist nature of many interpretations of the past in contemporary north India. Patricia Jeffrey, who has worked extensively

acknowledge that the pressure was on every poor man to get sterilised at the time and that if the pressure was greatest on Muslims this was only because their resistance was greatest—something of which most Muslims are proud. Ironically, it is young scheduled caste men who are the most prone to perceive the Emergency as a time of religious discrimination, arguing that it was Hindus who were discriminated against since Muslims refused to get sterilised. This is an interpretation buttressed by right wing Hindu organisations such as the BJP and Shiv Sena which encourage the view that the Hindu majority is under threat from the Muslim minority.

Most of the accounts we have heard so far have involved people trapped at the point of intersection between two uncompromising government schemes. They participated in the family planning scheme in order to lessen the crushing impact of the DDA scheme which threatened them either with eviction or homelessness. Such people can be identified as victims who, driven by circumstances, took on the role of agent of the state, perpetuating the family planning policy in their attempts to avoid its impact on their own lives. However conversations with local residents also revealed that there were some whose motivations were clearly more opportunistic than this formula implies. Instead of stopping short at using the family planning scheme to alleviate the effects of DDA policies, some appear to have gone one step further and used the scheme as a convenient means of accumulating plots. In the process, they reversed their victimhood entirely and converted family planning objectives into an instrument with which to maximise their chances with the DDA. One such category of people were those *jhuggi* dwellers who, after obtaining plots through self-sterilisation, sold the plots and returned to settle in *jhuggis*, knowing that the DDA would demolish their *jhuggis* a second time, thereby enabling them to obtain another plot in a different colony. Having already got sterilised themselves they would take the opportunity of giving a motivated case second time round. This was not difficult since they had cash available from the sale of their original plots and were still able to retain some profit after purchasing a sterilisation certificate. The immense scale of DDA demolitions made it impossible

---

in U.P., informs me that there is a tendency for Muslims there to link Partition, sterilisation and the destruction of the Babri Masjid into a narrative sequence demonstrating the persistent persecution of the Muslim community.

for officials in different colonies to monitor the thousands of names filling their files, so such cases generally went unnoticed. Although no one likes to openly confess to having adopted this strategy, there are many in the colony who claim to have witnessed it first hand. The frequency with which such behaviour is described suggests that it was not uncommon. One man estimates that at least a quarter of the inhabitants of his particular block sold their plots and returned to *jhuggis*, many during the Emergency period.

For those with greater wealth and ambition, the sterilisation drive seems to have been converted into little more than a cheap means of accumulating land, as one mechanic explained: 'Wealthy people wanted to give more and more cases because they found they could get extra plots from the DDA for less than Rs 1,000 and the value of a plot was much higher than the cost of getting someone sterilised.' Far from preventing such transactions, certain DDA officers seem to have helped make the arrangements 'because they too would get money from the deal' as well as filling their sterilisation quotas. The whole thing was done in such a way that the DDA records remained consistent with the rules. The entrepreneurs and property developers concerned would first obtain a plot either through self-sterilisation or through giving a motivated case. This plot would be registered in their own names. Since, according to the rules of resettlement, they were not allowed to register more than one plot, they had to find an alternative solution for the other plots they accumulated. This they did by finding an 'indirect method' of 'motivating others'—offering them Rs 500, not for the operation, but for handing over their plots after the operation. The 'motivated man' would register his case with the DDA as if it were a straightforward case of self-sterilisation. But once allocated a plot, he would be under obligation to sell it to his unofficial motivator with whom he had previously made a deal. Some of these unofficial motivators did this in order to obtain two adjacent plots, enabling them to have double the amount of space than their neighbours. But others are said to have made a veritable business out of it and would go on to sell the plots they accumulated, thereby entering the lucrative property market by using sterilisation certificates as a cheap means of obtaining plots. A survey conducted for the DDA in 1989 bears witness to the fact that some plots were immediately sold after their allocation in 1976. It is likely that these were the plots obtained by the unofficial motivators. Several people in the colony pointed out the grandiose house of one man with political connections who is said to have accumulated at least ten plots in Welcome by this method. Most of those who entered the property market were probably relatively prosperous men who had enough capital and political weight to motivate more than one person for sterilisation. Since the majority of people in the colony had difficulty motivating even one person, there probably were not many who made a full-scale business out of the trade in plots. However an extract from our conversation with two women neighbours suggests that some of those at the very bottom of the economic heap found alternative means of entering the market.

HINDU LABOURER

'Many women at that time allowed themselves to be sexually abused for they were very poor and were not in a position to give cases. This they did in order to get a plot...Some women were so innocent that they did not know what was happening until it was too late. First they were taken off and raped, then they were given sterilisation certificates.'

How do you know?

'Know? I *know* because one man tried to do it to me. He said he could help me obtain a certificate if I followed him. When I realised he was trying to take me off to a hotel, I hit him with my sandal which drew a crowd and he was made to apologise. Later that man started causing problems. After I had purchased cases, he tried to prevent me from getting them registered for the plot.'

MUSLIM NEIGHBOUR

'Some women went with *dalals* out of desperate need. They needed money for food so much that they were not in a position to refuse anything. But many more went voluntarily and made a business out of it. They were the ones who slept with *dalals* many times over in order to get plots which they then sold for money. In this way they made their fortunes.'

Did women help each other at all?

'At that time people did not know what was going on. Later when we got our plots then we used to leak out what had happened to each other bit by bit. But at that time the main concern was that if you did not speak with proper respect to the official in charge then he might cancel your allotment order.'

This brief extract raises a number of issues inherent in the study

of the motivation structure. Above all there is the problem of access
to certain types of participant in the market. We have already noted
the invisibility of the 'motivated' persons, the ones who sold their
infertility to others. But the same invisibility surrounds those who
abused the system to its maximum: the opportunists who are said to
have converted a cruel necessity into a thriving trade. Similarly the
dalal remains an elusive figure. The more we tried to press people
about his identity, the clearer it became that the *dalal* was not so much
a person as a function which could be performed by anyone who had
the will. There was a chilling nonchalance in some of the accounts we
heard of the market, reminding us that the commodification of the
body was neither so exceptional nor so specific to the Emergency as
such:

BRAHMAN RESIDENT
'No one ever has a fixed business in India. It keeps on changing all
the time. A man who is selling *angithis* [simple form of stove] one day
will start selling "stoves" the next. They change their business to keep
up with what is profitable at the time. The *dalals* [who sold sterilisation
certificates] were no different. They came into this business because
they felt they could make good money out of it...'

SOCK-FACTORY WORKER
'It was one type of business which even today is still going on. If
you go to Irwin Hospital then you will find people lined up on
the pavement to give blood or to sell a kidney for money. What's the
difference?'

An ethnography of the motivator

An ethnography of the motivation structure takes us one step further
from the simplistic stereotypes of the post-Emergency narrative in
which the poor feature either as helpless victims or as noble resistors
of state oppression. What we encounter here is a process of internal
differentiation as the poor themselves split into the three categories
of motivator, motivated and intermediary. By accepting to purchase
the sterilisation of others, many would-be victims of the Emergency
inadvertently became active agents of the state, perpetuating the very
policy they sought to dodge. In avoiding the direct impact of the
sterilisation drive they transferred their victimhood on to others, a

process facilitated by the market which became the key regulatory force.

In focusing on the active victims of the Emergency and on those who reverted their victim status by aggressively exploiting DDA policies, we are forced to acknowledge that the process of co-victimisation so often associated with the callous nature of bureaucrats has its parallel at the very bottom of the socio-economic scale. Here we do not so much encounter an alternative subaltern morality as pragmatism and at times blatant opportunism in the struggle for plots. By highlighting the active role of ordinary Delhi citizens in perpetuating state abuses, I do not intend to deny the state's responsibility, nor to underestimate the trials of those who reluctantly engaged in the regime, but rather to challenge the imbalances in the literature about the Emergency which tends to portray the intellectual as the emotional sufferer, the bureaucrat as the active participant and the poor as an undifferentiated mass of innocent victims. Such stereotypes are dangerous for they seem to mask the most frightening aspect of oppressive regimes; that is their ability to draw all kinds of people, through fear or greed, into participation. Just as disturbing as the state's coercion of its victims through so-called 'disincentives' was the readiness of so many victims to impose the burden of sterilisation on to others. Without their participation, it is unlikely that the sterilisation drive could have spread with such disconcerting speed, superseding government targets and expectations.

8

HEROES, HEROINES, VILLAINS
SUBALTERN PERCEPTIONS?

'The Great Janata Revolution that buried the emerging dynastic dictatorship of Indira Gandhi and re-established people's sovereignty in India is a development of far-reaching historic significance in this country. It has not merely saved Indian history from a dark tunnel of personal dictatorship of the mother and her son but also opened up a new chapter in the history of Parliamentary democracy itself...The most backward and abjectly poor people of the northern Hindi belt have shaped the history of India by throwing their powerful rulers with one hard stroke out there in the dustbin of history. The like has simply not happened in the entire course of Indian history since the Stone Age. To treat this revolution as a mere election is to diminish its historic importance and insult the people's achievement.' (*J.A. Naik*, 1977)

'After I had finished writing *All the Prime Minister's Men* in July 1977, I had shoved all my notes and clippings on Mrs. Gandhi into a large envelope, sealed it with cellotape and consigned it to the bottom of my filing cabinet, hoping it would never have to be brought out again, except to be thrown.' (*Janardan Thakur*, 1979)

Janardan Thakur and J.A. Naik were amongst the many post-Emergency authors who assumed that the Congress Party's defeat at the end of the Emergency in March 1977 marked not only the beginning of a new era in Indian politics but also the end of Indira Gandhi's career. Cast into the dustbin of history and the bottom drawer of filing cabinets, her demise seemed as total and uncompromising as her earlier rise to power. This is not to say that her defeat had been expected at the time. On the contrary, most post-Emergency authors reveal shock, not only at her calling a general election, but also at her losing it. None, it seems, credited the Indian population with the capacity to reject the Congress Party which had consistently dominated Indian politics both before and after independence. 'Not surprisingly', writes Ved Mehta, 'everyone concerned took it for granted that the elections would serve only to expose the impotence of the electorate.'[1]

The election results therefore led the post-Emergency writers to reflect on why they had been so unable to anticipate Indira Gandhi's defeat. They found their answer partly in the inscrutability of the Indian 'masses' whose preferences had been impossible to interpret during the election campaign. B.M. Sinha's observation is typical when he comments, 'Suppressed from all sides and denied any opportunity to seek justice from the court, the people presented the deceptive appearance of a man who has reconciled himself to his bad luck. It appeared that they had lost all strength to oppose the political dispensation Mrs Gandhi and her coterie had established; they seemed to have accepted her personal dictatorship under the garb of democracy...'[2] This inscrutability of 'the masses' was also considered one of the clues to understanding Indira Gandhi's decision to call an election. Along with other Congress notables, she was deceived into believing that the huge crowds that gathered to hear her represented a body of support even though these crowds had been organised in part by her own public relations machinery.[3] Similarly Bansi Lal, the notorious Chief Minister of Haryana, had mistaken 'the people's sullenness as a sign of submission'.[4] In a book titled *Miracle of Democracy in India*, Khanna explains the impossibility of anticipating a party's success from the crowds it attracts, arguing that in rural India people consider it wise to attend the meetings of both parties just in case, whilst in urban India many prefer to display the flags of opposing parties rather than express their voting preferences to the public eye.[5] What emerges from this literature is an image of a silent illegible electorate composed of poor and illiterate people who keep their opinions to themselves even as they cheer opposing parties.

However, if the people had seemed inscrutable before the famous election of 1977, their unanimous vote in favour of the Janata Party

---

[1] Ved Mehta, 1978, *The New India*, New York: Viking, p. 153.

[2] Sinha, 1977, *Operation Emergency*, p. 173.

[3] D.R. Mankekar and Kamla Mankekar, 1977, *Decline and Fall of Indira Gandhi*, Delhi: Vision Books, pp. 183–4.

[4] Ibid., p. 168

[5] N. Khanna, 1977, *Miracle of Democracy in India*, Delhi: Interprint, p. 35.

seemed to suggest that they were far more discriminating and politically aware than previously assumed. 'The greatest gain to the country stemming from the Emergency and its misuse and abuse of power,' write Mankekar and Mankekar, 'has been the political awakening it brought to this nation of 70 per cent illiteracy, which was only until the other day taken for a nation of sheep that could be made to vote at the bidding of a clever politician.'[6] Writing in a similar vein, Kuldip Nayyar asserts, 'The thundering victory of the Janata and the CDF...came as a great surprise to the intelligentsia in India and the people in the West—both cut off from the people. Little did they realise that the poor loved their liberty as much as anybody else did. Their approach might not have been sophisticated or ideologically pure but their faith in what they considered democracy was unflinching. A vote gave them the power to select the people they wanted and they used it to prove that they were the real masters; Mrs Gandhi and her party had taken away that right. This was their judgement against such high-handedness.'[7]

Central to this new notion of people's power was the idea that the people could not be duped beyond a certain point. If their ignorance that had led them to be taken in by Indira Gandhi in the first place, their discernment eventually threw her out. 'She had risen to great heights,' writes Janardan Thakar, 'but she could not keep herself there because her 'greatness' was a mere facade, a build-up. It lacked authenticity...She had lasted as long as she did mainly because of the lack of political judgement on the part of millions of dissatisfied, embittered individuals who submitted themselves to the redeemer cult that was systematically built around her person. Once the mask was off, she fell headlong in the eyes of the people.'[8] S.L.M. Prachand was not alone when he commented that the people were not so much anti-Congress as anti-Indira.[9] Such observations seemed to suggest that Indira Gandhi, once fallen, could never rise again. It was as if the very people who had at first swallowed her whole, had spat her out in one vast act of collective resistance.

I had been only partially familiar with the post-Emergency nar-

[6]Mankekar and Mankekar, 1977, *Decline and Fall*, p. 204.

[7]Kuldip Nayar, 1977, *The Judgement: Inside Story of Emergency in India*, New Delhi: Vikas, pp. 179–80.

[8]J. Thakur, 1977, *All the Prime Minister's Men*, New Delhi: Vikas, p. 174.

[9]S.L.M. Prachand, 1977, *The Popular Upsurge and Fall of Congress*, Chandigarh: Abhishek, p. 51.

Above left Drawing by Prabhakar Bhatlekar. (Courtesy of the artist)
Above right Indira Gandhi addressing a crowd, Haldighati, June 1976.
Below Indira Gandhi inaugurating a bridge near Kanpur 22 January 1977.
(Both: PD–PIB, New Delhi)

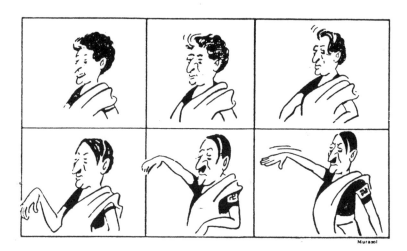

Above An alternative perception. (Cartoon by Murasol)   *Below* A jubilant crowd celebrates Indira Gandhi's defeat, New Delhi, 20 March 1977. (PD-PIB, New Delhi)

Left Election campaign, 1977.
(Courtesy Herblock)

Left Indira Gandhi returns to
power, 1980. *Above* 'Her
only problem was that she
bowed down too much to
her son.' Indira with Sanjay,
1976. (Both by PD-PIB,
New Delhi)

Right Poster by N.L. Sharma.
Below 'We were asked to
make a giant statue of Indira
Gandhi. It was paraded
around the whole Trans-
Yamuna area. The body was
destroyed, but we kept the
head.' Master Ram Nivas,
statue maker, Welcome.
Bottom Crowds outside the
Indira Gandhi museum at 1
Safdarjang Road, 1997.

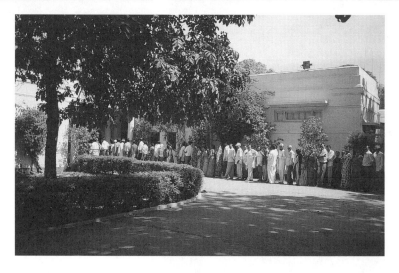

rative when I first began talking to people in Welcome about their experiences.

My own expectations had been built, not so much from the literature of the period as from the evidence my assistant and I had unearthed in the Slum Department files in Welcome. What we had seen was the systematic way in which the bodies of the poor had become a digging ground for sterilisation cases and once we had moved out of the records room and into the colony, we had found ample evidence of just how widespread and invasive the sterilisation drive had been. Given that so many people had suffered at the time, it seemed only logical that the people of Welcome would retain a negative image of the key figures associated with the Emergency regime. Reading the numerous volumes of the post-Emergency narrative as I progressed in my fieldwork served only to intensify our expectation of a discourse of resentment in which Indira Gandhi and her son, Sanjay, would feature as the villains of the piece. It was therefore with some surprise that I heard a government electrician explain that Indira Gandhi was 'the greatest leader the country had ever had' and that it was a pity that Sanjay Gandhi had not had an official post. When questioned further, he retorted, 'Had he been in the government it would have been better still because Sanjay cared about the poor.'

Although this man was one of the few who had successfully avoided a vasectomy, his praise of Indira and Sanjay Gandhi seemed particularly incongruous for it had been preceded by garish tales of forcible sterilisation in his native district of Pratapgarh where he claimed the police and local *pradhans* had been lifting people out of the fields and where local protests had resulted in a police firing. He had also talked at some length of how his colleagues in DESU had been made to get sterilised and had bemoaned the fact that it was the poor alone who suffered. He himself had only been able to avoid the operation because he was a temporary labourer rather than a permanent employee. He had not however been able to avoid the bulldozers; nor had he been able to obtain a plot since he had chosen to prioritise his fertility over shelter. This man's life had clearly been disrupted by the Emergency but when we asked him who was responsible for such disruption, it became quite clear that in his view it was neither the Prime Minister nor her son. '*Pradhans* and middlemen,' he replied. 'The government had a policy but these people undermined it out of greed for money. The policy was good, but these people made a business out of it. It was they who harassed the poor, leaving the rich untouched.'

The electrician's views on leadership and responsibility alerted

me to the fact that nothing could be assumed about people's opinions
of Indira and Sanjay Gandhi, the hated protagonists of the post-
Emergency narrative. I became curious to know how the people whose
bodies had borne the direct physical brunt of the sterilisation campaign
perceived their leaders. Were their opinions perhaps different from
the perceptions of those who had avoided sterilisation by becoming
motivators? What about those who claimed to have benefited from
the campaign? Was it possible to chart some kind of scale of perceptions
according to people's actual experiences of demolition and sterilisation?
From this time onwards, I began to make a point of introducing the
names of Indira and Sanjay into our conversations, often asking people
directly what they thought of them. It soon became clear that far
from being exceptional, the electrician's high opinion of Indira Gandhi
was widely shared:

HINDU SWEEPER
'Indira Gandhi? She was the best. If only there were others as good
as her!'

MUSLIM FACTORY WORKER
'She was a very great leader. Her main aim was to narrow the gap
between the rich and the poor. It was she who gave us our plots.'

MUSLIM IRON MERCHANT
'She was not only a great leader but very clever. It is no small thing
that the prime ministers of 101 countries attended her funeral.'

It did not seem to make any difference in which part of the colony
we were or to whom we spoke; the image of Indira Gandhi emerged
consistently untainted by the Emergency. Praise of her seemed to
sprout spontaneously from every tongue. When eventually we met
the Muslim toolmaker who had refused either to get sterilised himself
or to motivate his own relatives, I thought perhaps we had stumbled
across a fragment of counter narrative, for this man told us he had
been in jail in 1977. However, it soon turned out that he had been to
jail, not for his opposition to Indira Gandhi, but for his undying support
of her:

MUSLIM TOOLMAKER
'After the Emergency, the Janata Party came to power and they incar-
cerated Indira Gandhi. We were sent to jail because we tried to start

a movement for her release. It was called the 'Release Indira Movement'. The rally was stopped near the Odeon Cinema in Connaught Place. We were on our way to the Parliament building...Indira Gandhi was released but they kept us in for 14 days...She was an undisputed leader. A world-famous leader. If only there could have been two or three more like her!'

It was not that these Indira admirers had not suffered during the Emergency. Of the few cited here all had experienced the demolition of their properties, whether homes or shops. The factory worker and sweeper had both undergone vasectomy operations, the former to obtain a plot, the latter to get his salary. The iron merchant had paid his way out of the situation by becoming a motivator whilst the old toolmaker had lost his chances of getting a shop in Meena Bazaar when he refused to motivate others. All spoke of the Emergency as a time of fear and were highly critical of the way the sterilisation campaign had been carried out. Yet none associated their sufferings with Indira Gandhi, whose image remained above recrimination, beyond the realm of doubt. Their perceptions stood in staggering contrast to the post-Emergency narrative in which 'the people' were reported to be so embittered by the tortures of demolition and sterilisation that they would never again subject themselves to the tyrant who had caused their pain. Was it simply that time and subsequent events had changed 'the people's' perceptions? Alternatively, was it that the 'the people' of the post-Emergency narrative had never quite corresponded to the ordinary men and women living in places like Welcome?

One thing which came across clearly was that if today people systematically praised Indira Gandhi, it was not out of some more generalised respect felt by those at the bottom of the socio-economic scale for those at the top. Most residents of Welcome were deeply cynical about people in power: greed and ineptitude being the dominant themes:

What do you think of today's leaders?

BUS DRIVER, SC, BJP SUPPORTER
'What leaders? They are not leaders at all. They are only concerned with filling their pockets. Narasimha Rao has buried this country. His picture comes on TV but nothing else.'

JEANS MANUFACTURER, MUSLIM, ALI SENA SUPPORTER
'Previously only able and talented people were elected. Nowadays it is like stacking a load of books on the back of a donkey, then calling it knowledgeable. It has just become a game of money.'

EX-CONGRESS ACTIVIST, MUSLIM
'We have a maxim: earlier dacoits were found in *khadar* [the jungle]; now they are found in *khaddar* [hand-spun cloth].

Far from spreading to tarnish the image of Indira Gandhi, the squalor associated with present-day leaders seemed to serve only to intensify her superiority. As a result she often featured in our discussions of present and recent problems in the colony, the idea being that such things would never have occurred under Indira's firm but benign influence. This perception of her as powerful and protective seemed to be shared by young and old, Muslim and Hindu alike. At first sight such unflinching support might seem explicable in terms of the social and religious profile of the population of Welcome. Both Muslims and scheduled caste Hindus, the two largest categories of people in the colony, have conventionally been regarded as the bulwark of the Congress Party. Indeed critics of the party have often accused the Congress of pandering to Muslims and being too generous to scheduled castes in order to secure their mass votes. As the daughter of Jawaharlal Nehru, India's first and much respected Prime Minister, Indira Gandhi was well-placed for embodying the Congress heritage, which stretched back not only to the founding of the Constitution but right back to the early days of the freedom struggle. In fact, until its defeat in the 1977 elections, the Congress had been the only party to hold office at the national level. If the Congress Party seemed to fuse with the concept of the nation, so too did the identity of Indira Gandhi—a fact exploited in the popular phrase, first coined by D.K. Barooah during the Emergency: 'Indira is India, India is Indira!'

There is little doubt that the majority in Welcome were indeed Congress supporters up until the late 1970s. In addition, during the Emergency, most local *pradhans*, like the head of the iron market and the *pradhan* of QW2, were Congress supporters and activists whose strength lay in their ability to negotiate between prominent Congress officials and citizens at the local level. Even today, Welcome contains a number of Congress die-hards especially amongst elder generation men and women from scheduled caste backgrounds, and to a lesser extent amongst elder generation Muslims. Amongst such people, it is not uncommon to hear the phrase, 'I have voted Congress all my life and will carry on voting for them until I die.' However, much has changed in politics since the days when people of scheduled caste and Muslim backgrounds would vote, almost systematically for the Congress. Quite apart from the party's decisive defeat in east Delhi in 1977 when the Janata Party successfully wooed a semi-homeless, sterilisation-fearing electorate still licking painful wounds, there has been, since the late 1980s, a steady growth of support for the right wing BJP at both the local and national levels. Challenging the secular discourse of the Congress Party, the BJP has gathered support from a number of younger generation Hindus in Welcome with its militant Hindu nationalist discourse. The fact that Muslims are beginning to outnumber Hindus in the colony and have been highly successful in local industries such as the jeans trade, has made the Hindu-dominated areas of Welcome fertile new ground for the BJP and, to a lesser extent, the more militant Shiv Sena with its endangered majority rhetoric.

If Hindus have been gradually breaking away from the Congress, the exodus of Muslims has been far more sudden and systematic—precipitated by the demolition of the Babri Masjid and the subsequent violence of December 1992. Not only do Muslims of Welcome complain that the Congress Party failed to act to prevent or quell the growing tension following the demolition of the mosque at Ayodhya, but they also suspect that some Congress individuals may have been implicated in the violence, much of which showed careful planning. The fact that the vast majority of the looting and arson took place in Muslim-dominated areas and that the vast majority of people wounded, killed and arrested were Muslim confirms the feeling that the Congress Party totally betrayed the Muslim community in 1992, and that too after having enjoyed decades of Muslim support. As one Muslim ex-Congress activist put it:

'Earlier more than 70 per cent of Muslims used to vote for Congress and 30 per cent for other parties. Today its the other way round, with not even 30 per cent voting for Congress…It's not that they participated in the riots. But you tell me, the Prime Minister [then Narasimha Rao] was sitting just 10 minutes from here [during the 'riots']. Was he deaf and dumb that he could not hear our cries? Was he blind that he could not see what was happening here? I myself telephoned H.K.L. Bhagat[10] at the time our houses were being burnt. He told me, 'Make a file!' You tell me, was that the time for making files when our homes were burning down and our children being killed?'

Confirmation of the Muslim exodus from Congress was apparent during the 1997 Municipal elections when the Muslim vote was highly fragmented. Of the three Muslim *pradhans* we met who were standing in the elections, two were standing as independent candidates despite long histories of Congress activism and the other was standing for the Samajwadi Party. Since Welcome is divided into two different constituencies, the Muslim-dominated north side of the colony falls within the larger Hindu-dominated ward of West Goruk Park[11] where the BJP won the elections with a safe majority. However, the next most successful party was the Ali Sena, a new right wing Muslim militant party which has grown up in direct 'reaction' to and exploitation of the horrors experienced by Muslims in 1992. The president of this new party, a young and ambitious man with a dubious reputation, lives, not in Welcome, but in the nearby area of Jaffrabad. When we went to meet him, shortly after the 1997 elections, we found a man incapable of discussing any social or political issue that did not fit his violent schema of the necessity of a militant Muslim revenge. His principle line was to call on all Muslims to sacrifice their lives for the re-building of the Babri Masjid at Ayodhya. The party's symbol was a date palm tree with crossed swords and the name 'Ali Sena' (Army of Ali) had been chosen as a direct challenge to the Hindu militant organisation, the Shiv Sena (Army of Shiv). Had the Ali Sena candidate been able to buy the support of just one of the

[10]H.K.L. Bhagat, the Congress MLA (Member of the Legislative Assembly) for east Delhi at the time. He is a man with a formidable reputation, not least for his role as Minister of State for Works and Housing during the Emergency and for his alleged active involvement in the Sikh Massacre of 1984. He has long been involved in the politics of Welcome and is the principle person through whom local *pradhans* 'get things done'. This means that despite the high profile slurs on his character and suspicion regarding his actions in recent years, he is generally held in high esteem at the local level. One *pradhan* told us he used to be referred to throughout the colony as 'the King without a Crown'.

[11]Most Muslims in Welcome perceive this carving up of constituencies as a device designed to dilute the strength of the Muslim vote.

Muslim *pradhans* standing as independent candidates, he would have been able to win the seat in this ward. But despite their disillusionment with Congress, the two ex-Congress *pradhans* retain a secular discourse and refuse to lend support to a party whose principle orientation is blatantly communal and violent. As one of them put it, 'For me, both the Ali Sena and the Shiv Sena are the same. In my election campaign I argued, "Why are these two armies fighting here? Why not send them to the border if they are armies?"'

When we questioned the president of the Ali Sena, himself an ex-Congress activist, about the Emergency, it was clear that he was not very knowledgeable about the past but he did attribute sterilisation abuses directly to Indira and Sanjay Gandhi and is even reported to have once said in a speech that given the chance, he would have killed Indira Gandhi himself. But this man's main orientation was to rally Muslim forces by building on the wounds of 1992 and his popularity amongst Muslims in Welcome was based largely on the notion that Muslims needed a party of their own to protect their interests against the BJP since the Congress and others had failed them so badly. However, far from rewriting the history of Congress leadership as a gradual sliding decline, most Muslim defectors from the Congress Party preferred to draw a clear cut division between the present and the past, holding Indira Gandhi up as proof of how much better things used to be. When, on occasion, they invoked her name in relation to 1992, it was not to draw parallels with the misdeeds of contemporary Congress politicians but rather to reaffirm her unique greatness:

RETIRED SERVANT, MUSLIM, JANATA SUPPORTER
'Whilst she was alive we didn't face any problems. Under her, abnormal events would be calmed immediately. It is not that we didn't have riots in her day, but they were always brought under control rapidly and didn't cause too much disruption to people's business.'

CARPENTER, MUSLIM, ALI SENA SUPPORTER
'Indira Gandhi was not only sympathetic to the poor, she also knew how to keep everything in check. This Ayodhya affair could never have happened in her time.'

Where, then, did the people of Welcome direct their negative feelings about the Emergency? Whom did they consider responsible for the injustices they had suffered? If Indira Gandhi was exempt from responsibility in their accounts, who had occupied the role of the oppressor about whom we have heard so much but know so little? Discontent, blame, responsibility were much more difficult to locate than the positive aura that seemed to encircle the image of Indira Gandhi like a protective halo. Many, like the government electrician, placed the blame at the level of intermediaries, whether government servants, brokers or local *pradhans* whose functions often merged. These were the people with whom they personally had had to deal and whom they perceived as the main beneficiaries of the sterilisation drive:

FIRST HINDU MAN
'The police, the *dalals*, the doctors, the government officers; they were responsible. But Indira Gandhi was not responsible. Her intention was good. She just wanted people to have less children.'

SECOND HINDU MAN
'It is beneath the seat of power that you will find the traitors. Go to an important minister and he will not treat you badly. But go to his peon, and he will certainly abuse you all he can.'

HINDU WOMAN
'The main culprits were the petty officials and dealers. They were the ones who used force on others in order to get promotions and other benefits for themselves.'

OLD MUSLIM MAN
'There were many traitors from within—Muslims who went about trying to force people to be sterilised...They worked against our religion. They did anti-religious work for money.'

According to such assessments, Indira Gandhi had been unaware of the sterilisation abuses being perpetuated in the name of family planning. And despite the declining popularity of the Congress Party today, there were very few attempts to allocate responsibility at this level. 'We were abused by the workers,' a Muslim woman explained, 'The Congress wouldn't have wanted it. Why would they have wanted to spoil their own careers?'

Just as those at the top of the political pinnacle remained exempt from serious criticism, so individual high level officials were perceived as having been above malpractice on the one hand and ignorant of it on the other. When we asked people how they felt about K.K. Nayyar, the executive officer of the DDA who had signed all the DDA family planning allotment orders, replies indicated that he was held in considerable reverence in the colony:

SECRETARY OF THE IRON MARKET
'He was a very high up official in the DDA...He was a great and important man. He wanted to allot us plots just like that, but in the meantime, this sterilisation drive started up. Nayyar Sahib was pressurised by the government and so he told us we needed to give cases. In fact he himself wanted to give us plots without the sterilisation demand...but giving cases was something you could not avoid.'

HINDU WOMAN
'Nayyar Sahib was a good man but the people in-between would try their best to stop you meeting him. Nayyar Sahib was sitting inside. How could he possibly have known what was going on outside?'

MUSLIM MAN
'K.K. Nayyar was a very important man. He was directly responsible to Jagmohan. Everything was in his hands...There used to be a huge queue of people waiting to see him every day. He used to work very hard from eight in the morning to seven, eight, or nine at night giving out plots.'

Like Indira Gandhi, K.K. Nayyar seemed to be immune from criticism. He was perceived not as the purveyor of sterilisation but as the giver of plots. It was almost as if the people of Welcome felt it their duty to protect these 'high ups' from any negative conclusions that might be drawn, not least by the visiting anthropologist. If Nayyar Sahib had been forced to demand sterilisation cases, that was not his fault. He was under pressure from above and his personal magnanimity was contrasted with the cruel tactics of those below who tried to distort his noble efforts.[12]

However, such immunity from responsibility did not surround the character of Sanjay Gandhi over whom opinions split decisively along religious and often party lines. Sanjay's defenders were almost entirely Hindu. They included present-day supporters of the right wing BJP and Shiv Sena although there were some old Congress supporters who also put up a strong defence:

[12]I had hoped to interview K.K. Nayyar about his memories of the Emergency but was told he was deceased.

OLD HINDU, CONGRESS SUPPORTER
'Sanjay Gandhi lived by the maxim, speak less, work more. It was he who brought Indira Gandhi back to power. He should not have died like that. I don't know how educated he was but he was certainly a very wise man.'

MIDDLE-AGED HINDU, CONGRESS SUPPORTER
'Sanjay Gandhi was a good man. He should never have died so young. This country does not tolerate good people. It sends them to heaven early. Lal Bahadur Shastri ruled this country for only 14 months, then died. Nehru ruled for 14 years. Indira Gandhi was shot and she too was a very great leader.'

The admiration expressed for Sanjay Gandhi by BJP and Shiv Sena supporters centred less on his pedigree as Indira's son than around his capacity for firm, decisive action. In their accounts, Sanjay featured as a virile, aggressive man who had possessed the necessary physical strength to control the country, not least by 'clearing up' the Muslim-dominated old city centre:

YOUNG SWEEPER, BJP SUPPORTER
'You will not easily come across another man like Sanjay Gandhi. Had he been alive today he would have made India like Paris. He wanted to remove all *jhuggis* and to raise the standard of living, but this was not written in his fate...He wanted to destroy the whole of Old Delhi and make it into part of New Delhi, just as they destroyed the *kacha* houses of Turkman Gate and rebuilt them as new three storey flats...It was an excellent idea.'

RETIRED RICKSHAW DRIVER, SHIV SENA ACTIVIST
'He was a good man and a real hard worker. He worked well both in Delhi and Agra. For instance, he totally cleaned up the entire Jama Masjid area. The Jama Masjid was surrounded by such filth on all four sides that you couldn't even properly see it. Now you can see it; that was good work. Some speak ill of him but middlemen types always like to malign the image of a person who works. Even today, if you go to Agra, you will find people still pay him a lot of respect.'

YOUNG SC BUS DRIVER, BJP SUPPORTER
'The country needs a strong leader like Sanjay Gandhi. In my opinion if a man cannot run the country he doesn't deserve to be its leader...He

was not in fact the elected leader. He was just the son of Indira Gandhi but still he managed to do many good things for the country. It was his dream that every Indian should own a car like Americans...'

In contrast to this perception of Sanjay as an unsung hero who would have performed even greater works had he lived longer, was the common Muslim perception of him as one of the key agents of Emergency abuses.

OLD MUSLIM WOMAN, CONGRESS SUPPORTER
'He was a terrible man. He persecuted hundreds of people and that was why he died such a bad death. I would not wish this kind of death on anyone, but that was what Allah wanted...The way Sanjay Gandhi behaved was the very opposite of how his mother was.'

MUSLIM IRON MERCHANT, CONGRESS SUPPORTER
'He was part of an extremist group. He just did whatever he felt like doing. He didn't bother about whether or not people were suffering, or how much loss he was causing them. Property worth crores of rupees was destroyed by him.'

MUSLIM JAMAAT-E-ISLAMI [13] ACTIVIST
'He was just a very big pimp He wanted to rule this country. He didn't even want his mother there. He just used to consider himself the prime minister. Once he was beaten up in the street for misbehaving. The photographs of this were kept on display at Pragati Maidan.

Aren't such displays biased?

'There are two sides to every picture. They display such photographs to show what wrong was done to Sanjay Gandhi, but we interpret them differently. We say whatever wrongs appear to be happening to him, these are the results of his own wrong doings.'

Janardan Thakur, the journalist who in 1977 had buried his Indira Gandhi notes in the bottom drawer of his filing cabinet, later described the scene which prompted the photograph in question. It was 1 May 1979. Sanjay and his supporters had been stopped by the police whilst trying to lead a rally in Janpath. Sanjay had resisted arrest by defiantly

[13]Jamaat-e-Islami, a Muslim political organisation that was temporarily suppressed by Indira Gandhi during the Emergency.

but peacefully squatting on the ground and refusing to enter the police van. Photographers had made full use of the occasion. 'Within days', writes Thakur, 'huge posters appeared all about the city showing the great hero crouching before police *lathis*.' Thakur reads the circulation of Sanjay's image as the ultimate sign that his political rebirth was complete.[14] However, such an assessment rests on the idea that 'the people' were not capable of deconstructing an image placed before them. The interpretation given by the Jamaat-e-Islami activist in Welcome seemed to suggest otherwise.

One thing I found puzzling about these accounts from Muslims was the relationship between the indisputably positive images of Indira Gandhi and the negative images of her son Sanjay. Surely if Sanjay was perceived as a villainous thug, this would reflect to some extent on his mother who was, after all, prime minister at the time. That this was an area of tension in people's narratives was apparent in the fact that it was the only area in which any criticism of Indira Gandhi ever surfaced. Her one fault, according to such readings, was her inability to control her son:

THE SAME JAMAAT-E-ISLAMI ACTIVIST
'Sanjay Gandhi went out of control. She [Indira] couldn't control him because Sanjay knew some of her secrets, such as her illicit affair with Dhirendra Brahmachari. It was because of this that she couldn't stop him. And anyway, he didn't even listen to her.'

MUSLIM BAKER, JANATA SUPPORTER
'Indira Gandhi was very good but as far as I can see she had to bow her head before her son. That was wrong. She didn't control him properly.'

However, just as common as the image of Indira failing to control her son was the image of her sacrificing her son for the nation. According to this version of events, Indira found the ultimate means of curbing his activities. It was in conversation with two Muslim women who had been resettled from Dujana House that we first heard this interpretation:

FIRST WOMAN
'Nothing untoward ever happened under Indira. But Sanjay would have destroyed India if he had remained alive. In fact, Indira Gandhi

[14]J. Thakur, 1979, *Indira Gandhi and her Power Game*, Ghaziabad: Vikas, p. 79.

killed her son in order to save Hindustan [her choice of term]. It was his intention to wipe out the whole of Delhi. He only wanted to see his own house standing and nobody else's.'

SECOND WOMAN
'Yes, that's true. She certainly finished him off.'

But how?

FIRST WOMAN
'She tampered with the insides of his aircraft so that when he went up into the air his plane crashed.'

SECOND WOMAN
'He had to pay for his ill deeds.'

What did you feel about his death?

SECOND WOMAN
'We thought it was good, otherwise he would have ruined the whole of India. We celebrated that event. We felt happy at heart. He had done a lot of injustice to people.'

Sometimes the version of the story was more hesitant, as in the following conversation with a Muslim couple and a bystander:

HUSBAND
'Sanjay Gandhi was a bad leader...His politics was malicious, he never felt himself accountable to people, not even his mother...I have heard that he was a pilot and that he died in a crash. I also heard—I don't know if it's true—that he was killed by his own mother because Indira Gandhi did not like his ideas.'

To the wife: Do you think a mother could kill her son?

WIFE
'The time is such that there are tensions between mother and son, brother and sister and husband and wife'.

HUSBAND
'Wives sometimes kill their husbands.'

WIFE
'Sons sometimes kill their mothers.'

YOUNG MAN LISTENING
'And in politics anything can happen!'

Though by no means accepted by everyone we met, this version of events was not uncommon. It was an elegant means of converting the potentially negative undertones of Indira's close relationship with her son into a positive affirmation of her greatness. It was a story which confirmed her super human strength and at the same time served to boost her status as a great patriot. Such was her love of her country that she was even willing to sacrifice her own son for the greater good of the nation. With the murder theory, Indira's image as creator, destroyer and protector was complete.

Entangled narratives

This book began with two dominant narratives—both short-lived— one defending Emergency measures by promising a better future, the other exposing Emergency atrocities as evidence of a shameful past—both narratives truncated by the discourses and events which superseded them. If the cleaner, fairer, richer India promised by Indira Gandhi never did come into fruition, neither did the new era of people power promised by the Janata victory of 1977. Two old half-forgotten narratives and now a third, newly unearthed and given form. The question is, how does this third narrative fit with the previous two? More importantly, does it create an alternative vision altogether?

In encouraging people in Welcome to tell their stories and making these the emphasis of this book, I have, of course, been influenced by two academic traditions. One is an anthropological training which has taught me to place a high value on popular experiences and perceptions. The other is familiarity with recent trends in historiographical writing in which attempts have been made to rewrite history from a so-called 'subaltern' point of view.[15] That Indian history was, until the 1980s, dominated by an elitist perspective is nowhere more apparent than in the post-Emergency narrative itself with its facile concept of 'the people,' conceived as 'a nation of sheep' one minute and the valiant 'soldiers of democracy' the next, with very little evidence to support either perspective. What comes across very strongly from this narrative is the elite's 'ignorance' of ordinary people's lives and opinions—an ignorance which some authors go half way to recognising when they speak of their inability to interpret 'the people's' mood.

---

[15]The point of view of disadvantaged groups.

Whenever I find myself reading that expression, 'the people', I feel a cheeky desire to ask those authors who use the phrase what they are if not 'people' themselves? There is a level of 'us' and 'themness' in their accounts which is shocking to the contemporary reader—a shock no doubt related to the influence the subaltern studies project has had on contemporary understandings of how history is made. Yet the subaltern project has posed more questions than it has been able to answer. It may have convinced us of the need to incorporate the voices of a whole range of previously unrepresented sections of society, but it has been less convincing in demonstrating the analytical value of the category 'subaltern'. The proposition has of course gone through numerous transformations since Ranajit Guha first put forward the notion of an autonomous domain of subaltern resistance which exists outside the reach of the dominant ideology and practice.[16] Whilst nobody would dispute that the life and experiences of those in subaltern positions may be radically different from those of elites, the question of the extent to which they formulate a separate ideology is much less clearly demonstrated and has been challenged by numerous studies from within the subaltern school.[17] What can our tales of the Emergency add to this debate?

The first and most obvious thing to note is that the three sets of narratives uncovered here cannot be mapped in any clear-cut way into simplistic divisions between subaltern and elite categories of people. It is the post-Emergency narrative, rather than the accounts of men and women in Welcome, which presents a clearly identifiable discourse of resistance, but it is one which emanates from an elite position. True, many of its authors were subordinated during the Emergency through censorship and arrest, but their subordination was only temporary and context-specific. Like the authors of the Emergency narrative itself, the post-Emergency writers were from an elite segment of Indian society and were successful in imposing their interpretation of the Emergency in such a way that it became the dominant narrative for a brief period after the event. Despite its attempts to include the experiences and perceptions of the victims of slum clearance and sterilisation, this narrative on the whole failed

[16]See Ranajit Guha, ed., 1982, *Subaltern Studies I,* Delhi: OUP, introduction.

[17]For a good summary of these critiques see Arild Ruud, 1995, 'Caste Hierarchy and Resistance in Indian Village Politics', presented at the South Asia Anthropology Group conference, LSE, London, 18–19 Sept.

to capture the reality of their experiences[18] just as it failed to gauge popular perceptions of Indira Gandhi who was voted back to power just two years after her defeat of 1977.

At first sight the people of Welcome seem well-placed for developing a subaltern critique of the Emergency based on their first hand experience of oppression. As key targets of both demolition and sterilisation, they had felt the impact of the Emergency where it hurt—in their bodies, their security, their homes. They spoke not so much of the experiences of others as of their own personal experiences—clearly located within the structure of their everyday lives—their colony, their school, their workplace. They were not outside commentators but reluctant victims and perpetrators of government schemes. Yet what is most striking about their discourse on leadership and responsibility during the Emergency is its lack of self-reflexivity and its proximity to earlier dominant narratives of the past.

Indira Gandhi, the heroine, the great national leader, the daughter in an upright noble dynasty, protector of the nation, the one who really cared about the poor; this is just about as far as one can get from a subaltern discourse of resistance. It makes a mockery of the post-Emergency authors' retrospective attempts to detect a genuine hatred of Indira Gandhi in the people's silence and their vote. If anything, it justifies these authors' earlier perception of 'the people' as easily fooled by Indira Gandhi's benevolent mask. It seems to imply that the narratives and perceptions of the people of Welcome are not just 'tainted' by the master narrative of the Emergency, but saturated by it.

Take, for example, people's attempts to explain their negative experiences by locating responsibility and blame at the centre—with the government servants, middle men and *dalals*. This was precisely the view expressed by Indira Gandhi in her attempt to defend the family planning policy when she began to sense the murmurings of widespread discontent. If there had been any coercion, it was not, she argued, the policy but those who subverted it who were to blame—'over-zealous officials' and the like. When one Welcome resident had commented, 'it is beneath the seat that you will find the traitors,' he could almost have been quoting from Indira Gandhi herself.

Opinions of Sanjay Gandhi may have been more varied but they did not suggest an alternative ideological frame. Here, instead of finding

[18]Dayal and Bose's account, 1997, *For Reasons*, though somewhat melodramatic, is perhaps the exception here.

collusion with one dominant narrative we have a split collusion, with Hindu opinions tending to converge with the dominant Emergency narrative whilst Muslim ones converged with the post-Emergency counter-narrative in which Sanjay Gandhi is portrayed as a brutish and destructive brat.

Whilst the perception of Sanjay as unsung hero clearly fits current right wing Hindu preoccupations with a hard-line, hyper-masculine, muscle-driven approach to politics, there were no signs of the development of a new Sanjay-inspired ideology as such. On the contrary what people recounted stemmed directly from Sanjay's own simplistic maxims like 'speak less, work more' or his populist promises that Delhi would become like Paris or that every Indian would own a car. This was not so much a discourse *about* Sanjay as the discourse *of* Sanjay himself. Similarly, the critique of Sanjay Gandhi was little more than an underdeveloped reiteration of the dominant narrative of the immediate post-Emergency period. It was only in the portrayal of Indira as Sanjay's murderer that popular narratives about leadership departed from the mainstream but this was also the point when they were at their least plausible. Some of those who recounted the tale were themselves sceptical about its validity whilst others denied it altogether. Whichever the case, the story functioned not as the foundation for a critique of Indira's leadership but rather as confirmation of her right to lead.

But to take these saturated narratives as evidence of the futility of the subaltern studies project would be highly misleading. There is much in the narratives of the residents of Welcome which not only enriches our understanding of what went on during the Emergency, but which also fundamentally alters it. Here we find not an undifferentiated herd of passive victims nor fervent crowds of fiery resistors but individuals and families placed in difficult situations, negotiating their way around the system as best they can—some falling into the role of victim, others diverting the impact by becoming motivators and yet others subverting the system altogether by converting it into a profitable business or a cheap means of accumulating land. What these actions imply is something very different from a straightforward collusion with authority at the top. However much people might praise Indira Gandhi and her intentions, in reality they had done their best to avoid complying with the fate that she and her son had chalked out for them in such uncompromising terms.

It was not out of respect for others or belief in the family planning scheme that some men and women had accepted to have the operation instead of paying someone else. Rather—and all were adamant about this—it was through lack of choice. In the case of low-level government servants, it was threat of the withdrawal of salaries that drove them to the operating theatre. In the case of those who got sterilised for plots, it was lack of financial resources which prevented them from purchasing a case instead. When one man had told us, 'we would not have got sterilised ourselves if we had had the money to purchase cases,' he spoke for the majority. Whatever people's attitudes to sterilisation today, all were adamant that they had been deeply opposed to having the operation at the time. In short, if there was an obvious way of wriggling out of the situation, it was the root of non-compliance that was chosen even if that non-compliance ultimately resulted in perpetuating the system through the motivation structure. Similarly, when people were given the choice of voting for Indira Gandhi in 1977, they had voted against her. But what this vote signified was not so much the development of a new political consciousness as a desire to put a stop to sterilisation and demolition—the two features of the Emergency regime which were plaguing people's lives. What the post-Emergency authors had detected was not so much the inscrutability of 'the people' as their pragmatism.

Looking back at the post-Emergency narrative, it is possible to detect some of this popular pragmatism at work in descriptions of the 1977 general election campaign. It is especially recognisable in N. Khanna's observation that many people considered it wise to attend the political meetings of both parties or to display opposing flags during the election campaign. He also describes how in Delhi he came across a Janata Party worker manning the local Congress booth. The man was apparently delighted with the arrangement for it enabled him to be paid by the Congress whilst at the same time being in a good position for directing voters to the Janata booth.[19] Vinod Mehta describes a similar process in Sanjay Gandhi's constituency of Amethi, where, he claims, 'Congress' workers contributed to election malpractices and Janata supporters admitted that rigging did take place, but that it was not coercive but 'voluntary rigging'.[20] These were not so much soldiers of democracy leading an almighty revolution

[19]Khanna, 1977, *Miracle of Democracy*, p. 39.
[20]Vinod Mehta, 1978, *The Sanjay Story*, p. 171.

as J.A. Naik had claimed, as people who had pragmatically decided it was in their best interests to make sure that the Congress Party was halted in its tracks.

The question arises as to whether such pragmatism was peculiarly 'subaltern' or whether it is in fact found at every level of society. Returning to the family planning scheme of the Emergency, what seems to have occurred is that officials high up in the administrative system usually tried to avoid getting sterilised whilst compensating for their own non-participation by motivating others and that this process occurred at every level of the socio-economic structure—whether at the level of teachers trying to save their jobs by motivating the parents of their pupils or displaced slum dwellers trying to save or obtain a plot by paying someone else to take their place on the operating table. In fact, one of the key features of the Emergency was the reluctance of all but a few politically courageous people to oppose it in any decisive and effective way. Of course there had been Jayaprakash Narayan and his following, many of whom were students, as well as some journalists, intellectuals and political activists who took risks and often ended up in jail for their actions and views. But the vast majority of people at every level of society preferred to maintain a low profile—to lie low, keep silent and avoid trouble. And although most probably never wanted to victimise others, they nonetheless put the safety of themselves and their families before that of others and in so doing often found themselves diverting the impact of aggressive policies onto those less equipped to escape them. Since it was the poor who lacked the economic, political and symbolic capital with which to build protection in moments of crisis, it was on them that the weight of the system accumulated, and since they themselves were highly differentiated, they too participated in the processes of avoidance and transfer that were so common. Whilst informers and middle men certainly thrived in such an environment and opportunistic businessmen, officials and *pradhans* exploited the situation as best they could, most people seem to have responded much more ambiguously, taking refuge in silence and avoidance which represented neither resistance nor compliance in any clear cut way. It is this ambiguous response which Kuldip Nayar describes when he comments, 'One thing I observed during my tours and interviews [during the Emergency] is that however submissive almost everyone was, very few people had accepted authoritarian rule. There was fear, obedience, but not acceptance.'[21] This brings me back to my earlier point that if pragmatism and inscrutability were characteristics of 'the people' as post-Emergency authors imply, then we must include within this category not only the subaltern but also the elite and the people in-between.

Reframing the narratives of the Emergency at this broader level, the search for a specifically subaltern resistance seems somewhat futile. Strategies of avoidance and transfer become common features, not of subaltern behaviour but of a more general response to totalitarian regimes—a response which characterised India's Emergency but is by no means restricted to it as other explorations of human behaviour under conditions of oppression show.[22] If there are differences in popular and elite responses to the Emergency, these differences lie less at the level of impulse and behaviour than at the level of the relationship between behaviour and discourse.

One dominant theme of the post-Emergency narrative is that of guilt. Many authors, whether journalists, government servants, politicians, writers or activists, felt they could have done much more to oppose the Emergency. They were shocked at the ease with which powerful institutions like the press, the media, the government itself, allowed themselves to crumble under the draconian measures taken by Indira Gandhi. Many felt that if only they had had the strength to speak out, put their jobs on the line, breach censorship rules and so forth, they could have prevented the country from sinking into a state of silent but obedient submission. Many attribute this inertia or paralysis to a combination of shock and fear. They had been unprepared for such measures, were caught unawares and undefended. It was shock at their own incapacity to act and a desire to prevent a similar recurrence that motivated many of the critics of the Emergency to analyse the phenomenon after the event. In other words, their sense of guilt helped serve to integrate their experiences of the Emergency into a coherent narrative of resistance (albeit largely an *a posteriori* one) in which the entire political system came under critical assessment and review.

By comparison with the dominant post-Emergency narrative, the

[21]Nayar, 1977, *The Judgement*, preface viii.

[22]One of the most incisive and extreme accounts of such behaviour is found in Primo Levi's descriptions and analyses of life among prisoners in Nazi concentration camps. Levi reminds us that only those who have been placed under such oppressive conditions have the right to judge the behaviour of those who committed seemingly unthinkable deeds in the effort to save themselves. Primo Levi, 1979, *If This is a Man*, Harmondsworth: Penguin and, 1988, *The Drowned and the Saved*.

personal accounts of the people of Welcome sound almost casual and undramatic. People speak less in terms of insurmountable torture and blinding oppression than in terms of hardship and getting by. Despite the fact that orality lends itself well to high drama, there is a lack of sensationalism in these accounts which makes the dominant post-Emergency narrative read almost like the script for a Bollywood movie by comparison. This level-headedness can be attributed partly to the time gap of over 20 years which has served to push Emergency experiences into the background, smoothing over the edges. But the difference of tone can also be explained by the fact that for the residents of Welcome, being at the receiving end of aggressive government initiatives and being at the mercy of petty officials, policemen and local *pradhans* was nothing new. It was, and still is, part of everyday life in the colony. So whilst the sight of bulldozers razing whole areas to the ground was shocking to the elite, it was all too familiar to the inhabitants of slums and resettlement colonies. Well over half of the residents of Welcome had already had their homes demolished at least once before the Emergency and others had lived under the threat of demolition for several years. And although sterilisation was a new experience, and one which had incited considerable fear, suffering and resentment during the Emergency, people had survived it and had often been able to secure a plot of land or two in the process. Rather than turning their attention to a general critique of the system and the individuals who dominated it, they tended to place emphasis on the fact that at least under Indira Gandhi they had been given land which was more than they could say they had got from subsequent leaders. These were narratives dominated not by the idiom of shock or guilt but by the idiom of survival.

What the narratives of the people of Welcome offer is not so much a politicised discourse of resistance as a detailed account of personal experiences that lend insight into the texture of social and political relations at a local level. As such they not only open up a forgotten episode to analysis but also defy the stereotypes through which that episode was previously viewed. Taken together, these personal accounts offer some sort of collective critique of the Emergency, even if this critique is not explicitly formulated as such. In bringing together the voices of men and women ill-placed for writing their own history, I hope to have given shape to this critique without either undermining its complexity or smoothing over its contradictions.

BIBLIOGRAPHY

Secondary sources

Abraham, Abu, 1977, *The Games of Emergency*, Delhi: Bell Books.

Advani, Lal K., 1978, *A Prisoner's Scrap-Book*, Delhi: Arnold-Heinemann.

Ali, Sabir, 1990, *Slums within Slums: A Study of Resettlement Colonies in Delhi*, Delhi: Har Anand/Vikas.

———, 1995a, 'Typology of Delhi Slums', presented at the Delhi seminar at the Centre for the Study of Developing Societies, Delhi, 18 April 1995.

———, 1995b, *Environment and Resettlement Colonies of Delhi*, Delhi: Har Anand Publications.

Amin, Shahid, 1995, *Event, Metaphor, Memory: Chauri Chaura, 1922–1992*, Delhi: Oxford University Press.

Appadurai, Arjun, 1997, *Modernity at Large*, Delhi: Oxford University Press.

Barnouw, Eric and S. Krishnaswamy, 1980, *Indian Film*, New York: Oxford University Press.

Basu, Sajal, 1978, *Underground Literature During the Emergency*, Calcutta: Minerva.

Bhagat, Dhiren, 1990, *The Contemporary Conservative, Selected Writings*, Delhi: Viking.

Butalia, Urvashi, 1998, *The Other Side of Silence*, Delhi: Viking.

Chadha, Kumkum, 1981, *The Crucifixion*, Delhi: Ajanta Publications.

Chatterji, Saral K., ed., 1987, *The Meaning of the Indian Experience: The Emergency*, Madras: Christian Literature Society.

Chattopadhyay-Dutt, Purnima, 1995, *Loops and Roots: Conflict between Official and Traditional Family Planning in India*, Delhi: Ashish Publishing House.

Chib, S.S., 1978, *Nineteen Fateful Months*, Delhi: Light and Life.

Darbari, Janis and Raj Darbari, 1983, *Indira Gandhi's 1028 Days*, Delhi: Raj Darbari and Janis Darbri.

Das, Veena, ed., 1990a, *Mirrors of Violence: Communities, Riots and Survivors in South Asia*, Delhi: Oxford University Press.

———, 1990b, 'Our Work to Cry: Your Work to Listen' in Das, ed., *Mirrors of Violence*.

———, 1995, *Critical Events: An Anthropological Perspective on Contemporary India*, Delhi: Oxford University Press.

——— and R.S. Bajwa, 1994, 'Community and Violence in Contemporary

Punjab' in D. Vidal, G. Tarabout, E. Meyer, eds, *Violences et Non-violences en Inde. Purushartha*, vol. 16, Paris: EHESS.

Davis, J., 1992, 'The Anthropology of Suffering', *Journal of Refugee Studies*, 5, 2, pp. 149–61.

Dayal, John and Ajoy Bose, 1977, *For Reasons of State: Delhi Under Emergency*, Delhi: Ess Ess Publications.

———, 1978, *The Shah Commission Begins*, Delhi: Orient Longman.

Desai, Marakand, ed., 1978, *The Smugglers of Truth: Selections from Satyavani*, Vadodora: Friends of India Society International.

Dupont, V., E. Tarlo and D. Vidal, eds, 2000, *Delhi: Urban Space and Human Destinies*, Delhi: Manohar.

Foucault, M., 1982, *Discipline and Punish, The Birth of the Prison*, Harmondsworth: Penguin.

———, 1980, *Power/Knowledge: Selected Interviews and other Writings, 1972–1977*, ed. Colin Gordon, New York: Harvester Wheatsheaf.

Fuller, C. and V. Bénéï, 2000, *The Everyday State and Society in Modern India*, Delhi: Social Science Press.

Gandhi, D.V., ed., 1976, *Era of Discipline* (Documents on Contemporary Reality), Delhi: Samachar Bharati.

Gandhi, Indira, 1984, *Selected Speeches and Writings*, vol. III: *1972–1977*, Delhi: Ministry of Information and Broadcasting.

Ghose, S.K., 1978, *The Crusade: The End of Indira Raj*, Delhi: Intellectual Book Corner.

———, 1975, *Freedom is not Free*, Calcutta: Debooks.

Gluckman, Max, 1953, *Rituals of Rebellion*, Manchester University Press.

Guha, R., ed., 1982–9, *Subaltern Studies: Writings on South Asian History and Society*, I–VI, Delhi: Oxford University Press.

Gulati, Leela, n.d., 'Sterilisations and Family Planning', working paper no. 69, Trivandrum: Centre for Development Studies.

Gupta, Akhil, 1995, 'Blurred Boundaries: The Discourse of Corruption, the Culture of Politics and the Imagined State', *American Ethnologist*, 22, 2, pp. 375–402.

Gupta, Anirudha, 1977, *Revolution through Ballot*, Delhi: Ankur.

Gupta, Shiv Charan, 1991, *Focus on Delhi: Problems and Solutions*, Delhi: Jan Jagriti Samaj.

Gwatkin, Davidson R., 1979, 'Political Will and Family Planning: Implications of India's Emergency Experience', *Population and Development Review*, 5, 1, pp. 29–59.

Haider, Saraswati, 2000, 'Migrant Women and Urban Experience in a Squatter Settlement' in Dupont, Tarlo, Vidal, eds, *Delhi*.

Hartmann, B., 1987, *Reproductive Rights and Wrongs*, New York: Harper & Row.

Henderson, Michael, 1977, _Experiment with Untruth: India Under Emergency,_ Delhi: Macmillan.

Hendre, Sudhir L., 1971, _Hindus and Family Planning: A Socio-political Demongraphy,_ Bombay: Supraja Prakashan.

Jagmohan, 1975, _Rebuilding Shahjahanabad, the Walled City of Delhi,_ Delhi: Vikas.

_____, 1978, _Island of Truth,_ Delhi: Vikas.

Jeffrey, P., R. Jeffrey and A. Lyon, 1989, _Labour Pains and Labour Power: Women and Childbearing in India,_ London: Zed Books.

Kalhan, Promilla, 1977, _Black Wednesday: Power, Politics, Emergency and Elections,_ Delhi: Sterling Publishers.

Kapur, Jagga, 1978, _What Price Perjury: Facts of the Shah Commission,_ Delhi: Arnold Heinemann.

Khanna, N., 1977, _Miracle of Democracy in India,_ Delhi: Interprint.

Kothari, M.M., 1977, _Reflections during Emergency,_ Jodhpur: Hope Books.

Kripalani, Acharya J.B., 1980, _The Nightmare and After,_ Bombay: Popular Prakashan.

Lal, Kanwar, 1976, _Emergency: Its Needs and Gains,_ Delhi: Hittashi.

_____, 1977, _Thank You Mrs. Gandhi,_ Delhi: Anupam Publications.

Leacock, E., 1971, _The Culture of Poverty: A Critique,_ New York: Simon & Schuster.

Levi, Primo, 1995 (1958), _If This is a Man,_ Harmondsworth: Penguin.

_____, 1993 (1988), _The Drowned and the Saved,_ London: Abacus.

_____, 1995 (1989), _Le Devoir de Memoire,_ Paris: Mille et une nuits.

Lewis, Primila, 1978, _Reason Wounded,_ New Delhi: Vikas.

Malkani, K.R., 1978, _The Midnight Knock,_ New Delhi: Vikas.

Mankekar, D.R. and Kamla Mankekar, 1977, _Decline and Fall of Indira Gandhi,_ Delhi: Vision Books.

Marcus, George, 1995, 'Ethnology in/of the World System: The Emergence of Multi-sited Ethnography', _Annual Review of Anthropology,_ no. 24, pp. 95–117.

Mavalankar, P.G., 1979, _'No Sir'—Being the Collection of 24 Speeches in the Lok Sabha during the Internal Emergency of India,_ Ahmedabad: Sannishtha Prakashan.

Mehta, Ved, 1978, _The New India,_ New York: Viking.

Mehta, Vinod, 1978, _The Sanjay Story,_ Bombay: Jaico Publishing House.

Menon, Ritu and Kamla Bhasin, 1998, _Borders and Boundaries,_ Delhi: Kali for Women.

Miller, D., 1973, 'Holi-Dhulendi: Licensed Rebellion in a North Indian Village', _South Asia,_ 3, pp. 15–22.

Misra, Giresh K. and Rakesh Gupta, 1981, _Resettlement Politics in Delhi,_ Delhi: Institute of Public Administration.

Naik, J.A., 1977, _The Great Janata Revolution,_ Delhi: S. Chand & Company.

Nandy, A., 1980, 'Indira Gandhi and the Culture of Indian Politics' in *At the Edge of Psychology: Essays in Politics and Culture*, Delhi: Oxford University Press.

Naraismahan, V.K., 1977, *Democracy Redeemed*, Delhi: S. Chand & Company.

Narayan, Jayaprakash, 1977, *Prison Diary*, Delhi: Popular Prakashan.

Narayan, Kiran, 1998, 'How "Native" is the Native Anthropologist?' in Meenakshi Thapan, ed., *Anthropological Journeys: Reflections on Fieldwork*, Delhi: Sangam Books.

Nayar, Kuldip, 1977, *The Judgement: Inside Story of the Emergency in India*, Delhi: Vikas.

————, 1978, *In Jail*, Delhi: Vikas.

Oberoi, P., 1995, 'Recalling the D. School Research Room: The Emergency Years' in D. *School: Reflections on the Delhi School of Economics*, Delhi: Oxford University Press.

Panandikar, V.A. Pai, R.N. Bishnoi and O.P. Sharma, 1978, *Family Planning Under the Emergency: Policy Implications of Incentives and Disincentives*, Delhi: Radiant Publications.

Panandikar, V.A. Pai and Umanshankar, 1994, 'Fertility Control and Politics in India' in *The New Politics of Population, A Supplement to vol. 20 of Population and Development Review*, pp. 89–104.

Pandey, Gyanendra, 1995, 'Nation and Masculinity: Some Reflections on Gandhi and the Partition of India', presented at workshop, 'Gandhi and his Legacy', Centre of South Asian Studies, SOAS, October.

Perry, J.O., ed., 1983, *Voices of Emergency*, Bombay: Popular Prakashan.

Prachand, S.L.M., 1977, *The Popular Upsurge and Fall of Congress*, Chandigarh: Abhishek.

Qureshi, S.Y., 1995, 'Islam and Family Planning', *Towards Secular India*, 1, 1, pp. 1–30.

Rawla, N.D. and R.K. Mudgal, 1977, *All the Prime Minister's Men*, Delhi: Pankaj.

Roy, Beth, 1994, *Some Trouble with Cows*, Berkeley: University of California Press.

Ruud, Arild ,1995, 'Caste Hierarchy and Resistance in Indian Village Politics', presented at the South Asia Anthropology Group conference, LSE, London, 18–19 September.

Sampradayikta Virodhi Andolan/People's Movement for Secularism, 1992, *Seelampur 1992: A Report on the Communal Violence in Seelampur New Delhi*.

Scheper-Hughes, Nancy, 1992, *Death without Weeping: The Violence of Everyday Life in Brazil*, Berkeley: University of California Press.

Selbourne, David, 1977, *An Eye to India: The Unmasking of Tyranny*: Middlesex: Penguin.

Sen, G., A. Germain and L. Chen, 1994, *Population Policies Reconsidered*, Boston: HSPH & IWHC.

Singh, S. Jagat, 1977, *The Return of Democracy, Janata's Victory March*, Delhi: Pankaj Publications.

Singh, Shankar Dayal, 1978, *Emergency: Fact and Fiction*, Delhi: Prakashan.

Sinha, B.M. 1977, *Operation Emergency*, Delhi: Hind Pocket Books.

Sinha, Sachchidanand, 1977, *Emergency in Perspective: Review and Challenge*, New Delhi: Heritage Books.

Soni, Anita, 2000, 'Urban Conquest of Outer Delhi: Beneficiaries, Intermediaries and Victims' in Dupont, Tarlo and Vidal, eds, *Delhi*.

Spencer, Jonathon, 1992, 'Problems in the Analysis of Communal Violence', *Contributions to Indian Sociology* (n.s.), 26, 2.

Tarlo, Emma, 1996, *Clothing Matters: Dress and Identity in India*, London: Hurst/Delhi: Viking/University of Chicago Press.

———, 1998, 'Wasteland', *The India Magazine*, 18, 6, pp. 14–9.

———, 2000, 'Body and Space in a Time of Crisis' in V. Das, A. Kleinman, M. Ramphele and P. Reynolds, eds, *Violence and Subjectivity*, Berkeley: University of California Press.

———, 2000, 'Paper Truths: the Emergency and Slum Clearance through Forgotten Files' in C. Fuller and V. Bénéï, *The Everyday State and Society in Modern India*, Delhi: Social Science Press.

———, 2000, 'Welcome to History: A Resettlement Colony in the Making' in Dupont, Tarlo and Vidal, eds, *Delhi*.

Thakur, Janardan, 1977, *All the Prime Minister's Men*, Delhi: Vikas.

———, 1979, *Indira Gandhi and her Power Game*, Ghaziabad: Vikas.

Tyler, Mary, 1978, *My Years in an Indian Prison*, London: Penguin.

Thapar, Raj, 1991, *All These Years*, Delhi: Penguin.

Tipple, A. and K. Wills, 1991, *Housing the Poor in the Developing World*, London: Routledge.

Toofan, Brij Mohan, 1988, *When Freedom Bleeds*, Delhi: Ajanta.

Vasudev, Uma, 1977, *Two Faces of Indira Gandhi*, Delhi: Vikas.

Vicziany, Marika, 1982–3, 'Coercion in a Soft State: The Family-Planning Program of India, pt 1: "The Myth of Voluntarism" and pt 2, "The Source of Coercion", *Pacific Affairs*, 55, 3, pp. 373–401, and 4, pp. 557–93.

Vidal, D., G. Tarabout and E. Meyer, eds, *Violences et Non-violences en Inde*, *Purushartha*, vol. 16, Paris: EHESS.

Zur, Judith N., 2000, *Violent Memories: Mayan War Widows in Guatemala*, Boulder, CO: Westview.

Government records

Annual Reports of Ministry of Health and Family Planning.

'Hum Do Hamare Do', seminar on family planning, *Amrita Bazaar Patrika* and *Jugantar*, August 1976.

Preserving our Democratic Structure, Prime Minister Explains Reasons for Emergency, July 1975 (pamphlet containing speeches of Indira Gandhi).

Shah Commission of Enquiry, 1978, Interim Report I, Report II, Third and Final Report.

Souvenir on Emergency and Social Justice, November 1975, Delhi: Council of National Affairs.

Timely Steps, August 1975, Delhi: Ministry of Information and Broadcasting.

Will we let her do it again?, c. 1979 (Janata Party publication).

Unclassified papers and records of the Slum and Jhuggi Jhompri Department of the Municipal Corporation of Delhi, East Zone B.

Newspapers, magazines and specialist journals

Amrita Bazaar Patrika
Demography India
Economic and Political Weekly
Frontline
Hindustan Times
Illustrated Weekly
Indian Express
India Today
Pioneer
Population and Development Review
Seminar
Statesman
Times of India

Fiction

Mistry, Rohinton, 1995, *A Fine Balance,* Calcutta: Rupa & Co.
Narayan, R.K., 1976, *The Painter of Signs,* New York: Viking.
Rushdie, Salman, 1983, *Midnight's Children,* London: Cape.
———, 1994, 'The Free Radio' in *East, West,* London: Cape.
Verma, Nirmal, 1993, *Dark Dispatches* (Hindi: *Raat ka Reporter*), Delhi: Indus.

INDEX

Ali Sena Party, 208, 210–11
Amin, Shahid, 19, 20
Appadurai, Arjun, 13, 16
Ayodhya, 132–3, 209–211

Bansi Lal, 30, 203
Bharatiya Janata Party (BJP), 57–8,
   60–1, 197, 209–11
Butalia, Urvashi, 18, 22, 129

Congress Party, 25, 42, 53, 60, 95–8,
   202–4, 208–12, 222–3

Das, Veena, 6–7, 128–9
dalals, role in sterilisation, 182–190,
   193, 212, 220
Dayal, John, and Ajoy Bose: 21, 82–
   3, 158, 160 220; account of
   Turkman Gate massacre, 38–40;
   critique of Shah Commission,
   43–4; documents cited by, 83
Delhi Development Authority
   (DDA): 28, 39, 42, 74; involvement
   in sterilisation, 69–70, 79–93,
   96–119, 123, 150; denial of
   involvement in sterilisation, 43, 69;
   slum clearance, 4, 13–16, 71; *see
   also* demolition, resettlement,
   demolitions, 10, 11, 13; *see also*
   Slum Department; at Turkman
   Gate, 38–43, 56–8; at Dujana
   House, 137–45
Desai, Morarji, 59, 96
Dujana House, 38–9, 42, 55–6, 137–
   45, 174

elections, 30–1, 37, 42, 44, 47, 48,
   53, 59–61, 70, 95, 134, 139, 145,
   157, 202–4, 218, 220, 222

Emergency: arrests, 26, 35, 133, 134;
   as an anthropological object, 5–
   6, 16–17, ch.1; beautification of
   Delhi, 15, 28, 29; censorship, 2,
   3, 26, 27, 32–3, 35, 69; declaration of, 23–5, 35; end of, 30,
   41–2, *see also* elections; family
   planning policy, *see* sterilisation;
   foreign press reports of, 26, 30,
   32–5; interests in forgetting, 21–
   4; official documents pertaining
   to, 9–11, 68–70, 74–5, 78–91, ch.
   4; 20–point programme, 27–6,
   35, 53; 5–point programme, 27,
   53; personal narratives of, experiences during, 3, 16–19, 32–3,
   54–8, 123, 130–1, 139–42, chs 6
   and 7; propaganda of, 3, 24–9;
   resistance to, 29, 31–2, 35, 219–
   20, 225, *see also* Turkman Gate;
   silence surrounding, 2–3, 19, 21–
   2, 33, 69–70, 101; slum clearance,
   3, 4–5, 11–13, 28, 37–44, 58,
   130–2, 137–47, *see also* demolitions and resettlement; Youth
   Congress, 27; *see also* Jayaprakash
   Narayan, Indira Gandhi, Sanjay
   Gandhi, sterilisation
ethnography: of the state, 7–13; of
   events, 5–7; of personal narratives,